Georgia
GARDENER'S
GUIDE

The What, Where, When, How & Why
of Gardening in Georgia

Georgia
GARDENER'S
GUIDE

ERICA GLASENER
WALTER REEVES

COOL
SPRINGS
PRESS

Glasener, Erica
    The Georgia Gardener's Guide by Erica Glasener and Walter Reeves.

    p.   cm.
    Includes bibliographical references and index.
    ISBN 1-888608-08-0
    1. Gardening, Georgia   2. Georgia, Gardening, Guidebooks.
    I. Reeves, Walter.   II. Title.
635.09758--dc20
Gla/Ree

Cool Springs Press, Inc.
118 Fourth Avenue South
Franklin, Tennessee 37064

First printing 1997
Printed in the United States of America
10 9 8 7 6 5 4 3 2 1

DEDICATION

*T*O MY GRANDMOTHER "BUBBER," the first *gardener I knew who gardened for love.*

AND TO MY PARENTS, FRANK AND FRANCES, who fell in love as a result of their mutual interest in raising healthy plants and a healthy family.

—W.R.

*T*O MY MOTHER, CAROL L. REINSBERG, *for her nurturing spirit and loving guidance.*

—E.L.G.

ACKNOWLEDGEMENTS

*L*IKE A SEED, THIS BOOK COULD not have come to fruition without the care and knowledge of many individuals and groups. Many friends also indirectly contributed to this book. We thank them all for their suggestions and support. In particular, we thank Roger Waynick and Karen Wilson of Cool Springs Press, for their intuition that a book of this type would be useful for Georgia gardeners, and Andrew Bunting, for his mastery of plant nomenclature.

Erica especially thanks David Bennett for sharing his opinions about plants and design, Kathryn MacDougald for her support and her contribution of a personal space to garden, and Steve Wheaton for all of the plant trips we took.

The intriguing questions a garden "expert" is asked can help when deciding on the best way to explain and describe a garden topic to others. Walter thanks his friends and neighbors Gus and Lisa Callaway, Carl and Laura Greenberg, "Mr." Kim and "Mrs." Kim Cody, and especially Linda Garrett for the many gardening questions they all posed.

CONTENTS

Why Garden in Georgia?

GEORGIA GARDENERS ARE A COURAGEOUS BUNCH. We garden in conditions ranging from the tundra on Brasstown Bald to the tropics in the Okefenokee swamp. Plants that look wonderful on the pages of garden catalogs may wither in our summer heat. Garden solutions that are sometimes guaranteed to prevent diseases may turn out to be miserable failures in our humidity. And never forget the insects! Do gardeners in other parts of the country ever have to pick off Japanese beetles while standing in a fire ant bed?

Good Georgia gardeners are not dismayed by these challenges. We know that in many ways we live in a plant paradise. We have a very long growing season. With careful planning, our gardens can offer interest throughout the year, from early-blooming bulbs (like snowdrops) to late-blooming perennials (like Japanese anemones). Our winters are relatively mild and short and we have abundant sunshine. The solution to our garden predicament is simple: we just have to find the plants and garden techniques that are best suited to our own state.

For example, while a perennial like lady's mantle (*Alchemilla mollis*) may grow in full sun in Northern climates, author Erica Glasener discovered that what it really needs to thrive in Georgia is a half-shade location with cool, moist soil. Author Walter Reeves' blind determination to grow hostas in a site with a half-day of afternoon sunshine resulted only in good hosta compost!

Once we decide on the plants we want to grow, we must find the garden tricks necessary to meet the challenges presented by soil type, heat, and humidity. We must use the wisdom passed down to us by generations of Georgia gardeners combined with the latest research on the best ways to help a plant flourish.

Introduction

This is what our book is all about: the *what, where, when, how,* and *why* of Georgia gardening. You'll learn the best ways to make good soil, discover the tricks that thwart pests, and best of all, you'll acquire the skills needed to cultivate the plants that are proven performers in our part of the country.

The authors of this book have gardened for many years, both professionally and as a hobby. We garden because we enjoy it. Gardening is relaxing, intriguing, and nurturing. Gardening is an activity that is both profoundly simple and universally complex.

This book will introduce you to the wealth of ornamental plants that are suited for Georgia gardens. Whether you garden in Atlanta or Savannah, you will find every category of plant you need for a complete residential landscape. We have personally grown these plants or observed them growing strongly and healthily in gardens throughout the state. Some grow best in north Georgia, some flourish only in south Georgia, and some require experimentation with location. We have chosen not to include vegetables and fruits in the book, for that topic would demand another whole volume!

We often tell beginning gardeners that if they haven't moved a plant three times, it's probably not yet in the right place. We take comfort in what our friend, nurseryman Bud Heist, says: "Don't say we can't grow it, just say we don't yet know what it needs."

Before you consider the light, drainage, and exposure in your favorite garden spot, spend a little time learning about the soil, nutrients, pests, and plant diseases common in your area.

THE SOIL

Some roots are reputed to be able to crack a house foundation or to break up a sidewalk, but roots are actually quite tender. When you put a plant in the soil, whether it is Bermuda grass or a baby oak, the roots will grow in the direction where resistance is least. Roots grow in the parts of the soil that offer moisture, oxygen, and nutrients.

Plants prefer to grow in soil that is a blend of clay, sand, and organic matter. The water and oxygen required by roots are plentiful in such an environment and nutrients are available throughout. But few gardeners are blessed with perfect soil. The clay soil so abundant in north Georgia tends to have lots of moisture but little oxygen. The sandy soil prevalent along the coast has lots of oxygen but holds little water and few nutrients. The quickest way to make your soil better is to add more nutrients in the form of compost or other organic matter.

ORGANIC MATTER

Organic matter is found in manure, compost, and other materials. Ground pine bark is a common soil amendment found throughout the state of Georgia. Gardeners in the southern part of the state use ground peanut hulls. Peat moss is readily available, but it doesn't seem to persist in our soil as long as the coarser materials do. You may purchase your organic soil amendments, but if you learn how to produce them from good compost or if you find a good source of manure, you can have an unlimited free supply of organic matter.

COMPOST

Ever wonder why good gardeners wax eloquent about manure and compost? It's because either element, when added to a garden, can double the size and vigor of the plants. Some gardeners swear they achieve triple success when they add one of these materials to their ordinary soil. You might say that successful gardeners don't have green thumbs, they have black thumbs . . . from all of the manure and compost they've handled!

Introduction

The reason compost is superior to any other source of organic matter is that it is *alive*. Compost is the decomposed remains of leaves, lawn clippings, pruned branches, and discarded stalks. The billions of fungi, bacteria, and other living creatures in compost are important parts of any healthy soil. Unfortunately, if you are gardening in a spot that is hard and bare, the soil has very little life in it. Plants growing in hard soil can be made beautiful, but they require more fertilizer and water to keep them looking their best.

Compost is the lazy gardener's friend. It contains billions of living creatures that help roots absorb water and nutrients. These tiny gardeners can take over some of the tasks of fertilizing and watering your plants.

Making compost never has to be complicated. Mother Nature has been composting for millions of years, and she never used a pitchfork or compost bin or expensive compost starter. Some gardeners choose to compost on a large scale, lugging bags of their neighbors' leaves up the street to dump on their compost piles. Others just throw their own leaves and clippings onto a pile and let nature take its course. Either method is fine. But the forming of compost does take time. It takes approximately six months and a thirty-gallon bag of yard trimmings to manufacture one cubic foot of compost. Mixing and turning a compost pile once a month can make the process go a bit faster.

While it's easy to make compost, it might be even easier to buy soil amendments at a garden center. But how much of this supplemental material does one need to make a difference in the soil? Dr. Tim Smalley, Professor of Horticulture at the University of Georgia, recommends spreading a layer of compost two inches thick over a garden flower bed and then mixing it with the soil underneath. In practical terms, that's two cubic feet of soil conditioner for every eight square feet of flower bed. You can see why composters are caught "borrowing" their neighbors' leaves at night!

The organic matter should be mixed to a depth of six to eight inches in the soil. With the addition of organic matter the soil will loosen, and it will stay loose for years. Oxygen will penetrate to where the roots are growing. The organic matter will absorb excess water and hold it in reserve for the plant to use when drier times come.

WATERING

It seems simple enough to water an outdoor plant, but most gardeners either over-water or under-water their plants. Proper watering is accomplished differently in different parts of the state. Sandy soil drains so well that water must be applied twice a week during a blistering summer. Clay soil holds too much water. Plants in clay soil must be watered less often or they will succumb to root rot.

The amount of water to use also differs among plants. A shallow-rooted fern might need one-fourth gallon of water applied every other day. A densely rooted lawn requires six-hundred gallons per thousand square feet every week. A new tree might require three gallons twice a week for one month, and afterwards only need watering when a drought occurs.

Your own observations are best when you are determining when and how much to water. Here are some tips to get you started:

- Water container plants until the water runs out the bottom. Do not water again until the top inch of soil is dry.

Introduction

- Put a hose at the base of a newly installed plant and thoroughly soak the root ball once a week. As the plant begins to grow larger, take into consideration that the size of the root zone will also increase.

- Use shallow cans to measure the amount of water applied by your lawn sprinkler. Put six cans in the area being sprinkled and run the system for an hour. Then measure the depth of water in all of the cans. If the average depth of water is one-half inch, you will know the grass root zone has been irrigated. This may take one to two hours.

- If summer restrictions limit your watering, determine which plants would cost the most to replace, and water them first. It makes more sense to save a specimen maple tree than to keep ten dollars worth of petunias alive.

- An inexpensive water timer and a few soaker hoses can be a gardener's best friends.

MULCH

If a plant's roots are subjected to a long Georgia drought, even the toughest plant in the finest soil will suffer. Mulching will help you avoid this problem. Georgia's millions of pine trees give us two of the best mulches in the world, pine straw and pine bark chips. Mulch acts like a blanket. It keeps moisture in the soil, and it prevents plant roots from becoming too hot or too cold. Other good mulches include shredded fall leaves, wood chips, and shredded cypress bark. Few gardeners succeed without placing a one- to two-inch layer of mulch on top of the soil around all of their plants.

Introduction

Nutrients

Plants need nitrogen, phosphorus, and potassium in order to grow well. When you buy a bag of fertilizer, you will see three numbers on the label. These numbers indicate the amounts of nitrogen, phosphorus, and potassium in the fertilizer. The numbers represent the percentage of each nutrient in the mixture. For example, a bag of 10–10–10 fertilizer contains 10% nitrogen (N), 10% phosphorus (P), and 10% potassium (K). The other 70% is just clay.

Each nutrient serves a function in the overall good health of a plant. So how do you know which fertilizer to buy when your garden center offers dozens of combinations of the three nutrient numbers? Just look at the numbers on the bag and remember: Up, Down, and All Around.

Up: Nitrogen promotes leaf growth. That's why lawn fertilizer has a high nitrogen percentage. A common turf fertilizer is a 16–4–8, but some brands have even more nitrogen than this. Grass leaves are mowed off constantly, so nitrogen is needed to help grow more of them.

Down: Phosphorus is important in the formation of roots and is very important for flower, seed, and fruit growth. That's why so-called "starter fertilizers" and "bloom fertilizers" have high percentages of phosphorus.

All Around: Potassium increases overall cell health. When your plant is under stress from drought or from cold, adequate potassium helps the plant withstand the crisis. "Winterizer" fertilizer for lawns is a good choice for grass that must endure such conditions. Its potassium percentage is high to help the grass fight winter cold damage.

It is not necessary to buy a different fertilizer for each of the plant types you have in your landscape. You really can't hurt a plant by applying the wrong fertilizer. Your perennials won't be damaged by the application of "azalea fertilizer." The lawn won't be hurt if you fertilize it with 10–10–10. There may be some situations in which one type of fertilizer is marginally better; for example, a "slow-release turf fertilizer" might be especially desirable for some types of grass. But you can do quite well with the purchase of just three main types of fertilizer: 16–4–8 for your lawn, 6–12–12 for new plants, and 10–10–10 for everything else.

How do you know what amount of fertilizer to apply? How much nutrition does your soil already hold? Do you need any lime? To find out, you need to perform a soil test.

SOIL TEST

There are two ways to test your soil. You can purchase an inexpensive gardener's test kit with simple chemicals and test tubes and do it yourself, or you can take some of your soil to your local county Extension office for a low-cost analysis.

Test kits are economical and simple to use. To use one, you'll mix your soil with water, then add a few drops of indicator chemical that will cause the water to change color. If you feel confident that you can match the color of the water with the colors on the small color wheel that is provided, you can determine which nutrients you need to add to your soil. If you don't trust your powers of analysis, you might want to compare your conclusions with those of the University of Georgia Soil Testing Laboratory through your local county Extension Service office.

Having soil tested by the Extension Service is a simple process as well. Collect several scoops of dirt from different areas of your yard and mix them together. The Extension Service needs just one cup of this soil mixture for the test. Put the soil in a bag, take it to your local Extension office, and tell the Extension agent what you intend to grow in it. The soil will be shipped to a laboratory in Athens. Within ten days you will receive a mailed report describing the nutrients present in your soil, the amounts in which they are present, and specific recommendations for correct fertilizer use.

LIME

Though lime does not offer plant nutrients (aside from calcium, which plants need in small amounts), it helps plants absorb nutrients more efficiently. Georgia soils, particularly in the northern half of the state, tend to be acidic. In an acidic soil, plant roots can't collect the nitrogen, phosphorus, and potassium they need to function. Lime makes soil less acidic. Soil acidity is measured in numbers from 1 to 14 on what is called the pH scale. Most plants prefer soil that has a pH of 6.0 to 6.5. A hard clay subsoil may have a pH of 4.5. It takes a lot of lime to move the pH up to 6.5. Your soil test will determine the pH of your soil and the amount of lime it needs.

PESTS AND DISEASES

The same conditions that make our gardens so beautiful make Georgia a happy homeland for insect and disease pests. A long growing season means that insect populations have time to explode each year. Our high humidity and warm temperatures are perfect for the growth of fungi and bacteria.

It cannot be said often enough that a healthy plant is the best defense against pests. A plant that grows vigorously can quickly overcome insect damage. A plant that is not stressed by its environment can resist disease spores. Many of the plants included in this book were chosen because of their strong resistance to insects and diseases. If you follow our recommendations about the proper placement of your plants and how to care for them, your garden will rarely need pesticides. If you choose the plant varieties we recommend, you will have genetic allies in your fight against pests.

ORGANIC VS. INORGANIC GARDENING

I am literally the product of an organic garden. My mother purchased a small farm in order to grow vegetables using chicken manure for fertilizer. She had read that "trace-mineralized vegetables" would help her combat her incipient diabetes and her constant feeling of lethargy. She met my father—the local chicken farmer—at a house-warming party. They raised five children on a diet of home-grown vegetables, whole wheat flour, and all the well water we could drink.—W.R.

If you find pests attacking your plants, what should you do? Is the problem bad enough to use a pesticide? Which pesticide should you use? Should you rely on synthetic chemicals or should you choose pesticides made from organic sources? These questions trouble all of us. Some gardeners prefer to use only organic pesticides. Others are more pragmatic, sometimes using synthetic pesticides, occasionally preferring organic ones, but always striving to use the smallest amounts possible in every case.

There is no single correct answer to the question: *Which is best—organic or inorganic gardening?* Synthetic pesticides for home gardeners have been repeatedly tested for safety by their manufacturers and by the Federal government. Scientists and bureaucrats who advise us on environmental matters have declared that prudent use of approved pesticides offers fewer health risks that we would encounter if we avoided pesticides completely and endangered our food supply. Organic gardening does not always completely eliminate pesticide use, as it sometimes calls for the use of pesticides that come from organic sources. These organic pesticides may have risks higher or lower than synthetic ones. Fortunately, new gardening products with fewer risks appear on the market every year.

The choice between an "organic" or an "inorganic" garden is yours alone to make. You must decide whether the convenience of using synthetic pesticides offsets the hard work and constant vigilance required to completely eliminate their use.

INFORMATION ON PESTICIDE USE

If you need advice on which pesticides to use, the best resource for assistance is the local office of the University of Georgia Cooperative Extension Service. The agents there maintain the latest research data on the most effective and least potentially harmful pesticides to use. Ask them to tell you about all of the alternatives for solving your pest problem. Then you can use your experience and wisdom to make the choices that are best for your situation.

THE NAME GAME

Gardeners may wonder why they need to know the scientific names of plants. The answer is simple: you want to make sure the rose you purchase for your own garden is the same sweet-smelling rose you admired (and coveted) in your neighbor's garden. It's true that scientific names, which are derived from Latin or Greek, can be long and hard to pronounce. But unlike a common plant name, which often is applied to two very different plants, a scientific designation is specific and unique.

Introduction

When I moved to Georgia, I wondered what it was that people were fondly calling a "wild honeysuckle." Was it the weedy vine or the blooming bush with which I was familiar? It turned out to be neither! These native gardeners were referring to their native azaleas as "wild honeysuckle." When I design a landscape, I don't specify plants by their common names. What if I were to recommend "sweet box" and my client planted a boxwood instead of Sarcococca hookeriana?
—E.L.G.

Throughout this book we identify plants by both their scientific and common names. A plant's scientific name consists of the genus (the first word) and an epithet. For example, all maples belong to the genus *Acer*. The epithet (in our example, *rubrum*) identifies a specific kind of maple. *Acer rubrum* is a red maple. The genus and epithet are always italicized and the genus name begins with a capital letter, while the entire epithet is always written in lower case.

A third word in the name may refer to a special variety of the plant, called a cultivar. The cultivar name is important because it designates a superior selection known for bigger blooms, better foliage, or some other noteworthy characteristic. A cultivar name is distinguished by the use of single quotation marks, as in the name *Acer rubrum* 'October Glory,' a red maple with excellent fall leaf color. Most cultivars must be propagated by division or cuttings because they may not come true from seed.

A scientific name can change, but this happens only rarely, and there are certain rigid rules that apply to the practice of plant nomenclature. It is much easier to track down a wonderful plant if you know the full scientific name. Armed with a knowledge of both scientific and common names, you should be able to acquire the best plants for your Georgia garden.

Introduction

PROPAGATION

Once you become excited about gardening, you may develop "plant lust." You'll start to think that you must buy every new and exciting plant you discover. A much less expensive way to acquire your plants is to propagate them using seeds, cuttings, or divisions.

Growing annuals from seed works well, but it is usually the slowest method for propagating perennials, and is not always successful. The good news is that once they are well established in your garden, many perennial plants can be easily divided and transplanted, providing a constant supply of new plants.

When dividing a perennial, dig up the entire plant and separate it into pieces. You may dig up a mature clump and use a digging fork and your fingers to tease apart the roots, or you can make a clean cut with a straight-edged shovel to divide the large clump into smaller pieces. Make sure each piece has roots and buds. Remember, always have the new garden area prepared ahead of time for the new divisions, and don't let the roots dry out. Once all the divisions are planted, water them well. They'll grow large in no time!

Rooting stem cuttings is another option for propagating both perennials and annuals, as well as many shrubs. The important point to remember about cuttings is to take cuttings during the correct season. Timing is more important with shrubs than with herbaceous plants. Rooting stem cuttings provides a simple means to overwinter a piece of an annual that has grown too big to save in its present size; thus, it can be preserved and propagated again.

Another easy method for propagating plants, including most azaleas and hydrangeas, is layering. Penny McHenry, president of the American Hydrangea Society and a keen Atlanta gardener, propagates some of her favorite hydrangeas by bending young branches so that they touch the ground. Making sure to loosen the dirt at the point of contact, she places soil and organic matter on top of the stem and uses a brick to weigh it down. Within two months, Penny has a newly rooted plant that can be cut off from the main plant and transplanted to a new location.

These are just a few suggestions for ways to get more out of your garden or to share your bounty with friends. Some of the most wonderful gardens started with "a piece of this and a division of that." Who knows, you may develop your own favorite technique for propagating a special rose or that mildew-resistant phlox you discover in your garden!

HARDINESS

In this book, when we write of zones in which certain plants grow best, we are referring to the United States Department of Agriculture (USDA) hardiness zones. Years of collecting weather data have resulted in a map that divides the country into minimum temperature zones. For each plant, we have noted the zones in which it can survive winter.

The minimum winter temperatures that plants can tolerate may not be the main concern of a gardener who wants to grow plants in Georgia's hot, humid summers. But only recently have scientists made vigorous efforts to evaluate the ability of plants to withstand summer heat. The plants we recommend in this book are good performers in many parts of Georgia. Just remember, there is a wide range of weather conditions prevalent throughout the state. A plant suited for the Piedmont region may not be happy in a Coastal garden, and a plant that thrives in a Coastal garden may not do well in the Piedmont. On the other hand, you might be able to create a spot in your landscape that replicates conditions in another part of the state. Plants don't know geography—they only know if they are happy in the site you've chosen!

The location of a plant in your garden, soil type, and soil drainage are all factors that affect plant hardiness. Plants also need different amounts of sunlight. We have indicated the amount of sunlight suitable for each plant's growing requirements. The following symbols indicate full sun, partial sun, and shade.

Full Sun   Partial   Shade
          Sun

As noted earlier, simply moving a plant to another location may result in improved growth and long-term survival.

CONCLUSION

With these few tips you now have an overview of the basic information needed to become a gardener. To obtain the truly valuable skills of gardening, you will have to practice the 4-H Club motto: *Learn by Doing*. You will have to don your old jeans, take up your shovel, and *dig*!

If you keep your heart and mind open to the nuances of nature, you will cultivate more than just pretty flowers and strong trees. Both your plants and you yourself will grow in your beautiful garden. Fayetteville nurseryman Steven Stinchcomb may have said it best: "Some people are just gardeners in their heads and some people become gardeners in their hearts."

Good Gardening!

USDA PLANT HARDINESS MAP

Georgia

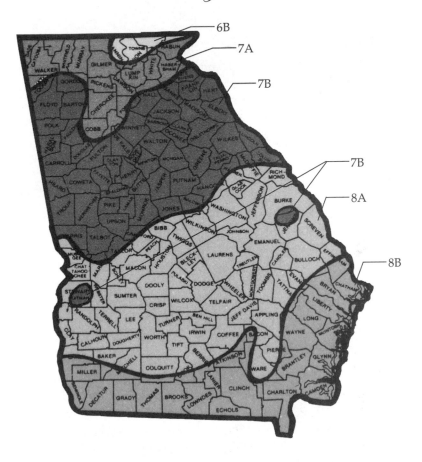

AVERAGE ANNUAL MINIMUM TEMPERATURE

6B	0° F TO -5° F
7A	5° F TO 0° F
7B	10° F TO 5° F
8A	15° F TO 10° F
8B	20° F TO 15° F

CHAPTER ONE

Annuals

ARLY IN MY GARDENING CAREER, WHEN *I heard people talk about annuals I would automatically assume they were referring to plants like red salvias and marigolds, which are so often planted around mailboxes. I dismissed annuals as too common. I wanted to grow perennials, which I considered to be much more sophisticated. It was after I moved to Georgia that I discovered a wealth of annuals that no good flower garden should be without. Now I have a whole new cast of plants that I have come to rely on for long season color. I use them in the gardens I design and in my own garden. —E.L.G.*

An annual is defined as any plant that completes its natural life cycle, from germinated seed through growth, flower, seed production, and death, in a single growing season. For this reason, USDA winter hardiness zones are not provided for annuals. In Georgia, gardeners have many annuals to chose from that will add long season color to the garden with a minimum amount of effort and cost. In addition, some reward us by reseeding freely, providing free plants for the following year, while others bloom almost continuously from spring until frost.

While perennials may provide the framework for the flower garden, annuals act as weavers and binders, tying everything together and bridging the gap between seasons. Imagine a shade garden without colorful impatiens or a sunny border without petunias. What would summer be like without sunflowers or winter without violas?

Most annuals are easy to grow from seed. Many can be sowed directly in the garden where they will grow. Others benefit from being started indoors and then transplanted to the garden after they have been hardened off (slowly introduced to outside temperatures). There are annuals for every garden situation, from the ground-hugging scaevola for full sun to the large tropical-like coleus for shade. Even if you purchase small plants, with annuals you get a lot of bang for your buck. Think about it: A cell pack of *Zinnia linearis*, six plants, may cost about $2.75 and will provide a two-foot square of flowers from early June until frost (in most parts of Georgia, first frost occurs sometime in November). Not many perennials can make the same claim.

GETTING THE MOST OUT OF YOUR ANNUALS

As with all types of plants, the secret to growing the most beautiful annuals is to start with good soil. Many of the annuals recommended in this book will tolerate less-than-ideal conditions such as poor soil and drought. However, ornamental plants, with a few exceptions, produce better growth and more flowers if they are planted in a soil that is well drained and amended with organic matter. Unlike perennials, annuals, which complete their entire life cycle in one growing season, benefit from regular applications of fertilizer. Liquid fertilizer is fine. Applied at recommended rates once every month, the fertilizer encourages vigorous plants and more blooms.

To prolong the flowering of many annuals, gardeners should know about deadheading. This is the practice of removing spent flowers before they have a chance to set seed. Some types of annuals respond to being cut back to encourage bushier growth and more blooms. Another technique that prolongs the show that annuals provide is to stagger the sowing of seeds. If you grow an annual that you particularly like, you may want to take cuttings so that you can hold over rooted cuttings for the next year. Grow them in the house in a sunny window, or in a greenhouse, if you're lucky enough to have one.

Whether you grow annuals in pots, use them as bedding plants, or select them for their unusual foliage, they play a critical role in the garden. Try new varieties, don't overlook the tried-and-true, and most of all, have fun with whatever you grow!

Antirrhinum majus

Snapdragon

Height: 6"–48"
Flowers: white, yellow, pink, red Blooms: early spring to frost

Snaps are favorites of many gardeners, and not only because of their child-hood memories of snapping the hinged flowers to make them look as if they are talking. Individual flowers open during a period of over two weeks, starting at the bottom of the spike and continuing upward. Whether grown in containers or in the flower garden, snapdragons make a nice complement to pansies. Young plants set out in the fall will bloom until they are hit by a hard frost. Then they rest over the winter and start blooming again in early spring once the weather warms up. Cutting off old flower stalks will encourage reblooming. In the warmest parts of Georgia, snapdragons act like perennials. In the rest of the state, during mild spells they will bloom on and off through winter. Described as "dragon-mouthed," these cheerful flower spikes range in size from dwarfs that only grow to 6"–10" tall and are well-suited for bedding plants, to the giant snaps that grow 30"–36" tall and make great cut flowers. The medium-height types like the Liberty series are good choices for cut flowers that don't need staking.

WHEN TO PLANT

Sow seeds indoors after the fear of frost has passed in the spring. Don't cover the seeds, as they need light to germinate. After the seeds germinate, in 1–2 weeks, thin them out and transplant them to pots. Harden them off before you plant them in the garden. If you start with young plants, they may be planted in spring or fall.

WHERE TO PLANT

Plant snapdragons in full sun or partial shade in a soil that is well drained. If the soil is too rich or fertile, plants will produce lots of foliage and fewer flowers.

How to Plant

Place plants in holes that are larger than their containers. Space them according to the needs of the variety. Large types will need more room than dwarf types. They can be used for borders or planted in large groups for cut flowers.

Care and Maintenance

Snapdragons will benefit from regular fertilization during the growing season, but make sure they don't get too much nitrogen. Check with your local Extension Service for recommended rates of fertilization. Deadheading (removing the spent flowers before they set seed) will encourage more blooms over a longer period of time. Keep plants well watered during periods of drought.

Additional Advice for Care

Snapdragons will often reseed themselves around the garden. To encourage this practice, let some plants set seed. This can result in interesting combinations, but some consider these plants "weedy." If they show up where they're not welcome, just pull them up.

Additional Cultivars and Species

If you want to grow snapdragons for cut flowers, the 'Rocket' series grows 30"–36" and comes in over 10 different colors. Among the earliest flowering are the dwarf 'Tahiti' hybrids. They have a compact habit and grow 7"–8" tall.

Begonia semperflorens

Wax Begonia

Height: 6"–12"
Flowers: pink, white, red or bicolor Blooms: spring to frost

Native to Brazil, wax begonias have long been popular in the South as bedding plants in the shade garden, for edging, for use in containers, and in window boxes. A profusion of flowers from spring until frost and the ability to thrive during the heat of Georgia summers make this annual popular with many homeowners and commercial landscapers. Sun-resistant varieties include the cocktail hybrids, dwarf types that only grow 5"–6" high. The colorful flowers are especially showy against shiny bronze foliage. Wax begonias are sensitive to cold and cannot survive frost, but they are easy to overwinter as houseplants. If you have limited space to grow plants indoors, you can take stem cuttings of your favorite types and root them in a small container like a paper cup. In the spring you will have new plants ready for the garden.

WHEN TO PLANT

Plant wax begonias after the last frost date and when the soil has warmed up. If you grow them from seed, start the seeds indoors, allowing 2–3 weeks for germination. After you transplant the seedlings and harden them off, plant them directly in the spot where they will grow.

WHERE TO PLANT

The best location for wax begonias is one where they will be in bright light or dappled shade, out of any hot direct sun. A soil rich in organic matter is ideal but they will grow in most soils provided they are not soggy. Avoid planting them directly under trees with lots of root competition. Wax begonias can be used as bedding plants, for edging, in containers, or window boxes.

HOW TO PLANT

When using as bedding plants, plant them 8"–12" apart, depending on the variety. Extra-dwarf types should be planted 4"–6" apart. If you use containers, be sure there is adequate drainage, as they resent it when the soil stays constantly wet.

CARE AND MAINTENANCE

Wax begonias that are planted in the ground should be watered weekly during the summer or during dry spells. Plants grown in containers or window boxes may need watering daily, especially during the summer, and in extreme cases they may require watering twice a day. As with most annuals, fertilizing with a liquid fertilizer such as 20–20–20 on a regular basis during the growing season (every 2–4 weeks) encourages maximum blooming. While you don't need to deadhead wax begonias, they can get leggy. If this happens, pinch them back so they will branch out and become better-looking, healthier plants.

ADDITIONAL ADVICE FOR CARE

A sea of wax begonias may be suitable for an office park landscape, but try mixing them with other annuals in your garden or containers for a more interesting effect. Mix some Osmocote™ with the soil mix when you first plant begonias in containers.

ADDITIONAL CULTIVARS AND SPECIES

'Pizzazz' hybrid offers 10" mounds of waxy green leaves with masses of bright blooms in shades of deep rose, pink, red, and white. 'Stara' hybrid is a vigorous plant that grows to 14".

Cleome hassleriana

Spider Flower

Cat's Whiskers, Needle and Thread

Height: 5'–6'
Flowers: white, white-pink, purple-pink Blooms: summer to frost

This vigorous plant has been passed from one gardener to the next for generations. Its common names include spider flower, cat's whiskers, and needle and thread. All three describe the unusual blooms atop tall, prickly stems with flowers that have stamens that stick out way past the petals, and long, thin seed pods. The large, rounded heads of flowers come in shades of pink, pink-and-white, lavender, and white. The pure white flowered form is easy to work into every type of color scheme. I first came to know this annual in north Georgia, but it grows almost anywhere that it is hot, humid, and sunny. Some people consider it weedy because of its tendency to reseed freely in the garden, showing up year after year in places you'd least expect. This is easy to remedy. Just pull up any that you don't want. You'll still have plenty to fill gaps in the flower border. During the dog days of summer and continuing until frost, few annuals can match the spider flower's height, texture, and color. Fairly drought-resistant, spider flower will grow in most well-drained soils. Deadheading will encourage longer blooming.

WHEN TO PLANT

Sow seeds early indoors a few weeks before the fear of frost has passed. Once they germinate, thin out seedlings and transplant them to peat pots. Let plants harden off, wait till the soil has warmed up a bit, then plant peat pots directly where you want plants to grow. Cleome seeds need light to germinate.

WHERE TO PLANT

Plant spider flowers in the middle or back of the flower border where they will add height. They should not need staking unless the soil is too rich. Combine spider flowers with other annuals and perennials. Underplant them with low-growing annuals like the white-flowered form of *Zinnia linearis*. It will cover some of the bare stems spider flowers tend to develop.

How to Plant

Plant spider flowers in full sun in a well-drained soil. Cut plants back if they get too leggy or woody. For best growth, fertilize plants with liquid fertilizer once or twice during the growing season. Check with your local Extension Service for recommended rates.

Care and Maintenance

Deadhead plants on a regular basis to encourage more blooms. Although they tolerate some drought, regular watering and applications of liquid fertilizer during the growing season will result in robust plants. Thin out seedlings and encourage the strongest to develop into big plants.

Additional Advice for Care

Cleomes make exotic cut flowers. They look good in almost every type of garden, from the overflowing cottage garden to the more formal garden.

Additional Cultivars and Species

C. 'Helen Campbell' grows to 48" tall and has white flowers. The 'Queen' series plants grow 4' tall and have 5"–6" wide flowers. They range in color from cherry, pink, rose, and violet to white and a mix of all the colors.

Coleus x hybridus

Coleus

Height: 9"–16"
Flowers: Coleus is grown for its colorful foliage.

It used to be that coleus came in dark red and a few other colors, and you used it when you couldn't think of anything else to grow in the shade. Easy to propagate from cuttings, it also made its way indoors where it often became leggy and forgotten as a houseplant. With the myriad hybrids available today, coleus is no longer a last resort when it comes to choosing annuals that offer beautiful foliage for shade and sun. Available in every color and color combination, and striped, spotted, splashed, and freckled, plants range in size from the dwarf and bushy to the tall and tropical-looking. Coleus is showing up in flower gardens, in exotic combinations in pots, and in window boxes. While most coleus are happiest in part-shade where their colors are more vivid, there are varieties that thrive in Georgia's summer sun. In a shade garden, coleus add easy-care seasonal color when planted with perennials like evergreen ferns. In the flower garden, they can serve as bold exclamation points, especially if the foliage is chartreuse or striped!

When to Plant

Plant coleus after fear of frost has passed. Plants can be easily propagated from stem cuttings and overwintered indoors or in a greenhouse. This is an inexpensive way to start plants which grow very quickly. Seeds can be started indoors in early spring. Germination takes 10 days to two weeks and the seeds need light to germinate.

Where to Plant

There is a coleus for almost every type of garden, whether you only have space for containers or you have a large, sunny flower garden or shady woodland. There are trailing varieties that you can grow in hanging baskets, too. Just check with your local nursery for either "sun" or "shade" types.

How to Plant

Coleus prefers a moist, well-drained soil. If you grow them in containers, make sure the soil mix is light but has enough organic matter to hold moisture. Be sure to site particular varieties according to their needs, i.e., shade, sun, trailing, tall, dwarf.

Care and Maintenance

Coleus is a fast grower and many types send out lots of branches, making them appear almost like miniature shrubs. Pinch plants and flower buds back regularly, once a month or more, to keep them full and bushy. All coleus benefit from regular watering. If you grow them in containers, add Osmocote™ to the planting mix and apply a liquid fertilizer once a month. Check with your local Extension Service for recommended rates. Stem cuttings root easily and offer an inexpensive way to save favorite varieties for next year.

Additional Advice for Care

Coleus is a versatile foliage plant that can be combined with annuals and perennials. The chartreuse types complement annuals like the magenta *Petunia integrifolia* and the black sweet potato vine, *Ipomea* 'Blackie.' The striped and mottled coleus blend nicely with evergreen ferns.

Additional Cultivars and Species

There are too many cultivars to list. Just look for either "sun" or "shade" types. 'Fairway,' extra-compact dwarf plants for shade, come in many colors. The 'Wizard' series offers large, heart-shaped leaves. With plants growing 12"–14", they are suited for hanging baskets, containers, and shady landscapes.

Cosmos sulphureus, C. bipinnatus

Yellow Cosmos

Cosmos

Height: 18"–36" or taller
Flowers: yellow, orange, pink, red, white Blooms: summer to frost

When you see them in bloom, it's easy to see why these colorful flowers get their name from the Greek kosmos, *which means harmonious. For drought-resistant beauty, yellow cosmos is hard to beat. This adaptable annual blooms for weeks, and once established, it requires very little moisture. In fact, if the soil is too rich, plants may become tall and lanky. Deeply divided, the feathery foliage adds to the overall fine texture of cosmos. Thriving in full sun, the bold flowers seem to dance in the breeze. Cosmos produces masses of 2½" flowers on 3'–4' plants that glow in the garden with yellow, golden, golden-orange and scarlet-orange. Plant them in flower beds, along roadsides, in disturbed areas, and in meadows. The largest flowered cosmos is C. bipinnatus. Its blooms measure 4"–6" across and come in shades of pink, red, white, and crimson. Sow seed directly in the garden. Cosmos attracts hordes of butterflies and thrives in spots where many other plants would perish.*

WHEN TO PLANT

Plant cosmos seeds in the spring after the fear of frost has passed and the soil has warmed up. By sowing a second group of seeds two weeks after you sow the first batch, you can help extend the season of bloom in the garden, in the meadow, or on the roadside.

WHERE TO PLANT

Plant cosmos wherever you want brilliant colors. They look good in the informal cottage garden in combination with other annuals and perennials, or in a big mass in more formal gardens. Plant them along roadsides, in meadows, or in the vegetable garden where they add color and can be used for cut flowers.

HOW TO PLANT

Cosmos almost seem to thrive with neglect. An average garden soil is best. If the soil is too rich, plants may become tall and lanky and may require staking. Plant cosmos in full sun and make sure the soil is well drained. If you plant in a meadow, it helps to prepare the soil first by tilling or, at a minimum, removing any weeds. Lightly cover seeds with 1/16" of soil. You can sow a few seeds in the same spot and then thin out the weaker seedlings as they start to grow. To have the earliest blooms, sow seeds indoors 2 to 3 weeks before the last frost date. Sowing them directly into individual peat pots will make it easier to transplant them to the garden when the time comes.

CARE AND MAINTENANCE

Once established in the garden, cosmos will thrive even during periods of drought. Starting with robust young plants is further insurance of this. Fertilize young seedlings with a dilute solution, 3/4 strength of the recommended rate for annuals, of 10–10–10. Water young plants until they are about 8" high. Remove spent flowers on a regular basis to encourage a longer bloom time.

ADDITIONAL ADVICE FOR CARE

Cosmos flowers are light and airy and look good when planted in combination with gray-and-silver foliage plants like lamb's ear or artemisia, or with spiky flowers like liatris. Its many different varieties are ideal for cut flowers of every color and height.

ADDITIONAL CULTIVARS AND SPECIES

C. sulphureus 'Ladybird' is a dwarf type growing to 12" with flowers that come in orange, scarlet, and a mixture. There are many different selections of *C. bipinnatus* that are gardenworthy. For unusual flowers, try 'Sea shells.' Its petals are fluted and come in creamy white, pink, and crimson. A tall selection growing 3'–4' is 'Early Sensation,' with flowers of crimson, rose, pink, or white.

Gomphrena globosa

Globe Amaranth

Height: 9"–24"
Flowers: purple, white, pink, yellow, orange Blooms: summer
to frost

An old-fashioned favorite, globe amaranth blooms all summer in Georgia gardens. In the autumn, when many annuals look tired and worn out, it blooms and blooms some more, until finally the plants are killed by a hard frost. The flowers hold their magenta color well, not only in the garden, but also in flower arrangements both fresh and dried. All this dependable annual requires is lots of sun and a well-drained soil. Unlike more demanding plants, it doesn't seem bothered by wind or rain. Whether you use it as an edging plant, in groups throughout the flower garden, or for cut flowers, globe amaranth adds interesting texture; it's hard not to touch its straw-like flower heads. Undaunted by our summers, it makes a good companion for heat-lovers like lantana and perennials like Verbena *'Homestead Purple.' For flower arrangers, the 'Woodcreek' series offers colors in shades of purple, silver, white, and pink; the plants grow 24"–30" tall. Seeds can be sown in clumps where you want them in the garden and thinned out as they develop.*

When to Plant

Plant young plants after the last frost. Sow seeds in the spring when the soil temperatures have warmed. For best results, start seeds indoors 6 to 8 weeks before the frost-free date. To expedite germination, soak seeds in water for 3 to 4 days before planting them. Be sure to cover the seeds with at least 1/4" of soil.

Where to Plant

Plant globe amaranth in the flower garden with other annuals and perennials for long season color. Use smaller varieties for edging or in containers. Larger types make good cutting flowers. The dark fuchsia-colored selection looks good in combination with purple foliage plants like *Alternanthera* 'Wave Hill.'

How to Plant

Globe amaranth likes hot sun and moist, well-drained soils. Amending the soil is not necessary unless it is heavy clay, but tilling in some organic matter will improve the drainage and overall health of the soil. Use 1/3 organic matter, 1/3 coarse sand, and 1/3 of the existing soil.

Care and Maintenance

Plants require no special care or fertilizer but will respond to liquid fertilizer applications during the summer. Check with your local Extension Service for recommended rates. If you want to dry flowers, harvest them just after they are fully open. Hang them upside down to dry and they will hold their color for years.

Additional Advice for Care

Globe amaranth is not a new plant to many gardeners, but the increase in the variety of colors and sizes available has made this tough annual well suited for all styles of gardens in Georgia.

Additional Cultivars and Species

The 'Buddy Series' offers 9"-tall plants for bedding, edging, or cut flowers in reddish-purple or white. 'Strawberry Fields' has bright red flowers and grows 24" tall.

Helianthus annus

Common Sunflower

Height: 2'–10'
Flowers: cream, yellow, burgundy, orange Blooms: summer

*Gardeners and artists alike have long been inspired by sunflowers.
Typically the species has been grown not for its ornamental flowers, but
for seed and seed oil. Yet there's nothing quite so magical as a huge field of
these tall flowers with cheerful yellow faces that follow the sun. Upon close
examination, each face is unique and charming. They are easy to grow, and
by staggering the time that you start seeds you can have sunflowers of all
sizes and colors blooming throughout the summer. With the many hybrids
offered to gardeners today, the flowers range from small flowers 1" across
to the 'Mammoth Russian,' which quickly grows to 12' or more. Large
types can be used to create a screen, a bold accent in the flower or vegetable
garden, or a background in a sunny landscape. Smaller sunflowers can add
bold splashes of yellow, orange, red, rust, or white to the perennial garden
or annual bed. All varieties make great cut flowers, and some produce seed
that is particularly appealing to birds. All gardeners agree that sunflowers
bring beauty to the garden and smiles to our faces.*

WHEN TO PLANT

Once the fear of frost is past and the soil temperatures have begun
to warm, sow sunflower seeds directly in the spots where you want
them to grow. If you start them indoors, sow the seed in peat pots
so you disturb them as little as possible when transplanting to
the garden.

WHERE TO PLANT

Sunflowers are tolerant of drought and heat, but starting them in a
soil that is moist and well drained and has been amended with
some organic matter will help ensure the best flower production.
Sunflowers like full sun and certain varieties need lots of room.
Plant accordingly.

HOW TO PLANT

Planting seed directly in the ground where you want sunflowers to grow and then thinning them out as they develop is the best method. Starting seeds of different types every few weeks will extend the period of bloom over the summer. If you have a problem with rabbits or other creatures looking for tasty young seedlings, be sure to plant extra seed so that you won't be disappointed by having just a few blooms. Planting extra seed is much less labor-intensive and frustrating than starting over.

CARE AND MAINTENANCE

When sunflowers are grown commercially, farmers till the soil, then water and fertilize on a regular basis. While this may not be necessary if you're growing only a few sunflowers, you will get bigger and better blooms if you apply the same principles to growing sunflowers in your own garden.

ADDITIONAL ADVICE FOR CARE

Once sunflowers finish blooming, don't be too quick to cut down the withering stalks. Provided the birds don't eat them first, spent flowerheads left to dry on the plant produce masses of seed which can be used for decorations or stored for next year's crop. Many of the hybrids don't come true from seed, but you can expect interesting flowers of various colors and sizes.

ADDITIONAL CULTIVARS AND SPECIES

A popular variety for the flower border, 'Italian White' grows 4'–6' and produces masses of 4" blooms that are a cream or ivory color. It also makes a good cut flower. For a different color, try 'Sonja' with its flowers that are a deep tangerine orange on $3^{1}/_{2}$'-tall stems. For large flowers, 'Large Flowered Mix' will produce flowers of red, yellow, and bronze that are 6" across on 10'-tall stems.

Impatiens wallerana

Impatiens

Sultana, Busy Lizzie

Height: 6"–18"
Flowers: single or double in all colors Blooms: summer to frost

Impatiens is one of the few annuals that you may actually be ready to pull out before it stops blooming. If the flowers are happy where they grow, next year you will probably be treated to volunteer seedlings that will plant themselves everywhere. Once they are 2"–3" high, impatiens plants are easy to transplant or to pull out. In Georgia and other parts of the South, there never seem to be enough plants that bloom in the shade. Impatiens grows under trees where it is often difficult to get anything to live, let alone bloom all summer. Some varieties grow in the sun and some have handsome variegated foliage. The 1"–2" flowers come in many different shades. The double forms look like tiny roses. The New Guinea impatiens is particularly exotic with its extra-large flowers and variegated foliage. Impatiens is ideal for containers and hanging baskets as well as for color in the shade or flower garden.

WHEN TO PLANT

Plant impatiens in the garden once the fear of frost has passed. Volunteer seedlings may appear in areas where these plants have been grown in the past. Impatiens is easy to propagate by stem cuttings that can be overwintered in the house.

WHERE TO PLANT

Impatiens is ideal for the semi-shade garden, at the edge of a woodland where the soil is rich in organic matter and isn't too dry, or in pots that can be moved around to wherever a spot of color is needed. Impatiens makes beautiful hanging baskets, especially if you keep plants full by pinching them back.

How to Plant

The secret to growing successful impatiens is to start with a moist, well-drained soil that has been amended with organic matter. This can make the difference between small plants and large robust plants. Amend the soil before you plant and you will be rewarded with almost non-stop blooms from summer until frost. If you have planted in a moist, well-drained soil, watered on a regular basis, and fertilized once a month, you will have small bushes of blooms!

Care and Maintenance

If plants get leggy, pinch them back to encourage a bushier habit. Don't let the soil get too dry or wet. Fertilize with a liquid fertilizer once a month. Check with your local Extension Service for recommended rates.

Additional Advice for Care

Impatiens is a good companion for ferns and hostas on the sunny edge of a woodland or in pockets in a semi-shady flower garden. It also looks good growing in combination with larger tropical plants in the garden or in pots. Some of the best varieties have been passed down from one generation to the next.

Additional Cultivars and Species

'Super Elfin' grows 8"–10" and comes in 15 different colors. 'Sun and Shade' series offers strong growers for pots, baskets, window boxes, and bedding plants; it comes in 17 different colors. Seed catalogues list many varieties. Plants with variegated foliage and double flowers are worth seeking out. *Impatiens* 'Rose Parade' has semi-double flowers, in brilliant colors, on 2'-tall plants.

Petunia x hybrida

Petunia

Height: 8"–15"
Flowers: many colors, white to deep purple Blooms: summer
to frost

*For bright color all summer long, petunias are unsurpassed. Georgia
gardeners now have a number of varieties to choose from with brilliantly
colored flowers of various sizes that bloom all summer and into the fall.
These petunias don't need deadheading, and best of all, the flowers hold
up in our heat, humidity, and rain. One of the most popular is the low-
spreading Petunia 'Purple Wave' with its brilliant rose-purple 3" blooms.
Growing only 6" tall, this vigorous hybrid quickly makes an effective
groundcover or hanging basket with long trailing stems up to 5' long.
Equally tolerant of hot, humid weather and full sun, though not as dramatic, is the small petunia Petunia integrifolia. This tiny flowered species has
1/2"–1" magenta blooms marked with deep violet centers and small foliage.
P. integrifolia is ideal for containers, window boxes, hanging baskets, or in
the garden for a spot of intense annual color.*

When to Plant

Start seeds indoors 5 to 6 weeks before the last frost date. Plant the
petunias outside after the fear of frost has passed.

Where to Plant

Plant petunias in hanging baskets, window boxes, containers, or in
the garden for bright annual color. Most varieties of petunia like full
sun, but the wild species will grow and bloom both in sun and in
shade. Hybrids like 'Purple Wave' make good groundcovers and
bloom all summer long.

How to Plant

Plant petunias in light, well-drained soils. The wild species type is
more adaptable to clay soils than the newer hybrids. Be sure to give
the groundcover types plenty of room to spread out in the garden.

CARE AND MAINTENANCE

In the past, most petunia varieties required regular deadheading, or removal of the spent blooms, to ensure long and continued blooming over the summer. Today many of the new hybrids require little deadheading and are better adapted to grow in heat, humidity, and rain. Fertilize these annuals once a month with a liquid both in containers and in the ground. Check with your local Extension Service for recommended rates. Many hybrids are bushy types with mounded growth and require no pruning. Long trailing types may be cut back if the plants get leggy.

ADDITIONAL ADVICE FOR CARE

The wild species are best acquired from seed collected from plants growing in your region or through sources like the *Georgia Farmer's and Consumer's Market Bulletin*. Petunias are easy to grow from seed or cuttings.

ADDITIONAL CULTIVARS AND SPECIES

There are many types of petunias, both single and double. A hybrid of the old-fashioned types, "The Pearl" petunia has single, fragrant 2" flowers that hold up to weather extremes and bloom all summer. In addition to 'Purple Wave,' look for 'Saul's Pink Wave.' *P.* 'Lavender Storm' was developed for its rain-resistant lavender flowers which grow 3" wide on 12" plants.

Portulaca grandiflora

Moss Rose

Height: 6"–8"
Flowers: rose, red, yellow, white, striped Blooms: summer to frost

Moss rose offers Georgia gardeners colorful blooms for hot, dry spots where few other flowers survive. Native to Brazil, this succulent grows happily along the Georgia coast and throughout the state as long as it gets lots of sun and heat. Left undisturbed in the garden, it will reseed freely, offering an ongoing source of plants in many colors. With their fleshy, needle-like leaves, these plants resemble moss plants when they clump together. With its dazzling 1"-wide satiny flowers, this prostrate creeper makes a bright carpet in the rock garden or a colorful edging plant in the flower garden. It is also effective spilling out of window boxes or containers. Fairly drought-tolerant, moss rose is a good companion for other succulents like sedums, hardy cactus, or ornamental grasses. The double-flowered selections look like tiny roses. Unlike some of the older varieties, many of the newer hybrids have flowers that stay open all day. Portulaca 'Afternoon Delight,' a double-flowered type, blooms all day and into the evening.

WHEN TO PLANT

Sow seeds indoors 6–8 weeks before the last frost date. Once they have germinated, thin them out and transplant them to small pots. Harden them off before planting them in the garden once the fear of frost is passed and the soil has warmed up. Seeds may also be sown directly in the garden where they will grow. This should be done once the soil has warmed up in early spring.

WHERE TO PLANT

Plant moss rose in hot, dry, sunny spots in the rock garden, the flower garden, containers, or window boxes. Because it is low and spreading, you can let it trail over a wall or use it as an edging plant creeping along a stone walkway.

HOW TO PLANT

Plant moss rose in a well-drained soil that is not too rich in organic matter. Sandy soils are fine too. Plant this creeper as a filler next to perennials that only bloom for a short time or in combination with other succulents like sedums.

CARE AND MAINTENANCE

Moss rose is a low-maintenance annual. To help young seedlings get started in the garden, make sure they don't dry out. Once it is mature, this tough annual requires no special fertilizer, pruning, or watering and is fairly drought-resistant. If plants are left undisturbed in the garden, they will reseed freely, offering interesting combinations of flower colors each year.

ADDITIONAL ADVICE FOR CARE

Finding annuals that hold up in Georgia summers without constant watering is a challenge. Moss rose is a reliable choice for bright summer color that survives even in the cracks of sidewalks or along the edges of a driveway. It makes a good groundcover on a sunny bank with bright flowers from early summer until frost.

ADDITIONAL CULTIVARS AND SPECIES

There are many cultivars available, both single and double, in every color from the brightest magenta to the softest melon. 'Afternoon Delight' offers many brightly colored flowers that stay open all day. 'Sundial' hybrids bloom earlier than other types, and the double flowers come in many colors. 'Minilaca Mixture' is a dwarf hybrid, and 'Sunglo' offers long-blooming double flowers in 10 shades.

Fan Flower

Height: 6"–1'
Flowers: purple or blue with yellow throat Blooms: summer to frost

When it blooms, fan flower looks like a profusion of tiny purple-blue fans marked with yellow. I think the flowers look more purple, but some describe them as blue. For long-season bloom and easy care, this Australian transplant gets my vote as one of the top ten annuals for Georgia gardens. In the most southern parts of the state, Zones 9 and 10, it may be perennial. In fact, the hotter it gets, the more it seems to thrive. For a striking combination, plant it with the magenta-flowered Petunia integrifolia. *Whether you grow it in hanging baskets, containers, window boxes, or the flower border, fan flower produces sprawling stems of flowering fans from summer until frost. Although it prefers sun, fan flower will tolerate some shade. Plant it in a well-drained soil and cut back plants early in the season if they get too leggy. Combine it with grays, yellows, pinks, and other blues.*
—E.L.G.

WHEN TO PLANT

Plant the fan flower in spring after the fear of frost has passed and the soil has warmed. Propagate it by stem cuttings taken in summer or early fall. Overwinter cuttings in a coldframe, greenhouse, or sunny window.

WHERE TO PLANT

Plant fan flower in containers with other annuals and perennials, in window boxes, in hanging baskets, or in front of the flower border as a border. Use it as a weaver between other annuals and perennials.

HOW TO PLANT

Plant fan flower in full sun or part-shade in a well-drained soil. Cut back plants in midsummer if they get too leggy. Mulch plants in the flower garden to keep the soil from baking in full sun.

CARE AND MAINTENANCE

Fertilize this annual with a liquid once a month. Consult your local Extension Service for recommended rates. If plants get leggy, prune them back in midsummer. This should encourage bushier plants and more blooms. Water during periods of drought.

ADDITIONAL ADVICE FOR CARE

Scaevola offers unusual flowers that bloom over a long period of time. Its diminutive flowers make it adaptable to many types of gardens and containers. With its sprawling habit, it is also suited to the rock garden.

ADDITIONAL CULTIVARS AND SPECIES

There are other ornamental species with similar habits but none are widely available to gardeners.

Purple Heart

Height: 12"
Flowers: violet-purple Blooms: spring to fall

The deep purple foliage of purple heart stands out in a garden. The challenge is where to plant this not-so-subtle showman. A low-maintenance plant, purple heart thrives in all types of soils from clay to sandy, provided they are well drained. This persistent plant tolerates salt spray, making it a good choice for Coastal gardens. One option is to grow it in a container that can serve as a focal point in the flower garden and then be moved around as needed. Sprawling and crawling, this fast spreader is an effective groundcover for a sandy slope. Grow it in hanging baskets, in window boxes, or as a houseplant. Perfect for a red border, it combines well with gray or silver foliage plants. Hardy in Zones 9 and 10, with reports of it being hardy in Zone 7, this tough performer is really more of a tender perennial than an annual. This means that while the foliage is killed back by cold weather, the roots survive and put up new growth the following spring.

WHEN TO PLANT

Plant purple heart in spring or early fall. Tip cuttings should root in a few weeks and can be taken any time during the growing season.

WHERE TO PLANT

With its strong foliage color, purple heart does not fit into every color scheme. Group it with other reds and purples or combine it with gray-and-silver foliage plants. Grow it in a container and move it around the garden wherever a strong color is needed. Use it as a groundcover in coastal areas.

HOW TO PLANT

You can start with new plants each year. Tip cuttings are easy to root. Stick the cuttings in the ground and in about two weeks you will have rooted plants. Purple heart will grow in a wide range of soils including those with a high percentage of clay and sand, provided they are well drained. Plants will rot in soggy soils. Plant purple heart in full sun or part shade.

CARE AND MAINTENANCE

Purple heart is a tough plant with no serious pest or disease problems. Plant it and forget it.

ADDITIONAL ADVICE FOR CARE

Although purple heart may act like a perennial, it is so easy to grow and the color is so strong that it can be treated like an annual and used for seasonal color in the flower garden or in containers. Just propagate new plants using tip cuttings and overwinter them in pots outdoors.

ADDITIONAL CULTIVARS AND SPECIES

A close relative of purple heart is the spiderwort, *Tradescantia* x *andersoniana*. Considered weedy by some, this hardy perennial grows in sun or shade. Unlike purple heart, it tolerates moist to soggy soils. The flowers come in violet-purple, white, pink, or red and are larger than those of purple heart. Spiderwort is a good choice for naturalized areas, wild gardens, and flower borders.

Tithonia rotundifolia

Mexican Sunflower

Torch Flower

Height: 4'–7'
Flowers: orange-scarlet daisies Blooms: summer

*I remember driving by an old country garden in South Georgia and marveling at some small flowering trees with intense orange daisies that seemed to be thriving despite the red clay soil. My impression was that the plants were larger than the house whose front door they framed. They looked like living torches. While in reality these Mexican sunflowers may have been only 7' tall, the effect was dramatic. This tall flowering annual has a coarse texture and colorful flowers that attract butterflies and provide brilliant color in the summer garden. Planted at the back of a flower border, it makes a good companion for black-eyed susans, Joe-Pye weed, and dark purple selections of the butterfly bush. This annual thrives in intense heat and dry conditions. When other annuals are finishing, the torch flower begins to put on its best show. It makes a good screen or background plant and holds up well as a cut flower. For long-season color, grow Mexican sunflowers with a variety of other annual sunflowers, starting seeds at two-week intervals so that you have plants blooming throughout the summer.
—E.L.G.*

WHEN TO PLANT

To sow seeds directly in the garden, wait until the fear of frost has passed and soil temperatures have warmed up. To start seeds indoors, use individual peat pots and sow seeds about 6 weeks before the last frost date.

WHERE TO PLANT

By sowing seeds directly in the garden where they will grow, you will get stronger plants. Plant Mexican sunflower about 2'–4' apart in the garden. Use it as a screen, create a summer hedge or a bold

accent in the flower garden, or use it in combination with other annuals and perennials. Site it at the middle or back of the border, where its large scale can be appreciated.

HOW TO PLANT

Mexican sunflower is not particular about the type of soil it grows in, but with a moderately fertile soil, plants will grow to great heights. Plant it in full sun where it will have plenty of room to grow.

CARE AND MAINTENANCE

A light application of liquid fertilizer once or twice during the growing season and watering during periods of drought will keep plants vigorous and blooming. On occasion, plants may need staking if they are not rooted well or watered thoroughly. If they are planted in groups, Mexican sunflowers can help support one another.

ADDITIONAL ADVICE FOR CARE

This plant is a must for attracting butterflies and hummingbirds to the garden. Planted in a group or as a single specimen late in the summer, it adds welcome color with which few other annuals can compete.

ADDITIONAL CULTIVARS AND SPECIES

There are a number of dwarf cultivars including 'Goldfinger,' which grows 2'–3', 'Torch,' which grows 3'–4', and 'Yellow Torch,' which grows 3'–4' and has yellow flowers.

Torenia fournieri

Wishbone Flower

Clown Flower

Height: 12"
Flowers: pale lilac-blue with velvety dark-purple blotched bottom lip; inside of throat is marked with yellow Blooms: summer to frost

The wishbone flower gets its name from the wishbone-shaped stamens found inside the flower's throat. It is also called the clown flower, as it has colorful, two-toned, spotted flowers. Reminiscent of snapdragons, a 1½"-long tubular flower is like a small tumpet with a pronounced flare. Both the flowers and seed pods look like tiny Chinese lanterns. This enchanting annual comes to us from Asia. It adapts to a wide range of growing conditions in our Southern climate. The wishbone flower grows in sun or shade and in dry or moist soil, but it prefers moist soil. If there is a prolonged period of drought, a little water quickly revives plants. When in flower, this profuse bloomer's foliage is barely visible. Use it as a bedding plant in the flower garden, in the shade garden, in pots, and window boxes. The wishbone flower is a viable alternative to impatiens for long-season color in the shade garden. It can also be used in full sun, and it loves humidity!

WHEN TO PLANT

Wait until the fear of frost is past and the soil temperatures have warmed up before you sow seed in the garden. The seed needs light to germinate. Plants normally begin to bloom in early July. For earlier blooms, start seeds indoors and transplant young plants to the garden.

WHERE TO PLANT

Plant the wishbone flower in the shade garden, in a sunny flower border, in containers, or in window boxes. They look good in a mass planting and bloom almost continuously through the summer until frost.

HOW TO PLANT

The wishbone flower will grow in sun or shade, but plants like humidity and a moist soil. A moderately fertile soil is best and plants respond to regular watering, especially during periods of drought. Plants reseed freely and are easy to move in any stage of development.

CARE AND MAINTENANCE

The wishbone flower requires no special care, but for maximum blooms use liquid fertilizer once a month during the growing season. Consult with your local cooperative Extension Service for recommended rates. Occasionally, plants will get leggy. Just pinch them back and they should produce new growth in no time. If plants dry out on a regular basis, the flowers will begin to look worn and faded.

ADDITIONAL ADVICE FOR CARE

Torenia is an old-fashioned plant that blooms in the summer garden with little or no care and thrives with a bit of attention. The colorful flowers are a welcome alternative to the impatiens that we see everywhere in Georgia gardens. They reward us by reseeding freely, providing sources of plants for next year and for years to come.

ADDITIONAL CULTIVARS AND SPECIES

The 'Clown' series offers colors of blue, blue-and-white, burgundy, rose, violet, and a mixture. 'Compacta Blue' grows to 8" tall and has blue flowers with violet-and-yellow blotches on the lips. The 'Panda' series has blue or pink flowers on plants that grow 8"–10" tall. *Torenia baillonii* 'Suzie Wong' grows to 8". Its flowers are an intense yellow with a deep purple-red, almost black, throat.

Viola x wittrockiana

Pansies

Height: 4"–8"
Flowers: usually 3 colors, many combinations Blooms: fall to spring

In Georgia, particularly in the middle and northern parts of the state, pansies are popular for the flower garden or for growing in containers. Planted in the fall, they bloom for months during the winter, their colorful faces providing cheer on all but the coldest of days. Even when plants look shriveled and wilted from extreme cold, with just a bit of warmth and sunshine they are quick to recover and continue blooming until well into spring. In early spring they become an elegant carpet for early bulbs such as tulips to pop through. For a different effect, combine them with edible and ornamental plants like red mustard greens, lettuces, ornamental cabbages, kale, and parsley. There are innumerable cultivars to choose from, but a few stand out as good performers. These include the 'Crystal Bowl' series with flowers that are 2" across and 8" tall; they are clear-faced, early-flowering heavy bloomers. Look for the species Viola tricolor*, the familiar johnny-jump-up, and other small flowered violas.*

WHEN TO PLANT

Plant pansies or violas in the fall for color through the winter and into spring. Summer heat will greatly reduce flowering.

WHERE TO PLANT

Plant pansies in containers, in window boxes, or in a flower border; or use them as bedding plants. They like full sun or part shade. For an interesting effect, combine them with ornamental cabbages, lettuces, parsley, and bright-colored dianthus.

HOW TO PLANT

Plant pansies in a cool, moist, well-drained soil. The larger types will spread and should be planted on about 3" centers. To encourage vigorous plants, pinch off the flower buds when you first plant them for fuller and healthier plants.

CARE AND MAINTENANCE

Pansies respond well to a moist, moderately fertile soil that is well drained. Fertilize them with a liquid fertilizer once a month during the growing season. Consult with your local Extension Service for recommended rates. If plants get leggy or suffer from stem rot, leaf spots, or anthracnose, just cut them back and they will put out new growth.

ADDITIONAL ADVICE FOR CARE

Pansies come in a wide range of colors and sizes and offer bright flowers intermittently through winter. *Viola tricolor*, johnny-jump-up, often reseeds itself. It delights us by showing up where we least expect it, blooming happily in lawns, beds, and borders. The tiny edible 1" flowers have a mild wintergreen flavor, making them perfect for use as a garnish in salads or to decorate cakes.

ADDITIONAL CULTIVARS AND SPECIES

Viola pedata, the bird's foot violet, is a hardy perennial that is native to Georgia. It requires a well-drained soil and occurs naturally along road cuts or rock outcroppings where the soil is coarse and gritty. Other ornamental selections of pansies include the 'Antique Shades' with flower colors in soft pastels and the 'Ultima Lavender Shades,' which have 2"-wide flowers that grow on 8" high plants.

Zinnia

Height: 6"–12"
Flowers: orange Blooms: summer to frost

Popular as bedding plants and in long-lasting bouquets, zinnias have long been grown for their brilliantly colored blooms. One of the drawbacks of growing zinnias is that often in our hot humid weather they are attacked by the powdery mildew which causes foliage to look gray and unsightly. With Zinnia linearis, this does not happen. A much smaller plant with a spreading habit, the flowers look quite different than those most of us know to be zinnias, but its vigor and long season of bloom make this gem worth seeking out. Effective as a groundcover or border plant, the 1½"-wide, intensely orange flowers look like minature daisies that glow in the garden, from late spring until frost. This tiny zinnia is also a good choice for containers and window boxes and for filling in places in the flower border where perennials bloomed earlier in the season. The strong orange color is not always easy to work into color schemes, but this heat-tolerant zinnia also comes in white and a softer yellow.

WHEN TO PLANT

Start seeds indoors in late April or early May. These plants resent having their roots disturbed, so sow seeds directly into peat pots. Plant them in the garden once the soil has warmed up.

WHERE TO PLANT

Plant zinnias in the front of the border, in window boxes, in containers, or in combination with other sun-loving annuals and perennials. For a striking contrast, plant them with 'Homestead Purple' verbena, or grow the orange and white forms together.

HOW TO PLANT

Although they will tolerate average garden soils, zinnias do best if planted in a moist, well-drained soil that has been amended with organic matter. For best flowering, zinnias need full sun and warm temperatures.

CARE AND MAINTENANCE

Zinnia linearis loves long, hot days and will tolerate some drought. It is true, however, that the better the soil is, the better the blooms will be. Apply liquid fertilizer once a month during the growing season to keep plants vigorous. Check with your local Extension Service for recommended rates. If plants get too large for an area, cut them back and they will quickly become bushy again. This should be done early in the summer.

ADDITIONAL ADVICE FOR CARE

Strains of the old-fashioned *Z. elegans* have been bred to resist powdery mildew. They make great cut flowers. While *Z. linearis* will never replace *Z. elegans*, it makes a good choice for a long-blooming, heat-tolerant annual to use spilling out of containers or as a groundcover. *Z. linearis* also makes a good cut flower and holds its color well as a dried flower.

ADDITIONAL CULTIVARS AND SPECIES

Each petal of *Zinnia linearis* 'Golden Orange' is highlighted with a lemon stripe. For pure white flowers, use 'Tropic Snow.' A mix offers a range of colors: white, primrose yellow, golden yellow, and orange.

Bulbs

*L*ONG BEFORE THE TERM "LOW-MAINTENANCE *gar-*
dening" was coined by writers and garden centers, many bulbs
had been providing years of blooms while requiring very little in return. I
have discovered and helped "rescue" heirloom varieties of daffodils thriving
in old abandoned gardens on back country roads throughout Georgia.
Planted by gardeners of times past, these daffodils provide confirmation of
the fact that, unlike many other types of plants, perennial bulbs have the
ability not only to survive but to thrive without much care.—E.L.G.

The treasures that we plant so hopefully in their dormant stage,
in anticipation of the flowers that will spring forth at another
season, are not all true bulbs. But all have certain characteristics in
common. Whether they are bulbs, rhizomes, corms, or tubers, all are
plants that go through a period of no foliage when the root system
may die away, only to be replaced by a new one. During the dormant period (when growth is slowed to a minimum), portions of
the plant underground contain stored food, leaves, flowers, and
seeds. The dormant stage can be extended if the bulbs are dug up
when they are leafless and rootless. Provided they are kept cool and
dry, they can be transported great distances with relative ease.
Because of this unique characteristic, we are able to import bulbs
from all parts of the world. While many of these are raised commercially in Holland, an equal number that grow in our gardens are
native to other countries, including some in Africa and some in the
Mediterranean. In Georgia, a great number of these bulbs naturalize
as perennials and reward us with flowers year after year.

PLANTING AND CARING FOR YOUR BULBS
When you receive your bulbs, make sure they are firm and dry.
Plant dormant bulbs like daffodils, crocuses, and alliums as soon as
you receive them in the fall. To encourage the best growth, plant
your spring-flowering bulbs when the ground temperature is at or

below 60 degrees F. In Georgia, this is usually in November or later. If you don't get your bulbs planted right away, store them in a cool, dry place. This will keep them from drying out or rotting. Even if you plant your bulbs in January, they may bloom the following spring; if they don't, they will probably catch up the following year.

As with all plants, the better the soil, the more vigorous the bulbs and the bigger the blooms will be. Amend soils with ample amounts of organic matter and make sure they are well drained, especially during the winter months. For the best results, fertilize every fall with a bulb fertilizer. Some gardeners mark their bulbs with golf tees, making it easier to see where to apply fertilizer in the fall when no foliage is visible.

The best time to divide many bulbs—such as daffodils—is after they have bloomed in the spring and the foliage has begun to turn yellow. You can replant them immediately or store them and replant them in the fall.

Fastidious gardeners have been known to tie their daffodil foliage into bunches when they finish blooming. Not only is this unsightly, it can hinder the bulbs in the process of taking in needed oxygen and sunlight they need to build essential food reserves for next year's blooms.

Brent Heath of the Daffodil Mart recommends that gardeners wait at least eight to ten weeks before cutting off the dying foliage. As an alternative to torturing plants unnecessarily by tying them up, interplant your daffodils and other bulbs with perennials whose foliage will help mask the awkward stage many bulbs go through. Whether you grow daffodils or ginger lilies, many bulbs are long-lived perennials that will provide years of enjoyment with very little effort.

Allium sphaerocephalum

Drumstick Allium

Height: 15"–30"
Flowers: white, yellow, lavender, pink, purple Blooms: May to July

Best known for its edible members—onions, leeks, chives, and garlic—the genus Allium *includes many types that have beautiful flowers. While it's true that all the members of this group have a distinct onion smell in foliage and bulbs, the rounded clusters of flowers exhibit a wide range of colors and sizes. From the small Naples garlic,* A. neapolitanum, *which has white flowers on 10"–20" stems in early spring, to the giant onion,* A. giganteum, *which produces 5"–6" wide globes of lilac-pink flowers atop 3'–4' tall stems in summer, ornamental onions represent a diverse group of bulbs. Many, like the drumstick allium, an heirloom variety introduced in 1594, make choice, long-lasting perennials in the flower border. The rich purple blooms of the drumstick allium arrive late, usually in June. The flowers seem to float in the air as if by magic on 2'–3'-tall erect stems. Drumstick alliums add welcome color when combined with lilies and daylilies or the large leaves and flowers of old-fashioned crinums.*

WHEN TO PLANT
Plant allium bulbs in the fall. In Georgia, it is a good idea to plant your bulbs between October and December.

WHERE TO PLANT
Plant drumstick alliums in the flower border, mix them in with other perennials or shrubs, or plant them in a mass. They make excellent cut flowers and many hold up well as dried flowers. Tip: use golf tees to mark where your bulbs are planted.

HOW TO PLANT
Plant your bulbs as soon as you receive them in the fall. If you have to store them, make sure they stay dry and have plenty of ventilation. As a general rule, plant bulbs at a depth of 3 times the height

ZONE
6,7,8

of the bulb, and space them at 3 times the width of the bulb on center. *Allium sphaerocephalum* bulbs are about the size of a quarter. Space them at a distance of about 10 per square foot. Prepare your beds ahead of time. Make sure the soil is well drained, and for best results, amend it with organic matter. Plant drumstick alliums in full sun or partial shade with other perennials for late-season color.

CARE AND MAINTENANCE

Bulb expert Brent Heath of the Daffodil Mart in Gloucester, Virginia, recommends topdressing bulbs in the fall after you plant them rather than putting fertilizer directly in the planting bed. By following his advice you will not have to worry about the tendency of fertilizer to burn bulbs and cause them to rot. He also stresses that, contrary to popular thinking, bone meal is not a complete fertilizer and for best results you should use a slow-release fertilizer like *Holland Bulb Booster* with a formula of 9–9–6. Broadcast the fertilizer in the fall after you plant the bulbs.

ADDITIONAL ADVICE FOR CARE

You may use organic fertilizers like *Bulb Mate* (5–10–12). Derived from cricket manure, it also contains rock phosphate, bone meal, dolomitic limestone, granite meal, and compost. Such organic fertilizers can be incorporated into the soil at the time of planting and broadcast every fall thereafter without fear of burning bulbs.

ADDITIONAL CULTIVARS AND SPECIES

A. caeruleum has clear, true-blue, rounded flowers on 12"–18" stems. It makes a good combination with yellow and orange-flowered perennials in May. For unusual flowers, try *A. christophii*. It has large, silvery, spider-like flower heads that grow 12"–20".

Caladium bicolor

Caladium

Height: 1'–2'
Flowers: grown for their colorful foliage

Splendid foliage plants in the summer, caladiums provide a long season of beauty with a minimum amount of effort. Relatives of the old-fashioned elephant ears, the flattened tubers quickly grow into lush plants in our humid Georgia summers. Caladiums need a rich soil, warmth, abundant moisture, and bright, filtered light to thrive. If they are set out too early in the spring, before the soil temperatures have warmed up, they will rot in no time. The foliage comes in shades of white, red, green, and various combinations of these colors. Some leaves are one solid color and others are marked with veins of another color like the hybrid 'Candidum' with its large, silvery-white leaves and dark green veins. This old-fashioned variety is a strong grower and tolerates direct sun better than many of the other hybrids. Dramatic as bedding plants or in containers, caladium leaves begin to flop with the first cool days of autumn. At this point you should reduce watering. When they have died down, the tubers can be lifted and stored for the winter. Be sure to keep them dry and warm until next spring.

WHEN TO PLANT

Plant caladium tubers in the spring after the soil has warmed up. Roots can be started in the early spring if they are potted and kept indoors near a warm, sunny window.

WHERE TO PLANT

Plant caladiums as bedding plants, in containers, or at the edge of a woodland garden for summer color. Caladiums thrive with bright, filtered light but there are varieties that will tolerate full sun. If they are planted in too much shade, the colors will not be as brilliant.

HOW TO PLANT

Caladiums need a soil that is well drained, rich in organic matter, and reasonably fertile. They also need abundant moisture during the growing season. The tubers have visible eyes on tops of the dormant roots, which contain buds of the flower spikes. Since caladiums are grown primarily for their showy foliage, cutting off the larger-growing points before they are planted will result in vigorous plants with more side branching. Since the roots sprout from the tops of the tubers, they should be planted at least an inch deep.

CARE AND MAINTENANCE

Make sure caladiums don't dry out, especially when they are getting established. Fertilize with a liquid fertilizer like 10-10-10 once a month during the growing season. Read the label for recommended rates, or check with your local cooperative Extension Service. After the leaves have died down in the fall, lift the tubers and store them in a warm, dry place until next spring. Remove the greenish flowers as they appear. This will help the plant use all of its energy to grow beautiful foliage.

ADDITIONAL ADVICE FOR CARE

Caladiums make good companions for autumn, cinnamon, and royal ferns. They provide long-season color and suffer from no serious pest or disease problems. Caladiums must be dug up and stored for the winter in all but the warmest parts of Georgia.

ADDITIONAL CULTIVARS AND SPECIES

There are numerous cultivars available. If you garden in full sun, be sure to choose varieties that have been developed to tolerate sun. 'Pink Beauty' has soft pink colors on a deep green background with rose veins. 'Red Flash' has waxy leaves with bright red centers, deep red veins, pink mottling, and green edging. 'Frieda Hemple' has solid red leaves with a green border and grows to 18".

Canna x generalis

Canna

Height: 1'–5'
Flowers: pink, orange, red, scarlet Blooms: mid- to late summer

In Victorian times, cannas were planted for their exotic tropical foliage. Still popular with Georgia gardeners, today there are hybrids that offer both striking flowers and luxuriant foliage. With leaves 2'–6' long, in shades of green, blue-green, and bronze, these perennials make a bold statement in the perennial border, in containers, as bedding plants, or as specimens. In Zones 8–10, canna rhizomes can be left in the ground all winter if they are mulched for protection against penetrating frost. There are two aquatic varieties that are native to Southern swamps, C. flaccida and C. glauca, both with yellow flowers. The hybrids range in size from the giant types like 'Red King Humbert,' growing to 7' with spectacular bronze-red foliage and brilliant red flowers, to the dwarf 'Tropical Rose' that only grows 2½'–3' at maturity. Canna flowers are usually divided into two groups, the orchid-flowered and the gladiolus-flowered. Both types are robust and free-flowering. While many are grown from rhizomes, annual types like the 'Seven Dwarfs Mix' can also be grown from seed.

When to Plant

Plant canna rhizomes in the spring after the fear of frost is over and soil temperatures have warmed. You can also start the rhizomes earlier in sand or soil and then transplant them outdoors after the frost-free date. If you grow them from seed, it is best to break the hard seed coats first. Then seeds may be soaked in water and allowed to swell before planting.

Where to Plant

Large types can be used for a colorful screen in the summer, in containers, or as a focal point in the flower border. Dwarf varieties can be grown as bedding plants in combination with other annuals, in containers, or in the flower border. Plant cannas in full sun.

HOW TO PLANT

While it's true that cannas are robust plants, for best performance plant them in a soil that is fertile, rich in organic matter, and well drained (except for the types which occur naturally in swampy areas). In the spring, cut the rhizomes so that they contain at least 2 or 3 eyes. These are the points from which new growth (buds, shoots and roots) will generate. Plant rhizomes 18"–24" apart, or more if you are planting clumps of established plants. Cover the roots with 4"–6" of soil.

CARE AND MAINTENANCE

For the best blooms, fertilize cannas with a liquid fertilizer once a month. Check with your local cooperative Extension Service for recommended rates. If the soil is amended before planting with an abundance of organic matter, established plants should need very little extra watering during the growing season. After the foliage is killed by frost, cut off the dead leaves, leaving 6"–8" of stem above the ground. This will make it easier to lift the rhizomes for storage or to mark where plants are so that they can be mulched for the winter. It is best to wait until spring to divide the rhizomes.

ADDITIONAL ADVICE FOR CARE

If you store canna rhizomes over the winter, make sure that they don't dry out or they will shrivel and rot. Store them in moist peat in a ventilated room at 45 to 50 degrees F. Some varieties of canna are worth growing just for their bold, architectural foliage. An old variety with bronze leaves, still found in some Southern gardens, is 'Robusta.' When grown in a rich soil it can reach a height of 9'–12'.

ADDITIONAL CULTIVARS AND SPECIES

There are many giant cannas to choose from. 'City of Portland,' with rosy pink flowers and green leaves, grows to 42". 'Wyoming' has golden-orange flowers and 5'–6' bronze-red foliage. The 'Grand Opera' series has gladiolus-like flowers in colors of rose, rosy peach, and canary yellow. 'Bengal Tiger' has variegated foliage and bright orange flowers.

Crinum

Height: 2'–3'
Flowers: pink to white Blooms: summer to fall

With their intensely fragrant flowers, lush foliage, and ability to tolerate poor soils and unpredictable weather, crinums have been a stalwart part of Southern gardens for generations. Established clumps thrive with equal abandon in antebellum estates and old country gardens. The large strap-like foliage is whorled in rosettes. Like giant rain lilies, crinums respond to the first rains of summer and continue throughout the year, sending out new foliage and flower stalks. Blooms occur as soon as ten days after a rain, with 15 or more per stalk and new buds opening each night. Long-lived perennials, they resent having their roots disturbed and produce more flowers if they are left in the same spot for several years. In their native habitat crinums grow in areas where seasonal flooding occurs, including swamps and coastal dune areas. In the garden, they will grow in heavy clay, but like many subtropicals they will reward you with more flowers if they are grown in a soil that is rich in organic matter.

WHEN TO PLANT

Plant crinums in the spring after the frost-free date. Containerized plants can also be planted in the summer, giving them enough time to establish roots before cold weather sets in.

WHERE TO PLANT

Crinums need lots of room. For this reason they make a bold accent or focal point in the perennial border. They will tolerate full sun or partial shade. In deep shade they will produce very few flowers. They also make an unusual groundcover for a bank or slope where their foliage provides interest year round. Crinums may also be grown in pots or at the edge of a pond where they will respond to extra moisture.

How to Plant

Crinums will tolerate heavy clay soils and grow in areas where the soil is subject to periods of wet and dry. For best results, amend the soil before planting with liberal amounts of organic matter. Plant bulbs at least 12"–18" deep, but make sure the necks are not buried. Mulch plants to keep the roots cool during the summer and to protect the bulbs from freezing in the winter. Plant crinums in full sun or partial shade.

Care and Maintenance

Fertilize bulbs with a liquid fertilizer to encourage lush growth and lots of blooms. Check with your local cooperative Extension Service for recommended rates. Dividing established plantings is a big undertaking, and you will need a strong back and a sharp spade. After they are divided, plants usually take several years to reestablish and produce flowers again, so it is best to divide them only every 3 to 5 years. Topdressing with organic matter in the fall helps to keep bulbs vigorous and encourages production of more flowers. Crinums require no pruning, but tattered leaves can be cut back if they become unsightly.

Additional Advice for Care

Interplanting crinums with the ornamental drumstick allium makes a stunning combination. Because it produces a great amount of seed, *C. bulbispermum* is responsible for a great number of hybrids and is the forerunner of many garden varieties of crinums.

Additional Cultivars and Species

Milk-and-wine lilies have flowers with a reddish stripeing. These popular flowers are the result of a cross between *C. bulbispermum* and *C. seylanicum*. *C.* 'Ellen Bosanquet' has rich burgundy flowers that first appear in June and continue on and off into the fall.

Crocus tommasinianus

Tommies

Height: 2"–3"
Flowers: reddish violet Blooms: January to March

Harbingers of spring, these tiny crocus, known affectionately as tommies, are happy and long-lived in Georgia gardens. While other species don't seem to like our climate and persist for only a year or two, tommies thrive for years. On sunny days in late winter to early spring, their spear-like silver-gray buds open to form a carpet of reddish-violet blooms. In March, the grassy green foliage appears and provides an accent for the colorful flowers. This gem will grow happily in the lawn, the front of the perennial border, or a rock garden. Because it spreads freely by seed, it is easy to have a large mass of color in no time. Tommies are also good to use in combination with other later-blooming bulbs like daffodils. Unlike many other crocus, tommies are squirrel-resistant. This makes them even more appealing to gardeners who have watched a brazen squirrel dig up other types of crocus even while they were blooming! With the exception of Coastal gardens, most parts of Georgia will allow tommies to thrive.

WHEN TO PLANT

Plant bulbs as soon as you receive them in the fall. In Georgia, it is best to plant bulbs after soil temperatures have begun to cool, usually between November and December.

WHERE TO PLANT

Plant tommies in the rock garden, perennial garden, or lawn, or force them in pots. Planted along the edge of a walk or atop a stone wall where they can be easily viewed, these tiny flowers are sure to delight.

HOW TO PLANT

Plant your bulbs as soon as you receive them in the fall. If you have to store them, make sure they stay dry and have plenty of

ventilation. As a general rule, plant bulbs at a depth of 3 times the height of the bulb and space them at 3 times the width of the bulb on center. Be sure to plant tommies in a soil that is well drained. Because they are small, planting them in groups of 10 to 20 bulbs per group makes for an effective display in the spring. Rather than planting individual bulbs, dig out an area, place them in a group, then cover them with soil. Plant crocus in full sun or partial shade. Deciduous shade is fine.

CARE AND MAINTENANCE

Bulb expert Brent Heath of the Daffodil Mart in Gloucester, Virginia, recommends topdressing bulbs in the fall after you plant them rather than putting fertilizer directly in the planting bed. By following his advice, you will not have to worry about the tendency of fertilizer to burn bulbs and cause them to rot. He also stresses that, contrary to popular thinking, bone meal is not a complete fertilizer and for best results you should use a slow-release fertilizer like *Holland Bulb Booster* with a formula of 9-9-6. Broadcast the fertilizer in the fall after you plant the bulbs.

ADDITIONAL ADVICE FOR CARE

Crocus can also be planted in combination with groundcovers like the tiny *Laurentia fluviatilis*, known as the blue star creeper, or the variegated creeping jenny.

ADDITIONAL CULTIVARS AND SPECIES

C. tommasinianus 'Barr's Purple' has larger flowers that are a rich purple color. 'Albus' has white flowers that are sometimes straw-colored on the outside. 'Lilac Beauty' has slender flowers that are pale lilac outside and violet inside. 'Ruby Giant' has reddish-purple flowers. It is one of the most vigorous and showiest of the tommies.

Hedychium coronarium

Ginger Lily

or Butterfly Ginger

Height: 3′–6′
Flowers: white, fragrant Blooms: late summer to frost

Just a few blooms of the powerfully fragrant ginger lily can perfume an entire garden and elicit praise from those not familiar with its intoxicating scent. The fragrance becomes even more intense in the evening. The rhizomes are also fragrant; some even use them in cooking as a substitute for commercial ginger. Considered charming in its native India, the ginger lily is equally popular in Southern gardens where it thrives in sun or partial shade. Producing eye-catching 2″-wide snowy blossoms from late summer to frost, once it is established in your garden you will have plenty to share with friends and relatives. With its large canna-like foliage, this easy-to-grow perennial adds an exotic touch to the formal or cottage garden. Just give it an average garden soil and plenty of moisture during the growing season. In most parts of Georgia, except for the very coldest parts, rhizomes should overwinter in the ground. Apply a good 2″–3″ layer of mulch. This plant is a survivor that is commonly found thriving in "old homesites" where the house and garden have long been abandoned.

WHEN TO PLANT
Divide and plant rhizomes in early spring just before growth begins and the frost-free date has passed.

WHERE TO PLANT
Plant ginger lily in a spot where you can appreciate its fragrant flowers in late summer to autumn. Give the plants some space to spread out. The canes grow 4′–6′ tall before they begin to produce flowers, and the rhizomes spread quickly to form large clumps up

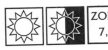

to 3' across. Plant them at the back of a flower border, as a focal point in a shrub border, or as a specimen. They make good understory plants.

How to Plant

For best results, plant ginger lilies in open shade or partial sun. They will tolerate more sun, especially if they are planted in a soil that is moist and rich in organic matter. When you plant the roots, don't plant them too deep. The soil should just cover the thick rhizomes. Ginger lilies love humidity and thrive in Georgia summers, coming to life late in the season when many other plants are tired and wilted.

Care and Maintenance

For best flowering, lift and divide clumps of ginger lilies every 3 or 4 years. It should be noted that clumps have been known to flower happily for years and years without any special care. Apply a thick layer of mulch in the fall to help protect the roots from freezing. Leaving the dried foliage on plants until the following spring is another way to help plants overwinter.

Additional Advice for Care

Ginger lilies are used to make perfume and as a lei flower in Hawaii. The scent of the flowers has been described as "a syrup of orange and honeysuckle that lingers even in wilting."

Additional Cultivars and Species

H. flavescens has yellow blooms with light orange-toned eyes. The flowers are larger than the ginger lily, up to 3" across, and very fragrant. Other fragrant selections to look for include *H.* 'Pink Beauty,' *H.* 'Lemon Beauty,' and *H.* 'Gold Flame.'

Hyacinthoides hispanica (Scilla campanulata)

Spanish Bluebell

or Wood Hyacinth

Height: 12"–16"
Flowers: blue, pink, white Blooms: April to May

*This heirloom bulb adapts well to shady Georgia gardens, where it natural-
izes easily in a deciduous woodland, or anywhere where it receives plenty of
moisture in the spring. In April, the 12"–16" spires are hung with 10–20
bell-shaped blossoms, each about 3/4" long. The flowers come in shades of
lavender, lavender-blue, lilac-pink, and white. The numerous shiny leaves
are about 8" long and 1/2" wide. The bulbs quickly seed and multiply to
form carpets of color under trees or in the perennial border. Although the
flowers come in different colors, confine mass plantings to one color for the
best effect. The flowers are fragrant. Spanish bluebells also make good cut
flowers. Tolerant of moisture, they also seem happy in full sun. Spanish
bluebells make an effective mass planting, or they can be planted with ferns
and other shade-loving perennials. The related English bluebell, H. non-
scripta, is less suited to the heat and humidity of Southern gardens.*

WHEN TO PLANT
Plant bulbs as soon as you receive them in the fall. In Georgia, it
is best to plant bulbs after soil temperatures have begun to cool,
usually between November and December.

WHERE TO PLANT
Plant Spanish bluebells in the deciduous woodland garden in
masses or in combination with other shade-loving perennials like
hostas and ferns. Plant them near a pond or stream that receives
lots of moisture in the spring. Plant them in rows in the cut-flower
garden.

ZONE
6,7,8

HOW TO PLANT

Plant your bulbs as soon as you receive them in the fall. If you have
to store them, make sure they stay dry and have plenty of ventilation. As a general rule, plant bulbs at a depth of 3 times the height of
the bulb, and space them at 3 times the width of the bulb on center.
Plant Spanish bluebells in a soil that is moist and moderately
fertile. Cover the bulbs with 3"–4" of soil and plant them 5"–6" or
10"–12" apart, depending on the effect you desire.

CARE AND MAINTENANCE

Bulb expert Brent Heath of the Daffodil Mart in Gloucester, Virginia,
recommends topdressing bulbs in the fall after you plant them
rather than putting fertilizer directly in the planting bed. By following his advice, you will not have to worry about the tendency of
fertilizer to burn bulbs and cause them to rot. He also stresses that,
contrary to popular thinking, bone meal is not a complete fertilizer
and for best results you should use a slow-release fertilizer like
Holland Bulb Booster with a formula of 9-9-6. Broadcast the fertilizer
in the fall after you plant the bulbs.

ADDITIONAL ADVICE FOR CARE

For a colorful combination in the woodland garden, plant Spanish
bluebells with ajuga, Japanese painted ferns, *Pulmonaria spp.,* giant
bleeding hearts, and the cardinal flower.

ADDITIONAL CULTIVARS AND SPECIES

'Danube' has dark blue flowers. 'Excelsior,' an heirloom variety that
dates to 1906, has deep violet-blue flowers and is larger than most of
the Spanish bluebells. Another heirloom variety is 'Rose Queen.' It
has pink flowers clustered at the top of the stem, slightly curved
petals, and yellow anthers. A robust white selection from 1944 is
'White Triumphator.'

Leucojum aestivum

Summer Snowflake

Height: 12"–18"
Flowers: white, green-tipped Blooms: April to June

Native to the Mediterranean, the summer snowflake benefits from excess spring moisture and a long summer baking, making it right at home in Georgia gardens. It grows happily in a range of soil types, including heavy clay and moist sand. Masses of lush green foliage set off the clusters of 2 to 5 flowers that spray out from the top about 12" high. The bell-like flowers are white and green-tipped, about 3/4" long. The large-flowered selection 'Gravetye Giant' originated in the garden of the famous English horticulturist William Robinson. A robust form, it has 5–7 flowers per stem and grows 18"–24". A great bulb for naturalizing, plant at least 6 bulbs in a group for the best effect. It grows with vigor in sun or shade and also tolerates moist soils. The blooms are slightly scented and make excellent cut flowers. Despite its name, the summer snowflake begins to bloom in spring and continues into the summer. The summer snowflake is a reliable early-blooming bulb that perennializes easily in Southern gardens, offering blooms for years to come.

WHEN TO PLANT
Plant bulbs as soon as you receive them in the fall. In Georgia, it is best to plant bulbs after soil temperatures have begun to cool, usually between November and December.

WHERE TO PLANT
Plant summer snowflakes in mass plantings, in natural areas, near ponds and streams, and in the woodland garden with other shade-tolerant bulbs like the Spanish bluebells. Summer snowflakes will grow in sun or shade.

BULBS

How to Plant

Plant your bulbs as soon as you receive them in the fall. If you have to store them, make sure they stay dry and have plenty of ventilation. As a general rule, plant bulbs at a depth of 3 times the height of the bulb and space them at 3 times the width of the bulb on center. Plant summer snowflakes 3"–4" deep, 5 to 6 bulbs per square foot.

Care and Maintenance

Bulb expert Brent Heath of the Daffodil Mart in Gloucester, Virginia, recommends topdressing bulbs in the fall after you plant them rather than putting fertilizer directly in the planting bed. By following his advice, you will not have to worry about the tendency of fertilizer to burn bulbs and cause them to rot. He also stresses that, contrary to popular thinking, bone meal is not a complete fertilizer and for best results you should use a slow-release fertilizer like *Holland Bulb Booster* with a formula of 9–9–6. Broadcast the fertilizer in the fall after you plant the bulbs.

Additional Advice for Care

While summer snowflakes are in general more robust than snowdrops, *Galanthus spp.*, there are a few types of snowdrops that are worth seeking out for their early blooms (January–March). Unlike most bulbs, the best time to divide snowdrops is immediately after they finish blooming. It is best to acquire these bulbs from another gardener in your area who has been successful growing them.

Additional Cultivars and Species

Both snowdrops and snowflakes are members of the amaryllis family. If you want to plant snowdrops, try *Galanthus* 'S. Arnott,' a larger and more vigorous hybrid.

Lycoris radiata

Spider Lilies

Surprise Lilies

Height: 12"–18"
Flowers: coral-red Blooms: September

One of the great things about gardening in Georgia is our long growing season. Just when we are ready to abandon the garden until spring, it seems to rejuvenate with the first days of fall, offering us colorful foliage, fruits, and flowers. Bulbs like the old-fashioned tried-and-true surprise lilies pop up out of the ground in late August to September. Planted in the woodland garden, the spidery, almost fluorescent, coral-red flowers stand out against nature's carpet of brown leaves. The foliage comes up after the bulbs have bloomed and persists through the winter. Imported strains of the spider lilies offered by many companies today may not be as vigorous as those that you get from old established gardens in the South. It appears that these older selections are better able to tolerate less-than-ideal soils and growing conditions. This is a good reason to share your plants with other gardeners: to help make sure that good selections of plants will be available to future generations. Surprise lilies look good when planted in masses or in combination with ferns and other shade-loving perennials.

WHEN TO PLANT

Lycoris radiata bulbs should be divided and planted in June. Often you will have blooms that same fall, but the bulbs may take a year to settle in before they produce flowers.

WHERE TO PLANT

Plant surprise lilies in the woodland garden in combination with native plants and shade-loving perennials. They can also grow in full sun. Planting them in a bed of ivy will highlight the flowers and help mask the foliage until it dies back in the spring.

How to Plant

Surprise lilies that have been passed down from generation to generation in Georgia gardens will tolerate heavy clay soils, but for best results plant them in a soil that has been amended with organic matter. A deciduous woodland with lots of leaf litter is ideal. Partial shade is ideal, but they will tolerate full sun. The flowers will last longer if they are protected from hot afternoon sun and winds.

Care and Maintenance

Bulb expert Brent Heath of the Daffodil Mart in Gloucester, Virginia, recommends topdressing bulbs in the fall after you plant them rather than putting fertilizer directly in the planting bed. By following his advice, you will not have to worry about the tendency of fertilizer to burn bulbs and cause them to rot. He also stresses that, contrary to popular thinking, bone meal is not a complete fertilizer and for best results you should use a slow-release fertilizer like *Holland Bulb Booster* with a formula of 9–9–6. Broadcast the fertilizer in the fall after you plant the bulbs.

Additional Advice for Care

Lycoris resent being disturbed and when they are divided and replanted, take at least one season before they are happy and blooming. They are members of the amaryllis family; therefore, they are pest-resistant.

Additional Cultivars and Species

Lycoris squamigera, known as the magic lily or naked ladies, does not adapt as well to all parts of Georgia; rather, it does well in the colder parts of the state. Warm soil temperatures may keep it from blooming. The magic lily puts foliage up in the spring, and the lavender-pink flowers, looking like small amaryllis, appear suddenly in late summer.

Daffodils

Height: 5"–20"
Flowers: yellow, white, bicolor Blooms: spring

Some of the best gardeners are confused by the seemingly complicated set of rules for naming daffodils. People will tell you that they don't grow daffodils, they grow jonquils, while others claim that they only grow Narcissus. *Keep in mind that all daffodils and jonquils belong to the genus* Narcissus—*so in a way, everyone is right! There are twelve different divisions of daffodils, each determined by physical characteristics and family tree or genetic background. There are literally hundreds of varieties to choose from for Georgia gardens, but a few that are well-adapted and persistant in our climate stand out. Just a drive through the country in early spring will introduce you to some of the more common varieties. All daffodils are poisonous and therefore resistant to pests such as rodents, which can eat other bulbs faster than you can plant them. Plant daffodils in an average garden soil that is well-drained, in full sun or partial shade, and they should reward you with flowers year after year.*

WHEN TO PLANT

Plant bulbs as soon as you receive them in the fall. In Georgia, it is best to plant bulbs after soil temperatures have begun to cool, usually between November and December.

WHERE TO PLANT

Plant larger types like 'Carlton,' a two-toned yellow, and 'Rijnveld's Early Sensation' in large groups. Interplant them with hostas or daylilies which will help mask the foliage as it ripens in early summer. Plant heirloom types like *N. pseudonarcissus* ssp. *moschatus* in areas where they can naturalize without being disturbed. Force minature types in pots like 'Tete-a-Tete' or plant them in the perennial border.

How to Plant

Plant your bulbs as soon as you receive them in the fall. If you have to store them, make sure they stay dry and have plenty of ventilation. As a general rule, plant bulbs at a depth of 3 times the height of the bulb and space them at 3 times the width of the bulb on center.

Care and Maintenance

Bulb expert Brent Heath of the Daffodil Mart in Gloucester, Virginia, recommends topdressing bulbs in the fall after you plant them rather than putting fertilizer directly in the planting bed. By following his advice, you will not have to worry about the tendency of fertilizer to burn bulbs and cause them to rot. He also stresses that, contrary to popular thinking, bone meal is not a complete fertilizer. Bulbs prefer a low nitrogen-moderate phosphorous-high potash fertilizer. A new slow-release fertilizer, 5–10–20 with trace elements, has been especially formulated for daffodils.

Additional Advice for Care

For organic nutrients use cottonseed or bloodmeal for nitrogen, bone meal for phosphorous, and calcium and wood ashes for potash. *Bulb Mate* is an organic fertilizer that Brent Heath recommends.

Additional Cultivars and Species

Other varieties recommended for Georgia gardens are 'February Gold,' 'Ice Follies,' 'Sir Winston Churchill,' 'Baby Moon,' 'Hawera,' and all jonquilla and tazetta daffodils.

Zephyranthes candida

Rain Lily

Height: 6"–12"
Flowers: white Blooms: late summer, autumn

*Some of the best plants in our gardens started out as roadside treasures.
The common rain lily, Z.* candida, *started as a wildflower that blooms
throughout much of the South. Undemanding in the garden, it grows in
clay or sandy soils as well as in the bog garden. With its grassy foliage
and small flowers, it is a choice addition to the perennial border. With every
fall rainstorm, clumps seem to burst into bloom. The white starry flowers
glisten in the garden and stand out against the dark-green, rush-like leaves
which persist through the winter. The small bulbs suffer from drying, so
it's best to acquire this plant when it is actively growing in a pot. A little
extra watering during the summer will help carry bulbs through. These
tiny wonders are easy to incorporate into the garden and offer delightful
flowers at a time when few others compete for attention. Growing along the
gulf coast is Z.* grandiflora. *This pink-flowered subtropical is a favorite of
many Southerners. Another popular rain lily for our gardens is Z.* citrina,
with golden flowers that put on their best show in fall.

WHEN TO PLANT

Plant rain lilies when they are actively growing in the spring or in
the fall. They bloom late in the season from September through
November.

WHERE TO PLANT

Plant them in areas where you can appreciate the small, colorful
flowers in late summer and through the fall. Plant them in combination with groundcovers like ajuga or evergreen vinca. Rain lilies will
tolerate full sun or partial shade.

 ZONE 7,8

How to Plant

For best flowering, plant rain lilies in a moist soil that is rich in organic matter. Plant them in groups of 10 or more for a good display. Fertilize them with a liquid during the first growing season. After they are established, they require very little care.

Care and Maintenance

Rain lilies grow in sun or shade, in clay or sand, without any special care. Watering the bulbs during periods of drought in the summer will help ensure they don't shrivel up and die before they become established. Planting them in a soil with an abundance of organic matter will help ensure good flowering. Planting them in combination with groundcovers will help keep the soil cool and moist.

Additional Advice for Care

If you follow the advice in this section, it will not be necessary to provide additional care for your rain lilies.

Additional Cultivars and Species

Atamascos, *Z. atamasca*, are rain lilies that are native to the swampy forests and coastal areas throughout much of the Southeast. They bloom in March or April and provide good companions for native azaleas and spring-blooming phlox in the woodland garden.

BULBS

Groundcovers and Ferns

*T*HOUGH HOME-BUILDING BOOMS ARE STILL going on
in some parts of Georgia, nothing can equal the frenzy of
hammering that occurred from 1970 to 1990. Baby boomers needed
homes, and developers were glad to oblige. Each home, of course,
came with a requisite landscape: trees, shrubs, turf, and maybe a
spot by the mailbox for flowers.

Two decades later, the landscapes around those homes have
matured. The maples that were twenty feet tall are now fifty feet
tall. The shrubs, first planted from one-gallon pots, are now large,
rounded, and mature. Both have encroached on the area once given
to the lawn. Shade has caused both grass and smaller shrubs to
decline. Larger areas have become devoted to perennial and
annual flowers.

If this sounds like your landscape, join the club! Homeowners all
over the state are discovering that shade, not sun, is a threat to their
original landscape. For many, the love affair with the lawnmower
has lost its bloom. The smell of new-mown grass is still as sweet . . .
but that perfume can be enjoyed from 1000 square feet of turf just as
easily as from 10,000 square feet!

Groundcovers and ferns can solve some of the problems of
maturing landscapes. Ivy, liriope, and other plants can grow in
shade and cover large areas that were once devoted to turf grass.
Ferns can add interest and texture to shaded flower beds. The plant
descriptions in this chapter will detail some of the best plants from
which to choose.

DETERMINING AREA

One of the mathematical problems facing a professional or amateur
landscaper is to determine how much area a site covers, measured
in square feet. This is important, whether it be a lawn or a bed of
seasonal annuals. You calculate the amount of fertilizer to apply or

the number of plants to purchase based on the approximate size of a site. Here are some tips to help you solve these problems.

You'll need several soft drink cans, a pencil, and a piece of paper. Roughly sketch the lawn or flower bed on the paper and divide it into rectangles. Outdoors, put a can on the four corners of each rectangle.

Walk from can to can. Count your paces between each can and mark down the figure on your sketch. Assuming your pace is 2.5 feet long, multiply the number of steps by 2.5 to find the length of each side in feet. For each rectangle, multiply the length of the short side by the length of the long side. That will tell you the number of square feet in that individual rectangle. Add all of the rectangles together to find the total square feet. Remember, you're not aiming for precision—just get "close"!

How Many Plants?

Once you know the area of the flower bed, how many plants should you buy? Rather than mark every spot or simply guessing, use this chart to calculate how many plants are needed for an area covering 100 square feet.

DISTANCE BETWEEN PLANTS	NUMBER OF PLANTS
6"	400
12"	100
18"	45
24"	25
30"	16

Example: If you want to plant pansies 12 inches apart in a bed that is 50 square feet, you will need 50 plants.

Adiantum pedatum

Northern Maidenhair Fern

Height: 12"–24" Width: 24"–36"
Deciduous

If ferns could dance, the northern maidenhair fern would be the prima
ballerina. *Wiry black stems hold the fan-shaped green blades parallel to the
ground. This is just the right angle for any wayward breeze to set a group
of these ferns bobbing and waving gracefully. Because the stems are dark
and hair-like, it is always a surprise to discover northern maidenhair ferns
growing in their usual spot in spring. While the green fiddleheads of other
ferns are quite noticeable, the green part of this fern does not reveal itself
for weeks. As warm weather progresses, the clump will appear to get larger
by the week until the fronds form a lacy green mound.*

WHEN TO PLANT

Maidenhair ferns transplant easily in fall or in early spring, just after
the green fronds have unfurled. A container-grown maidenhair fern
can be planted in midsummer if it is watered regularly.

WHERE TO PLANT

Rich, moist woodland, preferably next to a stream, is the perfect site
for maidenhair ferns. Full to partial shade is a must. Any more than
an hour of full sunshine and the fronds will begin to scorch. This
fern can form an attractive edge for a woodland walk or path, even
if only beside the chain-link fence in your backyard.

HOW TO PLANT

Mix soil conditioner 2:1 with garden soil in the spot where you want
to plant maidenhair ferns. They spread very slowly, so maidenhair
ferns can be planted 16" from each other and not become crowded
over time. A little crowding is preferable, in fact, to accentuate the
movement of the fronds.

ZONE
6,7,8

CARE AND MAINTENANCE

Spread a ¹/₂" layer of manure or compost over the bed each spring. The above-ground part of the plant will die back after the first frost, but the stems are so insubstantial that removing them is not necessary. If the soil is full of organic matter, maidenhair fern can survive periods of drought with little worry about watering.

ADDITIONAL ADVICE FOR CARE

Once your clump has been in one spot for a few years it can be divided very easily. The best time to do this is in spring right after the majority of the fronds have appeared. Dig your clump and use hand clippers to cut out several parts. Make sure each part has 3 or 4 fronds and some healthy roots.

ADDITIONAL CULTIVARS AND SPECIES

Southern maidenhair fern (*Adiantum capillus-veneris*) is sometimes found at nurseries, but it seems to be much more difficult to grow here than its northern counterpart. It is more low-growing than northern maidenhair fern and is not similar in appearance.

GROUNDCOVERS AND FERNS

Athyrium filix-femina

Southern Lady Fern

Height: 18"–30" Width: 24"–36"
Deciduous

Lady fern is one of the most common and reliable ferns for a shady Georgia garden. It spreads by a rhizome underground and is typically found in a colony of several dozen, if not hundreds of, fronds. It grows readily in moist woods and along streams. Given shade and moisture, it adapts easily to almost any situation. Although the coloration is subtle, from a distance the foliage of a grouping of lady ferns will appear to have a red/purple tint. Planted along the shady side of your house, lady ferns will grow just tall enough to hide the bare lower limbs of overgrown hollies. The epithet of the species, filix-femina, *means* fern-ladylike. *The gently arching fronds, moving lazily on a humid Southern day, recall stereotypes of the languid gestures of a visitor to Tara.*

WHEN TO PLANT

Lady ferns transplant easily in fall or in early spring, just after the fiddleheads have unfurled. A container-grown lady fern can be planted in midsummer if it is watered regularly.

WHERE TO PLANT

Rich, moist woodland next to a stream is the perfect site for a lady fern. Full to partial shade is a must. Any more than an hour of full sunshine and the fronds will begin to scorch. Make sure your lady fern is not in a spot where dogs might lie or children might play. The fronds break easily, although new fronds will quickly cover the damage.

HOW TO PLANT

Mix soil conditioner 2:1 with garden soil in the spot where you want to plant a lady fern. The planting hole should be 24" wide for a single plant, but if you expect it to spread, loosen the top 6" of soil

ZONE
6,7,8

throughout the planting bed. They spread slowly by underground roots, so lady ferns can be planted 16" from each other and not become crowded over time. A little crowding is preferable, in fact, to allow you to appreciate the graceful fronds of this fern.

CARE AND MAINTENANCE

Spread a 1/2" layer of manure or compost over the bed each spring. The above-ground part of the plant will die back after the first frost. The stems are generally not noticeable after they turn brown, but you can remove them if you need to tidy up a bed. If the summer is dry, plan to water your ferns once each week, thoroughly soaking the soil around them.

ADDITIONAL ADVICE FOR CARE

Lady ferns can have either red or green stalks in the same clump. Although this might appear to be a nutrient deficiency, it is accepted as a common occurrence.

ADDITIONAL CULTIVARS AND SPECIES

There are dozens of lady ferns selected for their different frond shapes. The tips of the greenery can be crested, comb-like, cross-shaped, or "frizzled." Unless you become a fern fanatic, crested lady fern (*Athyrium filix-femina* 'Cristatum') is the only one you are likely to find. Common lady fern is good enough for most Georgia gardens.

Athyrium nipponicum 'Pictum'

Japanese Painted Fern

Height: 12"–20" Width: 18"–30"
Deciduous

A Japanese painted fern as it unfurls its silver fronds in spring is an incomparable beauty! The central stem of each frond has a maroon stripe, while the rest of the blade is silvery white. Despite its delicate appearance, it is a vigorous grower and sends up new fronds throughout the summer. The light color of this fern draws the eye directly to its home in the shade, particularly when set against a blue-green hosta or deep-green vinca groundcover. Since this fern can be divided easily (see below) it can even be used as a border beneath the shade of rhododendrons or a group of camellias. Other good companions include foamflower (Tiarella wherryi), which will cover the ground around a fern with 8"-tall foamy white flowers in May, and hardy begonia (Begonia grandis). The pink flowers and red-bottomed leaves of the begonia accent the red coloration in a Japanese fern's frond.

WHEN TO PLANT

The best time to plant a Japanese painted fern in the spring so it can establish itself before the summer. It looks its best in the garden center in late spring, so that is when it is usually purchased and planted. Spring planting is usually successful if the soil around the fern is not allowed to dry out during the dry part of the summer.

WHERE TO PLANT

Shade and moist soil are necessities, of course, but the silver color of this fern makes it very useful compared to the green ferns. This fern looks its best when set among or in front of dark-green plants. The light color almost demands that it be the center of a shady grouping. The silver color will contrast very well with moss-covered granite rocks or a large log rotting along the edge of your property.

ZONE 6,7,8

How to Plant

Dig a hole 2′ wide and 10″ deep. Mix in 1 cubic foot (or 5 good shovelsful) of compost or soil conditioner. Put the fern in the center and water daily for a week. The root ball is not very large, so transplanting from another spot is easy. Once the plant is established, no further care is necessary other than watering occasionally during the summer.

Care and Maintenance

Japanese painted ferns can survive with no care if they are planted in partial to deep shade. If the summer is dry, pamper them with a deep watering each week. A shovelful of compost or decomposed manure spread over the frond before spring will supply all of the nutrients the plant needs.

Additional Advice for Care

A mature Japanese painted fern will have several "children" around the base of the original plant. When the fronds have unfurled in early spring, the fern can be dug up and divided. Carefully brush away the soil around the roots and tease away the young plants from the parent. Each group of fronds should have some roots and a few yet-to-emerge fiddleheads.

Additional Cultivars and Species

No crested fronds or other chance mutations have occurred to make a "special" Japanese painted fern. It is itself a superior selection of a species of fern found in Japan.

Cyrtomium falcatum

Japanese Holly Fern

Height: 12"–30" Width: 24"–36"
Evergreen

Most gardeners know the typical shape of a fern. Their mental image is probably not of a plant that is "thick, tough, and leathery" but that is exactly the appearance of the fronds of a holly fern. The fronds of a holly fern are held upright in a vase-like shape. The holly fern really looks nothing like a fern; its above-ground parts are more like holly leaves on a green stem. Sometimes you may see this fern being used as a foundation plant! Since the fronds of a holly fern are coarser than a "normal" fern, you can combine it with plants that have a more refined look. Certainly lady fern (Athyrium filix-femina) *and northern maidenhair fern* (Adiantum pedatum) *are good choices. Astilbe* (Astilbe x arendsii) *and columbine* (Aquilegia canadensis) *would add colorful blooms to the grouping.*

WHEN TO PLANT

Holly ferns can be planted or moved easily in fall or in early spring, just after the fiddleheads have unfurled. A container-grown holly fern can be planted in midsummer if it is planted in shade and watered regularly.

WHERE TO PLANT

A holly fern will grow in heavy clay soil but prefers a rich, organic site. With regular watering, it can tolerate direct sun for a few hours each day. The coarse texture of its leaves contrasts well with azaleas and hosta. If planted around a backyard pond, the fern will provide winter greenery in a moist spot. As a foundation plant, a holly fern looks very attractive beneath a shady picture window or when edging a low deck.

How to Plant

If possible, mix soil conditioner 1:1 with garden soil in the spot where you want to plant a holly fern. They spread very slowly, so holly ferns can be planted 24" from each other and not become crowded over time.

Care and Maintenance

Water occasionally during droughts, especially if the plant is exposed to full sun for more than 2 hours. Spread a 1/2" layer of manure or compost over the bed each spring. In spring, remove any brown fronds which have died during the winter.

Additional Advice for Care

Japanese holly fern can tolerate low humidity and can be used as an indoor house plant. It will grow best in a cool room in front of a bright window.

Additional Cultivars and Species

One improved selection of Japanese holly fern is sometimes found in nurseries. *Cyrtomium falcatum* 'Rochfordianum' is a bit smaller and does not appear quite as coarse as the common holly fern.

GROUNDCOVERS AND FERNS

Log Fern

Height: 30"–48" Width 20"–36"
Semi-evergreen

The word celsa *in this fern's Latin name means* held high. *The fronds of this fern rise strongly and vertically from the ground. George Sanko, curator of the DeKalb Botanical Garden, is a log fern enthusiast, but he admits that he has never seen one in nature growing from a log! This fern is evergreen in the southern part of Georgia but only semi-evergreen farther north. Several of them planted together make an excellent backdrop for some of the common shade-loving plants. Good companions might include* Hosta 'Frances Williams,' *astilbe (Astilbe x arendsii), and bleeding heart (Dicentra spectabilis). Other plants to consider include variegated Solomon's Seal (Polygonatum odoratum 'Variegatum'), foamflower (Tiarella wherryi), and wild ginger (Asarum shuttleworthii).*

When to Plant

Log ferns transplant easily in fall or in early spring, just after the fiddleheads have unfurled. A container-grown log fern can be planted in midsummer if it is watered regularly.

Where to Plant

A rich, moist woodland bed is the perfect site for log ferns. Full to partial shade is important, but a log fern can tolerate a few hours of full morning sunshine if it is fully shaded in the afternoon.

How to Plant

Mix soil conditioner 2:1 with garden soil in the spot where you want to plant a log fern. They spread very slowly, so log ferns can be planted 24" from each other and not become crowded over time. Because the ferns grow so vertically, a line of log ferns can form a solid green backdrop for smaller ferns or other plants in front.

ZONE
6,7,8

CARE AND MAINTENANCE

Spread a ¹/₂″ layer of manure or compost over the bed each spring. The above-ground part of the plant will die back if the winter is severe, but it will usually remain green. As the older fronds die out, remove them to allow young ones to push through in spring.

ADDITIONAL ADVICE FOR CARE

After your log fern has been growing in one spot for a few years, the clump can be dug and divided in spring. Once you have taken it from the ground, brush off the loose soil and look for places where you can cut the clump apart. Each section should have 2 or 3 fronds and some thick roots. The pieces should be planted immediately and watered thoroughly.

ADDITIONAL CULTIVARS AND SPECIES

Log fern is actually a fertile hybrid of Louisiana fern (*Dryopteris ludoviciana*) and Goldie's fern (*Dryopteris goldiana*). You could make an interesting botanical assemblage by planting the parents of a log fern slightly behind and on either side of it.

GROUNDCOVERS AND FERNS

Dryopteris erythrosora

Autumn Fern

Height: 18"–30" Width: 24"–36"
Evergreen

How can an autumn fern be compared to Rudolph the Red-Nosed Reindeer? The explanation is simple. Ferns are among our oldest-known plants. Even before the dinosaurs, ferns thrived throughout the world. They have had millions of years to evolve a special ability to grow and reproduce that allows them to take root wherever conditions are favorable. Ferns do not produce flowers and seeds. They reproduce by spores, which are formed on the backside of the fronds. The tiny brown spores are scattered by the wind; if one finds a bit of shade and damp soil, a new fern will appear. Autumn fern gets its scientific name for its distinctive spores. These microscopic reproductive parts are contained in red capsules on the bottom of the fronds. The capsules are called sori. Erythro *means* red. *It is easy to see why this member of the fern family could be called "Dryopteris the Red-Sori'ed Fern."*

WHEN TO PLANT
The best time to plant or move an autumn fern is in spring while the fiddleheads are still emerging. A container-grown autumn fern can be planted in the heat of midsummer if it is planted in shade and watered regularly.

WHERE TO PLANT
Autumn fern remains evergreen during most winters. One of its most distinctive features is the bronze-red color of the new fronds in the spring. This color remains for weeks, changing gradually to green as the frond matures. One of the best places to use this fern is in front of a large stone where the form and color change can be appreciated.

How to Plant

Dig a hole 2' wide and 10" deep. Mix in 1 cubic foot (or 5 good shovelsful) of compost or soil conditioner. Put the fern in the center and water daily for a week. The root ball is not very large, so transplanting from another spot is easy. Once the plant is established, no further care is necessary other than watering occasionally during the summer.

Care and Maintenance

Autumn ferns can survive with no care if they are planted in partial to deep shade. If the summer is dry, pamper them with a deep watering each week. A shovelful of compost or decomposed manure spread around the clump before spring will supply all of the nutrients the plant needs.

Additional Advice for Care

The fronds of an autumn fern are excellent for inclusion in a flower arrangement. They are stiff and leathery and not prone to become damaged. If your clump is large, a few fronds can be harvested at any time.

Additional Cultivars and Species

Autumn fern is native to China although other members of its genus are native to the United States. Autumn fern, like other *Dryopteris*, has sturdy fronds, so you can plant it among more delicate ferns such as lady fern (*Athyrium felix-femina*) or northern maidenhair fern (*Adiantum pedatum*).

JNDCOVERS AND FERNS

Pink Panda Strawberry

Height: 5"–8"
Semi-evergreen, spreading groundcover

Strawberries are not usually considered traditional groundcovers, but anyone who has had them in a vegetable garden has likely observed their potential. In the spring, a mother plant may send a half-dozen runner stems away from the central plant crown. Each runner will root 6"–12" from the main plant. These daughter plants will grow for a few months then send out more runners to form granddaughter plants. Obviously, a lot of ground can be covered in a hurry by one common strawberry. When a British plant breeder selected a strawberry plant that could grow in diverse conditions and simultaneously send out a dozen runners over a summer, 'Pink Panda' was born. The leaves of 'Pink Panda' are evergreen in most parts of the state. Multitudes of bright pink blooms cover the plants in spring and again when the weather cools down in September. Strawberry fruits are occasionally produced as a bonus from this attractive groundcover.

WHEN TO PLANT
Plant 'Pink Panda' strawberry in mid-fall after daytime temperatures have fallen below 75 degrees. Another good planting time is in the spring in late March.

WHERE TO PLANT
'Pink Panda' can be used as a groundcover in light conditions that range from semi-shade to almost full sunshine. It will spread and flower better in full sunshine. It is equally attractive in a hanging basket or around the edge of a large pot containing taller plants. 'Pink Panda' will cascade over a stone wall, dangling its stems and foliage for 24", but this part of the plant is sometimes killed by severe cold.

ZONE
6,7,8

HOW TO PLANT

To grow strongly, 'Pink Panda' strawberry should be planted in a
bed whose soil has been thoroughly mixed. Although the runners
display a remarkable ability to take root in hard soil, the soil must
be kept moist for them to thrive during the summer. When used as a
groundcover, position the plants 16" from each other. In a 16" hanging basket, 4 single plants will be plenty. Red stems and green leaves
will be hanging over the side of the basket in 4 weeks.

CARE AND MAINTENANCE

Because it can tolerate both sun and shade, 'Pink Panda' makes a
good groundcover for a mixed bed of shrubs and perennials. Plants
will take root wherever they find favorable conditions. In this case,
the fertilizer you apply to the other plants supplies plenty of nutrients for the strawberry. At planting, sprinkle 1 tablespoon of
10–10–10 around each plant. When growing in sandy soil or on a
dry, exposed site, plan to water the bed deeply each week during
the heat of the summer. Once the daughter plants have rooted near
your original plant, they can be dug up with a trowel and transplanted to other parts of the bed.

ADDITIONAL ADVICE FOR CARE

The name 'Pink Panda' comes from the original marketing cam-
paign for this ornamental in Great Britain. Its breeder licensed
the plant to Adrian Bloom, proprietor of Blooms of Bressingham,
one of the country's best known nurseries. Bloom pledged to
donate a portion of the early sales to the Worldwide Fund
for Nature, whose symbol is a panda.

ADDITIONAL CULTIVARS AND SPECIES

The garden strawberry is a hybrid of two or three species of strawberry. One of them, beach strawberry (*Fragaria chiloensis*), is also an
excellent groundcover. You can expect to see several superior selections of groundcover strawberry introduced at your local nursery in
the next few years.

Hedera helix

English Ivy

Evergreen vine and groundcover

Though it is not like the aggressive kudzu, English ivy can be a blessing in some garden situations and a curse in others. There are few spots so shady that ivy can't grow there. On the other hand, when ivy is left to its own devices, no nearby tree or wall is safe from its advances. Since it is ever-green, ivy is commonly used as a groundcover, particularly in deep shade or on steep banks. Some gardeners like the effect of English ivy growing up a home's brick wall, but this is discouraged by home repair experts. Ivy works very well when planted at the base of a chain-link fence and allowed to climb—it is opaque enough to give privacy, but natural enough to be "friendly" to your neighbors. It is interesting to note that the common three-lobed form of English ivy is its juvenile leaf shape. If you find a wall that has been covered with ivy for years, look for leaves that are a rounded oval. Sometimes this mature part of the vine will send forth clusters of small green flowers. If you are able to root a mature stem, the plant will be a bush, not a vine!

WHEN TO PLANT

Plant ivy in mid-spring or early summer. It will establish its roots faster if the soil is warming up, not cooling down. Don't worry if the vine seems to "just sit there" for months. Once the roots have become established, you'll wonder why you ever worried about slow growth.

WHERE TO PLANT

When all other flowers and shrubs have declined due to dense shade, ivy can be given the call to take their place. Already-rooted plants should be planted 24" apart. If you are trying to root cuttings of the vine, they should be placed 16" apart.

HOW TO PLANT

Like most other plants, ivy prefers to grow in moist, loose soil. That is not usually possible—at the very least, container-grown cuttings should be planted in an area of softened soil 12" in diameter. This may be difficult to achieve if you are planting under a tree—judicious use of a small, heavy shovel can help. To save money, plant pot-grown plants in the heaviest shade and try rooting cuttings in better sunlight. You can get 12" cuttings of ivy to root in place by making a 6" slit in the soil and burying half of each cutting while leaving 6" of stem and leaves exposed. Water the plot lightly every day for a month, then weekly for the rest of the summer.

CARE AND MAINTENANCE

Before you fertilize English ivy, ask yourself if the nutrients are really needed. Ivy can grow moderately with no fertilizer each year. If you want to speed up the growth of new plants, apply 1 pint of 10–10–10 fertilizer per 100 square feet of area in March, June, and August. English ivy should not be allowed to grow up the trunk of a tree. The leaves will eventually shade out the lower limbs of the tree and they will fall. If the ivy is already up beyond your reach, go around the tree trunk and cut out as much of the vine as you can. Ivy is not a parasite, so the vine above will gradually wither and die.

ADDITIONAL ADVICE FOR CARE

If your ivy becomes too rambunctious, you may be tempted to try to kill it with herbicide. Good luck! Weed-killer chemicals just bead up and roll off the waxy leaves. Mowing an overgrown bed in spring and then hand pulling the survivors is often the only way to eliminate ivy.

ADDITIONAL CULTIVARS AND SPECIES

There are dozens of different shapes and colors of English ivy leaves. *Hedera helix* 'Needlepoint' has small (2¹/₂") leaves. *Hedera helix* 'Aureo-variegata' has green leaves variegated with gold. *Hedera helix* 'Baltica' has small leaves and does not turn bronze, even during a frigid winter.

Liriope spp.

Monkey Grass

Liriope

Height: 8"–16"
Evergreen groundcover

Most gardeners recognize liriope in an instant. It is used to line sidewalks and to edge flower beds in landscapes from Dalton to Darien. It is also used as a groundcover in shady spots, from which it is much less likely to wander than English ivy. Though the strap-like leaves are attractive, liriope is also appreciated for its grape hyacinth-like flowers in June. Most of the liriope that you find growing in Georgia is Liriope muscari, *which forms clumps when it grows. Sometimes gardeners find a liriope that spreads rapidly but has narrow, light-green leaves. This is* Liriope spicata, *creeping monkey grass.*

WHEN TO PLANT

Liriope can be planted just about any time of year. It might dry out completely when planted on a scorching day in full sunshine, but it will find a way to survive most other planting conditions.

WHERE TO PLANT

Liriope is commonly used to line walks and beds and is a good substitute for turf grass in dense shade. Creeping monkey grass, in particular, can fill a site in just a year or two. If you prefer the deeper green of *Liriope muscari*, a clump can easily be divided and then planted in spring.

HOW TO PLANT

For best growth, plant liriope in thoroughly loosened soil. If this is not possible, try to give the roots of each plant an area 12" wide in which to grow. Unless you want a particularly attractive selection from a nursery, it should be easy to find a neighbor who will allow you to divide a liriope bed so you can have all you need. To divide

ZONE
6,7,8

liriope, dig a clump and soak it in a bucket of water for 30 minutes. Then use a hose to wash most of the soil from the roots. Use your fingers to separate the clump into individual plants. A clump 16" in diameter might yield 100 sprouts. Of course, you can always just slice a clump apart with a shovel!

CARE AND MAINTENANCE

Unless you need to accelerate the growth of a bed of liriope, it does not need fertilizer. For a new bed, apply 1 pint of 10–10–10 fertilizer per 100 square feet of area in March, June, and August. Water newly planted liriope once a week for a month. It should never need water again. After a severe winter in north Georgia, liriope will look brown and tattered in early spring. In February, raise your lawn-mower to its highest mowing height and cut off all of the liriope foliage. In a few weeks, dark green sprouts will appear and cover the base of the plant.

ADDITIONAL ADVICE FOR CARE

Parents sometimes wonder if the dark purple berries of liriope are poisonous to their children. While swallowing a number of berries might give a child a painful tummyache, the fruits are not considered truly poisonous.

ADDITIONAL CULTIVARS AND SPECIES

Liriope muscari cultivars have several different flower colors from which to choose. The flowers might be blue ('Big Blue'), lilac-pink ('Christmas Tree'), lavender ('Majestic'), or white ('Monroe's White'). The leaves might also be variegated ('John Burch' and 'Silvery Sunproof').

GROUNDCOVERS AND FERNS

101

Mondo Grass

Height: 3"–10"
Evergreen, grass-like, slowly spreading groundcover

Mondo grass and liriope are often confused for each other. Both are members of the lily family and both have evergreen, grass-like leaves. The easiest way to tell them apart is by their size: mondo grass leaves are rarely more than 1/4" wide while liriope leaves are rarely narrower than 1/4". A clump of mondo grass is not usually as tall as a clump of liriope. If you observe the two in July, the flowers are a dead giveaway: mondo grass flowers are hidden in the foliage while liriope flowers stand above the leaves.

WHEN TO PLANT

Mondo grass is very easy to plant or transplant at any time of year. If you need to plant it in the middle of summer, plan to water it a few times to help it through dry weather.

WHERE TO PLANT

Because mondo grass resembles turfgrass so closely, and because it is so shade-tolerant, it is often substituted for grass in dense shade. It does not grow tall or send up seedheads, but mondo grass cannot bear much foot traffic. This plant is very attractive when planted along the edges of a path or around the individual stepping stones in a path. It also makes a good filler plant among the rocks that surround a backyard pond.

HOW TO PLANT

Like liriope, mondo grass will grow best in thoroughly loosened soil. If this is not possible, try to give the roots of each plant an area 10" wide in which to grow. Mondo grass spreads slowly. You should be able to find a friend who will allow you to dig small clumps from a bed so you can have all you need. To divide mondo grass, dig a clump and soak it in a bucket for 30 minutes. Then use a

ZONE 6,7,8

hose to wash most of the soil from the roots. Use your fingers and a pair of hand clippers to separate the clump into several divisions. A clump 12" in diameter might yield 20 divisions.

CARE AND MAINTENANCE

Mondo grass does not require fertilization unless you are trying to speed up its growth. If that is the case, sprinkle 1 pint of 10–10–10 fertilizer over 100 square feet of bed in March and June. If the mondo grass is planted along a path, sprinkle 1 pint along 100 feet of length. Mondo grass may be damaged by winter cold, but the injury is not as noticeable as on liriope. If you need to renew a planting, mow it 2" high in February. Avoid mowing during the summer, as the cut edges of the mondo grass will turn brown and unattractive.

ADDITIONAL ADVICE FOR CARE

Another good placement for mondo grass is around and underneath a small Japanese maple. The shade of the maple won't faze the mondo grass, and in November its dark-green color will make a great canvas behind the marvelous red foliage of the Japanese maple.

ADDITIONAL CULTIVARS AND SPECIES

Dwarf mondo grass (*Ophiopogon japonicus* 'Nana') grows only 2" tall. Black mondo grass (*Ophiopogon planiscapus* 'Nigrescens') has leaves that are almost black. Landscapers are greatly divided about this foliage color. Some consider it an attractive contrast to light green plants; others believe it to be an abomination!

Osmunda regalis, Osmunda cinnamomea

Royal Fern and Cinnamon Fern

Height: 2′–5′ Width: 2′–4′
Deciduous

Both of these ferns are common at garden centers and are easy to grow in a moist site. The fronds of a royal fern do not look like a typical fern, resembling instead a branch of a locust tree. Cinnamon fern grows in practically every swamp in Georgia. The fronds are clustered around, and emerge from, a dark brown, wiry rootstock. This gives the appearance of a large green badminton shuttlecock when viewed from above. Both ferns belong to the Osmunda genus. Fossils show that this group of ferns has been around for millions of years. It is related to the large tree ferns on which you might see dinosaurs munching in displays in natural history museums. The most fascinating time for these ferns is in late spring, when light brown "cinnamon sticks" grow above the greenery. These are the fertile fronds; the spores on them are scattered by the wind during the summer, perhaps to land on fertile soil. In late spring, these cinnamon-colored tips are so unlike other ferns that the eyes are drawn to them.

WHEN TO PLANT

Plant royal or cinnamon fern in the fall or in early spring, after the fiddleheads have begun to unfurl. Since the fronds are "twice compound," the fiddleheads unfurl both upward from the ground as well as outward from the central stem. This is a fascinating process for young children, who can daily follow the progress of the young fern.

WHERE TO PLANT

Either of these ferns can grow happily in swamps and marshes. Don't worry that the spot you've chosen may be too wet! The drainage area of a backyard pond is ideal, but the ferns will also thrive in normal fern habitat: moist, shady, very organic soil.

ZONE
6,7,8

How to Plant

Dig a hole 2' wide and 10" deep. Mix in 1 cubic foot (or 5 good shovelsful) of compost or soil conditioner. Put the plant in the center and water regularly for a week. The root ball is not particularly large, so transplanting from another spot is easy. Once the plant is established, no further care is necessary except watering during summer.

Care and Maintenance

Both ferns can survive with no care if they are in partial to deep shade. If the summer is dry, pamper them with a deep watering each week. A shovelful of compost or decomposed manure spread over the dead fronds before spring will supply all of the nutrients either of these plants needs.

Additional Advice for Care

If you dig up the rootstock of these ferns, you'll find a large, prickly brown ball partially exposed in the soil. From this rootstock, new fronds arise each spring. The mass of old rootstocks and stems is commonly dug from swamps and bogs and then sold as osmunda fiber, an excellent potting media for orchids.

Additional Cultivars and Species

No superior selections of these two ferns are available except through specialized fern dealers.

Polystichum acrostichoides

Christmas Fern

Height: 20"–28" Width: 24"–30"
Evergreen

Few ferns are completely evergreen, but this one comes close! Christmas fern's name reputedly comes from its use by American settlers in Christmas decorations. This fern is one of the few green plants in a wintry forest. Extreme cold will freeze the fronds back to just a flat green pancake on the ground, but spring will bring silvery green fiddleheads curling up from the fern roots. Look for the brown spores on the back of the fronds. You'll notice that some fronds do not have spores on them at all. These are the sterile fronds—they are typically smaller and more erect. The spore-carrying fertile fronds are larger and are able to bend enough to touch the ground at their tips. Several companion plants grow nicely in the shade with this fern. Astilbe (Astilbe x arendsii) blooms in spring. White, pink, or red astilbe blooms can be selected. Toad lily (Tricyrtis hirta) will form white blooms with purple spots on top of its arching stems in September.

WHEN TO PLANT

Plant a Christmas fern in spring so it can establish itself before summer comes along. Early summer is not a bad choice for planting as long as the new plants are watered for the first few weeks. Make regular inspection visits during July and August to make sure the plants have not become too dry.

WHERE TO PLANT

Christmas fern will tolerate dry soil and heavy clay that would send other ferns to the compost heap. The clump will grow much larger in moist, loose soil, but a dry pine forest near a lake or stream will often have several seemingly happy clumps of this fern. Large clumps can be divided several times and used as a groundcover under oak and dogwood trees.

How to Plant

Dig a hole 2' wide and 10" deep. Mix in 1 cubic foot (or 5 good shovelsful) of compost or soil conditioner. Put the plant in the center and water regularly for a week. The root ball is not particularly large, so transplanting from another spot is easy. Once the plant is established, no further care is necessary.

Care and Maintenance

Christmas ferns can survive with no care if they are planted in partial to deep shade. If the summer is dry, pamper them with a deep watering each week. A shovelful of compost or decomposed manure spread over the clump before spring will supply all of the nutrients the plant needs.

Additional Advice for Care

A large, mature clump of Christmas fern is composed of several smaller plants. A clump can be dug and carefully divided in spring for planting in other spots or for sharing with friends. This is one of the least fussy ferns you can plant or transplant.

Additional Cultivars and Species

Polystichum acrostichoides 'Crispum' has ruffled margins on all of the fronds. *Polystichum acrostichoides* 'Cristatum' has toothed crests at the tips of fronds. *Polystichum acrostichoides* 'Multifidum' has deeply cut fronds. This fern is not as coarse as the species, looking much more "ferny."

Southern Shield Fern

Height: 36"–48" Width: 24"–48"
Deciduous

We usually think of ferns as inhabiting only dark corners of a garden. Southern shield fern can grow in very light shade or even full morning sunshine. The fronds of this fern are large and light green. Since it spreads readily by underground rhizomes, colonies of several hundred plants are commonly found in south Georgia. Besides its large size, another feature to aid in the identification of this fern is the rapid narrowing of its tip. A frond may be nearly 12" wide for most of its length up to 4" from the tip. At that point, it narrows drastically to the end of the frond. If you still have trouble identifying a southern shield fern, rub a frond gently on your cheek. It has tiny hairs on both the top and bottom of a frond which will feel simultaneously soft and raspy.

WHEN TO PLANT

You can plant or move shield ferns in spring while the fiddleheads are still emerging. A container-grown shield fern can be planted in the heat of midsummer if it is planted in shade and watered regularly.

WHERE TO PLANT

Shield ferns tolerate a wide variety of soil types, from sandy loam to clay. If given adequate moisture, they will thrive in almost full sun. Because it grows so tall, try planting a large hosta, like *Hosta* 'Sum & Substance' or *Hosta sieboldiana* 'Elegans,' in front of this fern.

HOW TO PLANT

The southern shield fern's rhizomes will spread into any soil that has been loosened around the original plant. If possible, mix soil conditioner 1:1 with garden soil in the spot where you want to plant

ZONE
7,8

a shield fern. The rhizomes stay within 3" of the soil surface, so the planting bed should be be dug wide rather than deep.

CARE AND MAINTENANCE

The fronds will wither after the first frost each year. Clip off the stiff brown stems at ground level. Spread a 1/2" layer of manure or compost over the bed each spring. Watering may be needed during a summer drought but a southern shield fern can tolerate several days of heat and dry weather without harm.

ADDITIONAL ADVICE FOR CARE

This fern can be dug and divided in early fall or in early spring. Carefully lift a clump from the soil and brush the earth from the brown rhizomes. The rhizomes can be cut into 6" sections with a hand clipper. Each section should have at least 3 frond stems growing from it. Plant as described above.

ADDITIONAL CULTIVARS AND SPECIES

Superior selections of southern shield fern have not been made, but there are two other members of the *Thelypteris* family which are attractive. Broad beech fern (*Thelypteris hexagonoptera*) grows to 12" tall and has a broadly triangular frond. New York fern (*Thelypteris noveboracensis*) grows 16" tall and is a strongly growing, clump-forming fern.

Vinca minor

Periwinkle

Myrtle, Vinca

Evergreen vine and groundcover

For years, neighborhoods in Atlanta fought the city and the state over the construction of a road connecting the downtown expressway and the Stone Mountain freeway. Right-of-way for the road was purchased early, and the houses standing on it were demolished or moved. As the legal maneuvering continued, yards where homes once stood began to blend into acres of weeds, kudzu, and honeysuckle. Sometimes the only way to know a house had once existed was by a green patch of periwinkle covering the earth near trees that once shaded a front porch. Periwinkle is a groundcover that has qualities that are even more appealing than those of English ivy. "Periwinkle blue" flowers emerge over the ground-hugging leaves in April and then occur sporadically for the rest of the year. Vinca can tolerate heavy shade. Periwinkle is one of those plants that would receive great praise if it were not so common and easy to grow.

WHEN TO PLANT

Periwinkle can be planted from pots in spring. You can transplant this vine from a neighbor's yard in fall or spring. Cuttings will root better from May through June.

WHERE TO PLANT

Like English ivy, periwinkle is often given jobs that no other plant can handle. Bare clay banks or dense shade under a low-growing tree do not faze it. An excellent use is under deciduous trees over an area where spring-flowering bulbs have been planted. The bulbs will bloom in spring and then their dying leaves will be hidden by the vinca foliage.

How to Plant

Periwinkle prefers to grow in moist, loose soil, but it can tolerate
heavy clay or sand. Good soil is not always possible, so at the very
least container-grown cuttings should be planted in an area of softened soil 12" in diameter. If you are planting under a tree, judicious
use of a small, heavy shovel is a good idea. To save money, plant
pot-grown plants in the heaviest shade and try rooting cuttings in
brighter sunlight. You can get 12" cuttings of vinca to root in place
by making a 6" slit in the soil and burying half of each cutting while
leaving 6" of stem and leaves exposed. Water the plot lightly every
day for a month, then weekly for the rest of the summer.

Care and Maintenance

Periwinkle will cover an area faster if it is fertilized lightly during
the growing season for a couple of years. Apply 1 pint of 10–10–10
fertilizer per 100 square feet of area in March, June, and August.
Watch for weeds that may pop up while the periwinkle is establishing itself. They should be pulled before they become established
or spread seed. After a few years, the periwinkle will be able to
smother weeds before they grow large.

Additional Advice for Care

If rainwater runs through your vinca bed, plants in the wettest
part of the site may turn brown and die due to fungal and bacterial
diseases. There is no cure for the problem other than correcting the
flow of water.

Additional Cultivars and Species

Vinca minor 'Alba' has white flowers. *Vinca minor* 'Sterling
Silver' has green leaves edged in white. Another species of periwinkle, *Vinca major*, has large leaves and is much coarser and less
tidy than *Vinca minor*. It can be used on steep banks where *Vinca
minor* can't quite hold on.

GROUNDCOVERS AND FERNS

CHAPTER FOUR

Lawns and
Ornamental Grasses

*W*HAT WOULD A LANDSCAPE BE LIKE without a lawn?
Though some landscape designers are promoting a "lawn-
less landscape," most Georgians prefer some grass to grow in front
of their homes. Although a lawn takes more time to care for than
any other part of the landscape, green turf is seen in front of homes
both grand and humble throughout the state.

The solid green of a lawn is but one use for the members of the
worldwide family of grasses. Several tall grasses have striking
foliage and blooms. Landscapers and homeowners are discovering
the hardiness and diversity of ornamental grasses. These plants
are excellent for landscapes where water and heat are a problem.
Because they originated in dry parts of the world, most ornamental
grasses provide beauty whether irrigated faithfully or never given a
drop of water.

The plant descriptions in this chapter will help you decide which
turf grass is best for your landscape. In addition, several ornamental
grasses that grow well in Georgia are discussed.

One of the most common problems that Georgia gardeners face
is managing plants that have grown out of their own place in the
environment. In other words, gardeners must constantly fight
weeds.

WEED CONTROL

A weed to one person may be a wonderful plant to another. Remember that kudzu was promoted as an ornamental arbor-covering vine
before it began trying to smother the South!

Weed control begins with the identification of the weed. They are
usually classified as grassy (i.e., crabgrass) or broadleafed (i.e., dan-
delions). Once this type is determined, the weed is categorized as

an annual weed (growing from seed each year) or a perennial weed (growing back from its roots each year).

Knowing what kind of weed you are dealing with will help you decide the correct way to manage it. You will have to decide whether you want to use a weedkiller chemical or just pull the weeds by hand. For a lawn, you might be able to simply increase the vigor of the grass so it will choke out encroaching weeds.

Annual weeds are easiest to control with herbicides. They come up from seed each year, and scientists have developed chemicals which prevent seed germination and rooting. Of course, these chemicals need to be applied before the weed seeds germinate. These herbicides are called pre-emergents. To control annual weeds which grow in summer (i.e., crabgrass), a pre-emergent should be applied in mid-March, before warm weather makes the seeds ger-minate. Some annual weeds (i.e., chickweed) sprout in October and grow rapidly in early spring. To control them, a pre-emergent must be applied in early October. Read the labels on every product you consider to make sure it will control the weed you want to fight.

Perennial weeds grow from their roots each year and may spread further and further by seeds or by underground roots. To control them, a post-emergent herbicide is used after the weed leaves have emerged. This is a situation in which it pays to observe whether the plant is grassy or broadleafed. Chemicals which kill grassy weeds are usually ineffective on broadleafed weeds, and vice-versa. Again, read the product label to determine if it will do the job you desire.

Non-selective plant killers are just that. When sprayed on the green leaves of a plant, whether dandelion or dahlia, the plant will be killed. Several non-selective herbicides have been marketed in the last few years. Most of these chemicals do not linger in the soil, so you can spray a weedy lawn one weekend and plant grass seed the next. Since the chemical can't read your mind, use care when employing these herbicides.

Calamagrostis spp.

Feather Reed Grass

There will be a "whole lotta shakin' going on" if you plant feather reed grass. The tall, light-red, upright flower spikes emerge from the green foliage in early June. The spikes rise 3' to 4' above the foliage and gradually dry to a golden, then buff, color by autumn. Planted in a group, a sea of feather reed grass flower spikes will bend and sway with every breeze of summer. There are two species of feather reed grass that are useful in Georgia landscapes. Calamagrostis acutiflora *is sun-loving and typically will make few blooms in the shade. In south Georgia, it is semi-evergreen, but from Atlanta northwards the winter foliage is first yellow, then brown.* Calamagrostis brachytricha *blooms in late summer and can tolerate considerable shade. It can be an asset to woodland plantings and to areas too shady for other grasses. The flowers are denser than those of* Calamagrostis acutiflora. *The foliage will turn brown in winter in all parts of Georgia.*

WHEN TO PLANT

The best time to plant feather reed grass is in the spring, when days are warm and nights are cool, so that it can become established before summer. Feather reed grass can be divided in March after it has been cut back. A large clump can often be divided with a shovel into three or four separate plants.

WHERE TO PLANT

Plant *Calamagrostis acutiflora* in full sun, preferably where it is breezy. In a perennial flower bed, put it towards the back with *Sedum* 'Autumn Joy' or fall asters. You may wish to place some blue veronica in front. While *Calamagrostis brachytricha* can grow in shade, it will certainly do better in full sun. Try placing it in front of a camellia or an evergreen hedge of wax myrtle.

How to Plant

Dig a hole 3 times as wide as the root system of the container. There is no need to mix in soil amendments unless the grass is being planted in a large grouping or in an island with other plants. Spread the roots a little, by hand, before placing them in the hole. Tamp down the soil around the roots and water thoroughly.

Care and Maintenance

Fertilize a clump of feather reed grass late in the spring, when the leaves have begun to grow vigorously. New plants should get 1/8 cup of 10–10–10 fertilizer in May and the same amount in late June and late August. Mature clumps should receive 1/4 cup of 10–10–10 in May. Water weekly for a month after planting. Feather reed grass prefers a moist root system, even in full sun, so be ready to uncoil the water hose if summer rains do not appear weekly.

Additional Advice for Care

As with other ornamental grasses, feather reed grass has very few pests or problems. Beetles may chew briefly on the edges of the grass blades, but no control for them is necessary.

Additional Cultivars and Species

Calamagrostis arundinacea 'Karl Foerster' looks almost identical to *Calamagrostis acutiflora*, but it blooms a few weeks earlier. Rumor has it that because the two are indistinguishable, they are commonly sold interchangeably. If one of your plants doesn't bloom in synchronicity with the others, this could be the reason!

Cortaderia selloana

Pampas Grass

Pampas grass is ranked among the most durable landscape plants. It has few pest problems, grows well in a wide range of soils and requires little fertilizer—making it perfect for someone who hates yard work! But it does require a little care; without it, pampas grass will become just a big haystack. This grass is a perennial, native to Brazil and Argentina, and is hardy in all but extreme north Georgia. A mature plant may reach a height of 8'–10', with a spread of 6'–8'. The silvery-white plumes that are produced in late September look like cotton candy on a stick. There are both male and female pampas grass plants. The female plumes are broad, with many silky hairs covering the white flowers. The male plumes are narrower and do not have the tiny hairs. Don't worry that you'll be disappointed if you have a male plant; the differences are noticeable only when the two kinds grow side-by-side. It is not even necessary to have both sexes near each other. Plumes will form regardless of planting arrangement.

WHEN TO PLANT

The best time to plant pampas grass is in the spring, when days are warm and nights are cool, so it can become established before summer. Pampas grass can be divided in March after it has been sheared. A large clump can often be divided with a shovel into 6 or 8 separate plants.

WHERE TO PLANT

Pampas grass grows and flowers best in full sun. It will grow very slowly and may not produce plumes if it is planted in the shade. It makes an excellent screen plant at the edge of a lawn, but it should not be planted at the end of a driveway where it can obscure vision. The grass blades have very sharp edges, so don't put a clump in a spot you pass frequently.

How to Plant

Dig a hole 3 times as wide as the root system of the container. There is no need to mix in soil amendments unless the grass is being planted in a large grouping or in an island with other plants. Spread the roots a little, by hand, before placing them in the hole. Tamp down the soil around the roots and water thoroughly. Pampas grass tolerates salt spray and is an ideal plant for coastal Georgia landscapes. In sandy soil, watering may be necessary for the first year.

Care and Maintenance

Pampas grass requires a yearly pruning to look and grow its best. This should be done in February so that you can enjoy the plumes and dry foliage all winter. Since the grass blades are sharp, wear leather gloves when doing this chore. Tie a rope very tightly around the clump 4' from the ground and use a carpenter's saw or power weed trimmer to do the cutting at 12" to 18" high. A new clump should receive 1/2 cup of 10–10–10 in March, May, July and September. A mature clump needs only 2 pounds of 10–10–10 fertilizer in March.

Additional Advice for Care

Pampas grass makes a dramatic sight when the sun can shine through the foliage and plumes. The cloud-like plumes make excellent components of dried flower arrangements. Collect them just before they have fully opened, preferably in the morning. Older plumes tend to shatter. Just for fun, try dyeing them with food coloring!

Additional Cultivars and Species

Cortaderia selloana 'Rosea' has plumes that are rosy-pink instead of snow-white. *Cortaderia selloana* 'Pumila' is a dwarf form, barely reaching 5' tall. *Cortaderia selloana* 'Silver Stripe' grows to 5' tall and has a white stripe along the edge of each blade. *Cortaderia selloana* 'Gold Stripe' is similar but has a gold stripe.

Cynodon dactylon

Bermuda Grass

This warm-season grass is green in summer and buff/brown in winter. It is supremely adapted to Georgia, so it is sometimes cursed by gardeners though revered by golfers. The original Bermuda grass was brought from Africa around 1750. Development and improvement occurred in Arizona; the name for Bermuda seed is Arizona Common. But any grass that grows so rapidly has vast potential for improvement as gardeners select the plants that stay low and produce fewer seedheads. 'Tifton 419' (Tifway) and 'Tifton 328' (Tifgreen) Bermuda grasses are sterile hybrids, available only as sod. They produce no viable seed but a sprig of Tifton 328 sod will grow to cover a 12" by 12" square in only one summer. Laid in a checkerboard pattern over bare earth, Bermuda sod transforms a red clay eyesore lawn into a green eye-pleaser in just a day. As you might imagine, Bermuda seed costs less per square foot to establish than does Bermuda sod. On the other hand, the common Bermuda sends up multitudes of seed heads quickly after mowing. The seeded Bermuda is also a very common uninvited guest in flower beds!

WHEN TO PLANT

Common Bermuda seed can be planted anytime during the summer. The hybrid Bermuda sods are best laid in early summer. The sod will be thick and lush by September. It is even possible to plant dormant Bermuda sod in winter—as long as you don't mind the stares of neighbors when you water it in December!

WHERE TO PLANT

Bermuda grass is very much a sun-loving turf. It grows well in full sun and tends to thin out in partial shade. But with good, deep tilling before planting, Bermuda will grow even in the deep shade of a southern magnolia tree. If the grass becomes thin under a maturing shade tree, consider covering the area with mulch rather than fighting to get Bermuda grass to grow where it would rather not.

How to Plant

At the very minimum, use an aerator to loosen the earth before planting seed or sod. The best practice is to use a tiller to thoroughly soften the soil. (Pray for a cloudy day and stock plenty of lemonade if you are contemplating tilling a large area!) The tiller gives you the opportunity to mix in lime and starter fertilizer before grass covers the tract. If you are planting seed, use 1 to 2 pounds of seed per 1000 square feet. It is best to mix 1 pound of seed with 3 pounds of dry play sand before putting the mixture into a seed spreader. If you lay sod, put the pieces firmly against each other as you cover the earth. Use a hatchet to carve sod pieces to fit around a curb or flower bed.

Care and Maintenance

Fertilize Bermuda after it has turned 50 percent green in the spring. Don't be tempted to put out fertilizer any earlier, for a late freeze could wipe out the tender "forced" sprouts. Fertilize every 4 to 8 weeks during the summer. Four-week intervals make an intense green lawn . . . but you'll need to mow every five days! A September application of "Winterizer Fertilizer" will help the grass survive the winter. Bermuda grass will adapt to extreme drought by going semidormant. If water is given, it should be applied deeply and thoroughly. Thirty minutes with a sprinkler is not nearly enough.

Additional Advice for Care

Mow Bermuda grass at a height of 3/4" to 1 1/2". Weeds are not a big problem if the grass is strong. If weeds appear, correct your maintenance of the grass before you bring out the herbicides. Green winter weeds show up easily on a brown lawn in January. If the grass is dormant, use glyphosate herbicide to wipe out the invaders.

Additional Cultivars and Species

'Cheyenne' and 'Yuma' are introductions of improved Bermuda seed. They tend to be deeper green than common Bermuda and are reputed to resemble a sodded Bermuda. All Bermudas are very tolerant of wear. Whether in a stadium or between backyard soccer goals, no grass is better for sports turf.

119

LAWNS AND ORNAMENTAL GRASSES

Eremochloa ophiuroides

Centipede Grass

"This is the poor man's grass: never needs fertilizer, never needs lime, just mow twice a year!" *If this were true, every lawn in Georgia would be made of centipede grass and the fertilizer companies would be out of business. In fact, centipede can be a very attractive turf, but it has advantages and disadvantages just like any other grass. In the first place, centipede is a warm-season grass. It is green in the summer but goes dormant in the winter. Some homeowners prefer the year-round greenery of fescue. In the second place, centipede turf is a gray-green color. Some people prefer the deep green of a sodded Bermuda lawn. In the third place, centipede* does *require care and nutrients . . . so don't sell your fertilizer company stock yet! Centipede certainly has two advantages: it spreads rapidly by above-ground runners and it doesn't grow very tall. Mowing is needed, but less frequently. Centipede is a good alternative for some landscapes but a poor choice for others. Your choice of turf should depend on what you like and can maintain in your own personal space.*

WHEN TO PLANT

Centipede grass seed and sod can be planted in early summer. It is important to plant the seed before the hot, dry days of July. The seeds are slow to germinate and the seedlings require constant moisture to thrive. There is more leeway in planting sod. During the first month, regular irrigation is critical for the sod to become established.

WHERE TO PLANT

Centipede grass requires moderate to full sun. Light shade under pine trees is fine, but in deeper shade your centipede will become thin and weedy. Establishing centipede from seed has exacting requirements. Do not attempt it unless daily observation and care is possible. Centipede will not choke out other turf grasses, so the site should be completely cleared in preparation for seeding or sodding.

HOW TO PLANT

Planting centipede seed successfully is possible—but not everyone who attempts it will be successful. The soil must be tilled first, to give the seedling roots a chance for rapid growth. Spread only 1/4 pound of seed over 1000 square feet of soil and lightly rake to cover the seed with earth. Lightly mulch the area with wheat straw and begin daily watering. It is imperative that the upper 1" of soil be moist for the first two weeks. Depending on the weather, watering twice per day may be necessary. Though more expensive than seeding, centipede sod is much easier to establish successfully. If seeding fails, sodding is a backup alternative!

CARE AND MAINTENANCE

Contrary to popular opinion, centipede grass grows much better in limed soil. It is true that centipede can tolerate acid soil, but liming can make a big difference. If a soil test shows the pH to be less that 5.5, add lime to bring it up to pH 6.0. Centipede is sensitive to excessive phosphorus in the soil; the typical centipede fertilizer is 15–0–15. Apply 6 pounds of fertilizer per 1000 square feet in May, after the grass has turned green, and repeat in July. Mow centipede to a height of 2". Centipede grass tolerates drought by going semi-dormant. If you can't water in the summer, don't worry; when rain does come, the centipede will be green.

ADDITIONAL ADVICE FOR CARE

If you insist on trying to plant centipede seed, you'll find the seeds are quite tiny. A good sneeze might waste a lot of your landscaping budget! To help spread the seed evenly, mix 1 part seed with 8 parts dry sand. Set the seed spreader to its smallest opening and plan to push it over the lawn in several trips rather than just one.

ADDITIONAL CULTIVARS AND SPECIES

There are no improved varieties of centipede commonly available. One sod producer explains this by saying, "The secret of my success is knowing how to avoid fixing what ain't broken. Centipede grass hasn't broken on me yet!"

Festuca arundinacea

Fescue Grass

Fescue is a fast-growing turfgrass that stays some shade of green year-round. It looks its best fall through spring, but has problems trying to grow on hard soil or in full sunshine. It is usually planted from seed rather than grown from sod. Originally an excellent pasture grass, Pennington Seed Company saw fescue's potential as a lawn grass. For decades, 'Kentucky-31' fescue was the answer for homeowners who wanted a green lawn all year long. 'Kentucky-31' does tend to become "clumpy," however, and it has a rather coarse texture. In the last decade, seed companies have improved the old standard with numerous introductions of "turf-type" tall fescue. 'Rebel,' 'Anthem,' 'Tribute,' and several other selections have become desired brand names. The "turf-type" tall fescues usually rate higher than 'Kentucky-31' fescue in comparison trials. However, no one brand stands head and shoulders above all of the others in all situations. For this reason, it is much more important to establish and care for fescue properly than to look for the miracle fescue seed that will solve all of your lawn problems.

WHEN TO PLANT

The best time to plant fescue is in the fall, between September 15 and the end of October. The seedlings will have plenty of time to become strong in preparation for the summer heat nine months hence. Fescue can also be planted in early spring between mid-February and mid-March. This planting time can lead to problems with summer survival, however, so plant in fall if possible.

WHERE TO PLANT

Fescue is the most shade-tolerant grass for northern Georgia. If the ground is tilled before planting, it will tolerate full sun and summer drought. In hard clay and baking heat, though, fescue will thin out and need overseeding the next fall. Lawns with a mixture of shady and sunny spots are prime candidates for fescue. Dappled shade is excellent, but the grass will thin considerably in constant deep shade.

How to Plant

When planting a new lawn, till the entire area to a depth of 6 inches. This is also a good time to dig in lime and starter fertilizer as recommended by a soil test. Spread 6 pounds of "turf-type" seed evenly over 1000 square feet of earth. Rake the seed lightly to cover it with soil, then spread wheat straw over the area, one bale per 1000 square feet. Water lightly each day for a week, until tiny green "hair" begins to emerge from the ground. If no rain falls, water every other day until the entire lawn is green. Then begin watering twice each week until the grass seems deeply rooted. The wheat straw can be left to rot or it can be gently raked up.

Care and Maintenance

Fescue should be fertilized during its season of rapid growth, from fall to early spring. You should usually apply fertilizer 3 times: in September, in early November, and in mid-February. Use any brand of turf fertilizer at the rate recommended on the bag. Turf fescue looks best when mowed 2" high. In dry summers and when growing in heavy shade, mowing to 3" high helps the grass tolerate its environment. Water weekly during droughts if possible. Use empty soup cans to measure the water applied: don't stop the sprinkler until the water in the cans averages 3/4" deep.

Additional Advice for Care

Take care when using weedkiller chemicals close to the time when fescue seed is planted. Some chemicals take as long as 6 weeks to disappear in the soil. Read the herbicide label thoroughly before you spray your lawn. Brown patch disease is particularly prevalent on fescue fertilized during the summer.

Additional Cultivars and Species

Planting a blend of fescue seed has certain advantages over planting a single variety. The different seed in a blend should be able to adapt to different conditions in your lawn. The varieties in a blend change from year to year to take advantage of newer, improved selections of fescue grass.

123

LAWNS AND ORNAMENTAL GRASSES

Imperata cylindrica 'Red Baron'

Japanese Blood Grass

Don't let the name put you off. The upper half of its green foliage is blood red, but Japanese blood grass is not suitable for use in a Halloween horror house! In the southern part of the state, the leaves grow 12"–18" tall in a slowly spreading clump. Although blood grass is listed as hardy up through Zone 6, it seems to have a hard time surviving winter in north Georgia. The alternating periods of relative warmth and freezing cold during the winter along with soggy clay soil usually spell doom for a planting of Japanese blood grass. Even when grown as an annual, Japanese blood grass is exciting to see during the warm season. The foliage emerges green, with just a speck of red on the tip. As the grass grows, the red progresses down the blade, nearly to the ground by fall. Unlike other grasses, Japanese blood grass does not have flowers. The color of the foliage more than makes up for the lack of reproductive parts.

WHEN TO PLANT

Japanese blood grass is planted in spring in all but extreme south Georgia, where it is relatively perennial. In all parts of the state, afternoon shade is important. The thin foliage loses water rapidly and readily wilts under a hot sun.

WHERE TO PLANT

By all means, plant Japanese blood grass where the sunlight can stream through its thin leaves in morning or afternoon. The red-and-green-colored leaves waving back and forth in front of each other will be mesmerizing. Japanese blood grass makes an excellent centerpiece for a large pot on your patio or deck. Try combining it with blue and white petunias or blue scaevola for a feast of color.

How to Plant

The planting area should be very well drained, with little clay. Make sure the clump is not below the surrounding soil—excess water on the roots means quick death. A clump of Japanese blood grass in a container will look relatively small when purchased. The leaves are predominately vertical and do not arch like maiden grass or black fountain grass. Plan on planting 3 to 6 clumps 12" from each other in one spot for a good effect. In a half-barrel planter, 2 or 3 clumps will make a nice statement when surrounded by other plants.

Care and Maintenance

Japanese blood grass requires little fertilizer. Apply 1/8 cup of 10–10–10 at planting and another 1/8 cup in June. Strive for a lightly moist but not soggy soil. If the grass is seen to wilt in late June, move it to another, more shady spot. Unless you like the challenge of keeping Japanese blood grass alive over the winter, you can enjoy the brown foliage until it becomes tattered, then cut it all down. From mid-Georgia southwards, a light mulch of pine straw might help it survive the winter.

Additional Advice for Care

Like most ornamental grasses, Japanese blood grass has no important pests except the weather.

Additional Cultivars and Species

Like a character in a Gothic Southern novel, Japanese blood grass is the saintly member of a family of outlaws. *Imperata cylindrica*, its African cousin, is an aggressive weed which is forbidden for import into the United States. Observe your clump for blades which never turn red. A solid green leaf means you have a potential rival to kudzu on your hands!

Miscanthus sinensis

Maiden Grass

Among the showiest and most beautiful of ornamental grasses, a clump of maiden grass will grow to 7' tall by late summer. The top of a clump is decidedly wider than the bottom. The top may be 8' wide, emerging from a 24" diameter base. The stiff, arching leaves extend on all sides. Various cultivars have been introduced with variegations which contrast with the green leaf tissue. The beauty of the leaves in summer is supplanted by the magnificent tan-to-red seedheads which appear in late August. Winter brings another period of beauty to maiden grass. The leaves turn buff brown and the seedheads fade to silver. The plant surfaces seem to attract frost. Few things are more eye-catching than a frosted clump of maiden grass set in front of a tall evergreen hedge. By spring, the leaves and stems will have become broken and tattered. Then it is time to cut off all the foliage to a height of 6"–8" and allow the new blades to grow. By May, the "crewcut" will be hidden in greenery. Maiden grass is a terrific addition to a landscape. Its texture is unlike any other plant, so it is a striking accent plant next to tall, bold plants like Black-eyed Susan or purple coneflower.

WHEN TO PLANT

The best time to plant maiden grass is in the spring, so it can become established before the heat of summer. Clumps are always purchased in containers. Even if you have to plant in summer, maiden grass will probably do well if it is watered occasionally. Wait until the new grass blades have grown 12" before dividing it in the spring.

WHERE TO PLANT

Miscanthus can be used as a background to a perennial flower border, as a specimen plant in the middle of a lawn, or even as a hedge between properties. Its advantage when used as a hedge is that you can walk between adjacent plants without being cut, as you would with pampas grass. The variegated cultivars are particularly eye-catching. Maiden grass tolerates both very dry and very wet sites.

ZONE
6,7,8

How to Plant

Dig a hole 3 times as wide as the root system of the container. There is no need to mix in soil amendments unless the grass is being planted in a larger island or flower bed. Spread the roots somewhat, by hand, before placing them in the hole. Tamp down the soil around the roots and water thoroughly. Make sure the grass is not planted too deep. If water stands on the clump after a rain, root rot can ensue.

Care and Maintenance

Fertilize a fall-planted clump late in the following spring, when the leaves have begun to grow vigorously. New plants should get 1/4 cup of 10–10–10 fertilizer in May and again in late June and late August. Mature clumps should receive 1 cup of 10–10–10 in May and in late August. Except at establishment, watering is rarely needed. The foliage can be removed any time after it has turned brown. The feathery seedheads can be collected and used in dried arrangements, but unless they are cut early in the fall, they will become dry and fall apart indoors.

Additional Advice for Care

When the center of a mature clump of miscanthus becomes open or hollow, it's time to bring out the shovel and saws to divide it. Dig up the whole root ball, then plunge a sharp shovel through the center. Most likely, each half can then be halved again. Plant one section in the original hole and look for other places where the grass can flourish.

Additional Cultivars and Species

Miscanthus sinensis 'Gracillimus' is the most common cultivar. Look for the stripe of silver running up each blade. *Miscanthus sinensis* 'Variegatus' has leaves edged in white. *Miscanthus sinensis* 'Zebrinus' is very striking, with bands of yellow variegation that cut across the blade every 6" from the base to the tip.

Pennisetum spp.

Fountain Grass

The choice of purple fountain grass (Pennisetum setaceum 'Rubrum') for landscapes and planters during the 1996 Games in Atlanta was a huge success. The purple foliage and the tan bottlebrush seedheads gave just the right texture and height to many beauty spots without taking up a lot of room. Clumps of Pennisetum setaceum 'Rubrum' grow to 4' tall. The base is very narrow and only in late summer will the blades arch outward and shade neighboring plants. Unfortunately, this grass will be killed at temperatures below 20 degrees, but it is readily available in garden centers as an annual grass each spring. Another fountain grass commonly used in landscapes is Pennisetum alopecuroides. It has green, not purple, foliage. The dark, almost black, seedheads are almost as striking as those of purple fountain grass. This species of fountain grass seeds itself readily wherever it is planted. Don't try to use it as a specimen plant, but try it as a groundcover for a slope. Another idea is to use it as a groundcover in an island in the center of your yard, with a dogwood or small maple in the center. Turf grass growing around the island will keep this fountain grass at bay.

WHEN TO PLANT

The best time to plant pennisetum is in the spring, when days are warm and nights are cool, so it can become established before summer. Seedlings of *Pennisetum alopecuroides* will show themselves, in desired as well as undesired places, by May. They can be pulled like weeds or transplanted to new spots.

WHERE TO PLANT

Plant pennisetum in full sun. Since the grass does well without watering, similarly low-maintenance plants make good companions. The purple foliage of *Pennisetum setaceum* 'Rubrum' contrasts with yellow flowers. Try planting it in front of perennial sunflower (*Helianthus atrorubens*) or behind *Lantana camara* 'New Gold.'

How to Plant

Dig a hole 3 times as wide as the root system of the container. There is no need to mix in soil amendments unless the grass is being planted in a larger island or flower bed. Spread the roots a little, by hand, before placing them in the hole. Tamp down the soil around the roots and water thoroughly. A mature clump of *Pennisetum alopecuroides* might need to be divided every 3 years to keep it looking its best. This can be done in spring, after the green blades have emerged but before the summer arrives.

Care and Maintenance

Fertilize a clump late in the spring, when the leaves have begun to grow vigorously. New plants should get 1/8 cup of 10–10–10 fertilizer in May and again in late June and late August. Mature clumps should receive 1/4 cup of 10–10–10 in May. Except at establishment, watering is rarely needed. The foliage can be removed any time after it has turned brown. The spiky foxtail seedheads can be collected and used in dried arrangements, but unless they are cut early in the fall, they will become dry and fall apart indoors. Some gardeners have reported good results by spraying them with hair spray to hold the seeds to the stems.

Additional Advice for Care

Fountain grass is attractive in mass plantings or you may plant just 2 or 3 together. Try not to crowd them beside sheltering plants—the slightest breeze sets the foliage and flowers in motion. Fountain grass is a good choice for a mixed perennial flower bed along the edge of a building. It will give height and motion to the scene.

Additional Cultivars and Species

Black fountain grass (*Pennisetum alopecuroides* 'Moudry') has exceptionally dark seedheads. They are very attractive in contrast with the glossy green foliage. *Pennisetum* 'Burgundy Giant' is not hardy in the northern half of the state, but it is perennial in south Georgia. As its name implies, it is very large, possibly 10' tall with 3' seed spikes.

Lawns and Ornamental Grasses

St. Augustine Grass

Where would south Georgia lawns be without St. Augustine grass? Indige-nous to the West Indies and common in tropical Africa, St. Augustine grass is an excellent choice for the sandy soils of the lower half of the state. Locals have no need to try anything else when St. Augustine does so well. St. Augustine is common from Macon up to Atlanta, though it is not the predominant turfgrass choice. North of Atlanta, only a gambler would plant a grass that will suffer cold injury in most winters. This low-growing warm-season grass goes dormant in cool weather but recovers quickly. It endures sun and shade and is very tolerant of close clipping. The grass blades are quite broad. St. Augustine is much more coarsely textured than Bermuda grass. It grows so aggressively that a lawn feels slightly "spongy" beneath your feet. On a warm fall day, nothing is better on which to play tag football!

WHEN TO PLANT

Seed is not commonly available. St. Augustine sod can be planted any time from late spring through early fall.

WHERE TO PLANT

St. Augustine grass is very tolerant of shade. The wide blades are efficient in gathering sunshine underneath shrubs and trees. It is also an excellent full-sun turf and will crowd out most weeds. In the northern third of the state, winter injury is the main danger for St. Augustine grass. The center of a lawn may die completely, though areas along a warm driveway or in the shelter of shrubs may survive.

HOW TO PLANT

Sod is easy to lay. Simply clear the area of weeds, dig the soil with a tiller, and rake it smooth. Using a hatchet to cut smooth curves around landscape islands and concrete curbs, place the pieces in a

pattern like a bricklayer's. St. Augustine grows very rapidly. You can plant 3" by 3" plugs 12" apart in spring and they will grow together by fall. The plugs can be planted in an existing lawn and the St. Augustine will eventually crowd out the original grass.

CARE AND MAINTENANCE

St. Augustine grass responds well to regular applications of "slow-release" turf fertilizer. Apply a good quality turf fertilizer when growth begins in spring and again in June, July and September. Mow at a height of 2" to 3". In sandy soil and extreme heat, St. Augustine grass needs watering once each week. Use soup cans to check how much water is being applied. To make sure the soil under the grass is wet deeply, don't stop watering until there is about ³/₄" of water in the cans.

ADDITIONAL ADVICE FOR CARE

Infestations of chinch bug are common on St. Augustine lawns. These bugs chew foliage and spread disease. To determine if you have them, cut out both ends of a gallon tin can. Press one cut end into an area of the lawn and fill it with water. If chinch bugs are present, they will float to the surface. Check with your local Extension office for an effective control.

ADDITIONAL CULTIVARS AND SPECIES

'Floratam' is an improved selection of St. Augustine grass, resistant to chinch bug and to St. Augustine Decline virus. 'Raleigh' St. Augustine grass is more cold-tolerant than other selections. If you really want to turn heads and stop traffic, try to locate 'Variegated St. Augustine Grass.' You'll be the first on your block with a bright yellow lawn!

LAWNS AND ORNAMENTAL GRASSES

Zoysia spp.

Zoysia Grass

Zoysia is a slow-growing but extremely thick and durable turfgrass. It is green from spring through fall, then changes to a golden-brown in winter. The grass is well adapted throughout the state. It spreads by above-ground stolons and by rhizomes beneath the ground. Zoysia grass arrived in the United States in the early 1900s. It was among the thousands of plants found by biological explorers in Asia who shipped their finds back to the United States for study. Although thick and carpet-like, zoysia grass is slow to establish in a new lawn. Seed is very difficult to harvest; zoysia is almost always established by laying sod. Two sod varieties are commonly available: 'Meyer' and 'Emerald.' 'Meyer' zoysia has a wider blade and is coarser than 'Emerald' in appearance. 'Emerald' is a deeper green and has fine blades. Both can tolerate light shade. Another technique for planting zoysia is to plug 2" by 2" pieces into an existing fescue lawn that is struggling to survive in full sun. If the lawn is mowed lower than 2", the zoysia will choke most of the fescue out in 5 years.

WHEN TO PLANT

Lay zoysia sod in early summer when the earth is very warm. Unlike Bermuda sod, laying zoysia sod in the fall simply tempts fate and courts failure. If the ground is hard, the roots will not be able to grow into it before cold weather comes. The shallow-rooted zoysia sod is easy prey to severe cold and drying winds.

WHERE TO PLANT

'Meyer' zoysia is more more tolerant of winter than 'Emerald,' while 'Emerald' is more shade-tolerant than 'Meyer.' Neither can grow in deep shade, and both look their best in full sun. South of Atlanta down to the Florida line, either grass is acceptable, but north of the city, 'Meyer' gets the nod. 'Meyer' can survive temperatures below zero degrees, but periods of warm weather in winter weaken it considerably.

How to Plant

Use a tiller to thoroughly dig the soil. This is a good time to mix in lime and fertilizer, if recommended by a soil test. Rake the area smooth, then run a lawn roller once over the area to reveal any low spots. Correct these with added soil. Lay the sod pieces tightly together, in a pattern like a bricklayer's. Use a small hatchet to chop sod to fit around curbs and flower beds. When all of the sod is down, push the roller over it again to put the roots in close contact with the soil. Water regularly for two weeks to keep the sod and the earth moist. Use soup cans to check how much water is being applied. Don't stop watering until there is about 3/4" of water in the cans.

Care and Maintenance

Zoysia does best with less rather than more fertilizer. It tends to form a layer of thatch under the green grass if too much fertilizer and water are used. Spread fertilizer in spring when the zoysia is mostly green, and repeat in midsummer. Use any brand of turf fertilizer that contains "slow release" nitrogen, at the rate recommended on the bag. Mow the turf no higher than 1½". This will help prevent thatch and cold injury. Zoysia will go semidormant during a drought but will spring back green when rain returns.

Additional Advice for Care

'Meyer' zoysia is sometimes advertised as 'Amazoy' zoysia. Plugs of this turf are sold by mail. Consider the cost versus the size of the shipped plugs before you buy. Since zoysia is slow to establish, plugs should be no smaller than 2" in diameter and should be planted no more than six inches apart. Mail-order plugs are usually smaller than this.

Additional Cultivars and Species

'El Toro' zoysia is similar to 'Meyer' but is reputed to be much faster at establishing itself. Zoysia seed is occasionally found in garden centers, but it is difficult to get a thick stand in one year by planting seed. Weeds quickly take advantage of the initially thin grass. It may take years to have an acceptable zoysia lawn planted from seed.

133

Perennials and Herbs

ERENNIALS, PLANT THEM AND FORGET THEM. *Well, almost. I remember working at Barnsley Gardens in Adairsville, Georgia, and installing a 120-foot long herbaceous border. Most of these plants were perennials, but we learned that some took several years to bloom, some needed staking, and others quickly outgrew their allotted spaces, making it necessary to move them so that other plants would have room to grow. In fact, it was during this time that I came to appreciate the expression I had heard from other gardeners: "If it hasn't been moved three times, it's not in the right place."—E.L.G.*

The good news is that, unlike annuals, which must be replaced each season, most perennials will grow and bloom in the same spot year after year. With just a minimum amount of care, perennials may outlive the gardeners that plant them. Perennials, often referred to as herbaceous plants, produce fleshy stems which die down each winter, but their roots stay alive and send up new growth in the spring. In some parts of Georgia, certain perennials remain evergreen all year round. There are even perennials like hellebores whose flowers brave the cold days of winter.

Another advantage of growing perennials over annuals is that many are easy to divide and transplant, providing you with additional plants in very little time. There is a wealth of perennials that thrive in Georgia gardens, including many for sun and shade and many that have striking foliage or dramatic flowers.

HEAT HARDINESS

When a book tells us that a plant is hardy from Zones 4 to 8, what it often doesn't say is whether the plant will tolerate hot, humid summers like those that we experience in Georgia. Plants like the much-loved delpheniums are perennials in the North, but they rarely survive our summers and are best treated like annuals here. In recent years, more perennials that actually seem to enjoy our weather have become available to gardeners in Georgia.

Soil, Siting, and More

As with all plants, the key to growing successful perennials is having the right soil for the right plant. The best insurance for growing healthy perennials is to begin with a soil that has been amended with organic matter and that holds moisture but is well drained. Once they are established, perennials should not need to be fertilized regularly, especially if the soil is topdressed with an organic mulch in the spring and the fall. Though certain perennials do tolerate our hot summers, soil that stays wet in winter will lead to their quick demise.

When choosing perennials for your own garden, consider what they will look like even when they're not blooming. Certain perennials like hostas are grown more for their foliage than for their flowers and offer a long season of interest in the garden. Be sure to consider all the seasons: include in your garden not only spring-flowering perennials but those that bloom in summer, fall, and winter. If you want perennials that require the least amount of maintenance, be sure to choose varieties that won't require staking, or site the plants so that other plants will help support them.

Perhaps the most important thing is to have fun. Try a few perennials and add more as you find out what does well in your garden and what you like. And remember that perennials are only part of the garden and should be combined with annuals, shrubs, and trees for the best effect.

Allium schoenoprasum

Chives

Height: 12"–18"
Flowers: pale pinkish-purple Blooms: late spring to early summer

Although best known for their uses in cooking, chives are a fine perennial for edging a flower or herb garden. In cooking, they are used as an alternative to the stronger onion, adding a mild garlicky-onion flavor to many different foods. The green, hollow, grass-like foliage looks good all season, and showy flowers add a spot of pale color when they bloom. For optimum flavor, harvest chives before they flower while the stems are young and slender, being sure to cut back the clumps to a few inches in height. This will encourage new growth and healthy plants. Chives will tolerate a range of growing conditions, but for best results plant them in full sun in a well-drained soil. If you want to establish a clump of chives quickly, sow about 20 seeds together in a 4" pot. When they are several inches high, set the whole clump out in the garden. Chives, like other alliums, are extremely cold hardy, so they can be set out as early as a week or two before the frost-free date. You can also make new plants easily by dividing mature plants.

WHEN TO PLANT

Plant chive seeds in the early spring. If you want to establish a clump quickly, start them indoors in pots with about 20 seeds per 4" pot. Transplant them to the garden when they are several inches tall. This can be done as early as two weeks before the frost-free date since chives are very cold hardy. Divide clumps in the spring or the fall. You can transplant as few as 3 to 6 of the small bulbs.

WHERE TO PLANT

Plant chives in the flower garden, in the herb garden, or in containers. A tough perennial, chives make a good edging plant. The plants increase in size in no time. Plant them in combination with other herbs like thyme, basil, parsley, or oregano. Considered a deterrent

ZONE
6,7,8

to Japanese beetles and several leaf diseases, it is recommended
by some that chives be planted with roses, tomatoes, carrots,
and grapes.

HOW TO PLANT

Plant chives in full sun in a well-drained soil. Dividing clumps
every other year or so will keep plants looking full and healthy.
Avoid areas where soil is wet or soggy. If you use chives as an
edging plant, space them about 12"–18" apart.

CARE AND MAINTENANCE

Chives are easy-care perennials. Once you establish a clump in the
garden, you will be able to easily divide and transplant these small
bulbs to other areas or give them to gardening friends. They require
no special fertilization, but they do benefit from shearing back to a
height of about 2" when their leaves are harvested. You may want to
harvest every other plant so that they won't all look unsightly at the
same time.

ADDITIONAL ADVICE FOR CARE

To make a colorful salad, harvest chive flowers and chop them into
small pieces. Mix them with various lettuces and other fresh herbs.
Chive flowers are also pretty in small summer bouquets. Alliums
are a large group of plants, including bulb types and some with
more fibrous roots. They are tough garden plants; once planted,
many will flower year after without any special care.

ADDITIONAL CULTIVARS AND SPECIES

Allium giganteum has lilac-pink flowers, 5"–6", borne on 3'–4'-tall
stems. *Allium caeruleum* offers beautiful true-blue flowers on
12"–18" stems.

Amsonia hubrichtii

Arkansas Blue Star

Height: 2½'–3' or more
Flowers: pale sky-blue Blooms: late spring

Because blooms are often "here today and gone tomorrow," it is important to consider foliage when choosing perennials for our Georgia gardens. Both local and mail-order sources have begun to offer more perennials that will not wither in our heat. One of these gems is the little-known Amsonia hubrichtii *which offers delicate, blue, star-shaped flowers in late spring and handsome foliage throughout the growing season. Almost needle-like, the leaves whorl around the stem. The effect is like that of a small willow. In the fall, these delicate leaves turn golden-yellow, sometimes orange. This Southeastern native likes full sun, but can tolerate some light shade. A slightly acid, moist, well-drained soil is ideal, but this* Amsonia *is a tough, carefree sort that adapts well to a wide range of growing conditions. Its fine texture provides a good contrast for plants like chrysanthemums, iris, black-eyed susan, purple coneflower, bee balm, and some of the more sun-tolerant hostas such as 'Sum and Substance.' In just a few years, this perennial will form large clumps that grow as wide as they do high.*

WHEN TO PLANT

Plant *Amsonia* in early spring or fall. It can be grown from seed, divisions, or cuttings taken in the spring.

WHERE TO PLANT

Plant this Arkansas blue star in full sun or light shade. If planted in too much shade, the clumps will be open and floppy. A moderately fertile soil that is evenly moist is ideal, but an average soil is fine.

HOW TO PLANT

If you plant young divisions, take them in early spring or fall. Plant them as soon as you divide them and water them well. If you buy a

| | | ZONE 6,7,8 |

container-grown plant, dig a hole 2 to 3 times larger than the container and plant the blue star to a depth equal to what it was in the container. There is no need to regularly divide this perennial. Its large clumps look good in the garden.

CARE AND MAINTENANCE

This perennial should not need fertilizer or pruning unless you want to cut it back immediately after blooming to keep the plants bushy. Water during periods of drought.

ADDITIONAL ADVICE FOR CARE

For a dramatic effect, plant this perennial in groups to present masses of finely textured foliage. You may plant it in combination with other summer-blooming perennials. It also complements asters.

ADDITIONAL CULTIVARS AND SPECIES

Perhaps better known and slightly more cold-hardy is *Amsonia tabernaemontana*, which also grows to about 3'. The leaves are much wider and the effect is not the same. If you have room for only one blue star, I would recommend *A. hubrichtii*.

Anemone x hybrida 'Honorine Jobert'

Japanese Anemone

Height: 3'–4'
Flowers: white Blooms: early fall

One almost never gets too much of the color white. In the garden it can either soften intense hues or help show them off. An elegant fall bloomer, the white Japanese anemone brightens up the garden at the end of the day when the light is low in the sky. Popular since before the Civil War, 'Honorine Jobert' is still a favorite selection of gardeners who do not live in coastal areas. A strong grower, it produces a large mound of foliage with leaves divided into 3 leaflets. As the summer progresses, its bright green leafy mass gives no hint of what's to come in fall, when the slender sturdy stems shoot up to 3' or more. Loaded with buds for what seems like weeks, they finally open to beautiful white flowers that dance in the autumn breezes. The silky flowers are 2"–3" across. A. 'Honorine Jobert' makes a good cut flower.

WHEN TO PLANT

Plant Japanese anemone in the spring or fall. Divisions should be taken in the spring; root cuttings should be taken when the plant is dormant.

WHERE TO PLANT

Plant this perennial in the middle or back of the flower border where the blooms can arch over other plants. Morning sun combined with shade during the hottest part of the day is ideal. If you plant in full sun, be sure to keep the soil moist. Avoid areas where the soil does not dry out or drain well during the winter, the plant's dormancy period.

HOW TO PLANT

Planting this perennial in a site that has rich, moist, well-drained soil, morning sun, and shade from the hottest part of the day will result in its rapid spread. Wet feet in the winter will lead to its quick

ZONE
6,7,8

death. Plant Japanese anemones so that they have at least 2'–3' to spread and grow. Locating them next to gray foliage plants or bright colors will show off their flowers.

CARE AND MAINTENANCE

Amend the soil before you plant by mixing 1/3 organic matter, 1/3 coarse sand, and 1/3 of the existing soil, which usually has a high content of clay. Topdress with organic matter in the spring and fall. Keep plants watered during the summer months. No pruning is necessary. If you plant this perennial in a windy area, it is best to stake the stalks before they begin to flower.

ADDITIONAL ADVICE FOR CARE

Japanese anemones look good in combination with gray foliage plants such as artemisia or lamb's ears. They also contrast well with rich purple asters.

ADDITIONAL CULTIVARS AND SPECIES

One cultivar with semi-double white flowers is *A.* 'Whirlwind.' Not nearly as elegant as the white forms but still worth growing is the pink-flowered cultivar of the related species *A. hupehensis* 'September Charm.' It grows 2'–3'.

Aquilegia canadensis

Columbine

Height: 2′–3′
Flowers: red and yellow, bell-shaped, nodding Blooms: early spring

This columbine grows throughout much of eastern North America, mostly in woodland areas. Although its flowers are not as showy as are those of some hybrid columbines, this vigorous native seeds itself freely and delights us when it appears in the most unlikely places: between rocks, in tiny crevices, or in the cavities of dead trees. About an inch in size, the delicate flowers bloom on and off for several weeks. When growing any type of columbine, a gardener may encounter damage done by leaf miners, though A. canadensis *seems more resistant to leaf miner than some of the larger-flowered selections. Leaves riddled with tunnels of a light color are a sign that leaf miners have invaded your garden. A simple and nontoxic remedy is to cut back the foliage as soon as you see damage. Plants will soon put out a flush of fresh dark-green leaves that will look good until frost. Use this columbine to achieve spots of color in a bright woodland garden or in a more sunny location. In the hottest parts of Georgia, columbine may perform like an annual.*

WHEN TO PLANT

Plant columbine in early spring or fall when the soil is warm. Plants grown from seed sown in the spring may not flower the first year.

WHERE TO PLANT

Plant columbine in a woodland garden where it gets plenty of light but not full sun all day long. If you plant it in a place that gets full sun, make sure the soil is rich and moist. Columbine growing in dappled shade will bloom over a longer period of time.

ZONE
6,7,8

How to Plant

Plant in early spring or fall. Seeds sown in the spring may not bloom the first season. Divisions can be taken in late summer or early fall. Columbines prefer a rich, moist, well-drained soil.

Care and Maintenance

Water during dry periods and cut back foliage if the plant is attacked by leaf miners. No other special care is needed. If mature clumps of columbine need to be divided, it is best to do this after they finish blooming. Dig up the entire clump and carefully tease apart sections of the main plant with a digging fork. Make sure that each division has buds and some roots. Replant, mulch, and water well.

Additional Cultivars and Species

A. canadensis 'Corbett' is a yellow-flowered cultivar 12"–24" tall. A good dwarf columbine is *A. flabellata* var. *nana*. It grows less than 12" tall and is good for the front of a border or for a rock garden.

Powis Castle Artemisia

Height: 2'–3'
Flowers: insignificant

Long before they became popular as garden plants, the leaves and flowers of
Artemisia *(wormwood) were grown for their medicinal and healing properties.* Artemisia absinthium, *thought to be one of the parents of
'Powis Castle,' was used to make the drink absinthe, a potent stimulant
that can cause mental illness. Because of its toxic properties, wormwood is
not recommended for use in home remedies! This plant may be too successful, sometimes taking over other plants. Placed in the right location, its
finely textured silver-gray foliage offers interest year round. The divided
leaves, 2"–5" long, have a silver cast which makes the plant a good candidate for planting next to harsh colors, or for combining with plants like
roses. Its height can cover the ugly knees that roses so often develop. One
word of caution: 'Powis Castle' can grow to the size of a small car in just a
few seasons! Although you can cut it back, for best results propagate this
plant from cuttings every 2 or 3 years. If you must cut it back, do not do so
until early spring just before new growth begins.*

WHEN TO PLANT

Plant 'Powis Castle' in the spring when soil temperatures begin to
warm or in the fall when soil temperatures are still warm.

WHERE TO PLANT

Plant *A.* 'Powis Castle' in a location where it will get lots of sun.
Allow it some space; it grows 2'–3' high and wide very quickly.

HOW TO PLANT

Plant in well-drained soil. If necessary to improve the drainage, add
sand. This artemisia is a happy companion for roses or other perennials like coneflowers, salvias, and chrysanthemums.

ZONE
6,7,8

CARE AND MAINTENANCE

There is no need to fertilize. Cut the plant back in late spring if it gets leggy and open. This hardy perennial becomes woody after one season of growth. Any cutting back should be done in late spring or early summer so that plants can recover before winter.

ADDITIONAL ADVICE FOR CARE

This perennial may suffer during wet weather, but is quick to recover, unless the soil remains wet.

ADDITIONAL CULTIVARS AND SPECIES

This cultivar has proved to be one of the best for our hot, humid summers, but is probably not suited for Coastal gardens.

Mottled Wild Ginger

Height: 2' by 2' clumps
Flowers: purple brown Blooms: in early spring

Discovered at Callaway Gardens in Pine Mountain, Georgia, this vigorous
selection of wild ginger has evergreen, heart-shaped, shiny green leaves
with lighter cream markings. The leaves look something like those of hardy
cyclamen. Planted in a woodland, in a moist but well-drained soil, this
selection of wild ginger forms evergreen clumps that look good year round,
even during the heat of our summers when other plants look wilted and
worn out. A good companion plant for hellebores and ferns, it will brighten
up any shade garden. Slow to spread, it can be easily propagated by divid-
ing the underground rhizomes in late winter. Children will have fun
discovering "little brown jugs," the inconspicuous flowers hidden under
the leaves. Mottled wild ginger gets its common name from the ginger-like
scent released by bruised or cut roots. It is truly an aristocrat, worth seek-
ing out for a shade garden. It is not related to Zingiber officinale, *the*
exotic plant whose rhizomes are the source of the gingerroot used for
cooking and medicine.

WHEN TO PLANT

Plant mottled wild ginger in spring or early fall. Take divisions in
late winter or early spring.

WHERE TO PLANT

This native ginger needs a moist, well-drained woodland area. Plant
it with other woodland species such as ferns and hellebores. It also
makes a good companion for spring-blooming woodland phlox and
small bulbs like dwarf iris. Although A. 'Callaway' is an evergreen,
it is not fast-spreading like ivy or vinca and is perhaps best used as
a specimen plant.

ZONE 6,7,8

HOW TO PLANT

Plant in a rich soil, avoiding areas where there may be competition from tree roots. Topdress with mulch in the spring and fall. Keep plants well watered.

CARE AND MAINTENANCE

No special fertilization is needed. Just be sure the soil is rich in organic matter. If the soil stays too dry, plants will look wilted and unattractive. Apply a layer of mulch in the spring and in the fall.

ADDITIONAL ADVICE FOR CARE

To create a tapestry effect in the garden, plant this woodland gem in combination with more aggressive groundcovers such as ajuga or foamflower.

ADDITIONAL CULTIVARS AND SPECIES

Asarum canadense, the Canadian wild ginger, has broad, heart-shaped leaves up to 7" across. It grows 6"–12" high. Although it is not an evergreen, it tolerates the extreme heat that we experience in Zone 8.

Asclepias tuberosa

Butterfly Weed

Height: 18"–36"
Flowers: orange, lipstick red Blooms: late spring to midsummer

Butterfly weed is a familiar wildflower often seen growing along the same roadside ditches and open sunny fields that later display asters and golden-rods. Individual plants in one field may bloom in a whole range of colors, from yellow to orange to deep red. A native wildflower, butterfly weed makes a good ornamental for the flower garden. Because it competes so well with grass, it also makes a good meadow plant. The blooms are especially attractive to Aphrodite and Fritillary butterflies. Be sure you remember where you place this plant in the garden; it comes up late in the spring and might be mistaken for a weed by the uninformed. It is both illegal and destructive to dig plants from the wild, although there are exceptions to this rule. In order to successfully transplant butterfly weed, dig deeply to avoid cutting the tap root. The name Asclepias comes from the Greek: Askelpios was the god of healing.

When to Plant

Plant divisions in the fall. Use fresh seed to start new plants. Container-grown plants can be planted in the spring once new growth is visible, or they can be planted in the fall.

Where to Plant

Plant butterfly weed in a hot full-sun spot where the soil is well drained. Avoid wet areas. Because it is a short plant, locate it toward the front or middle of the flower border where its flowers can be appreciated.

How to Plant

Sow seeds in the spring. Plant transplants immediately after you divide them. Keep as much of the original soil with each division as possible.

ZONE
6,7,8

CARE AND MAINTENANCE

Hot temperatures and dry soils are all this tough perennial needs to thrive in your garden, but it does require watering during periods of drought. It requires no special care and is virtually free of pests and diseases.

ADDITIONAL ADVICE FOR CARE

This perennial makes a good cut flower. The dried seed pods are ornamental and used often in dried arrangements and in wreaths.

ADDITIONAL CULTIVARS AND SPECIES

Asclepias incarnata, swamp milkweed, grows to 3' tall and has clusters of mauve, pink, or white flowers. This species will grow in dry or wet soils and attracts hordes of butterflies. It is hardy from Zones 3 to 9.

PERENNIALS AND HERBS

Aster tartaricus

Tartarian Daisy

Height: 6'–7'
Flowers: lavender daisies Blooms: late September–November

After the dog days of summer, the fall garden can delight us with its brilliant foliage and flowers that suddenly appear like old friends with whom we can pick up right where we left off. A native of Siberia, Aster tartaricus *grows happily in Georgia gardens in full sun or part shade. Tough and adaptable, this perennial comes into bloom in late autumn just when many plants such as iris, loosestrife, and bee balm have packed up for the season. After one year in the garden, the slender but strong flower stalks can reach up to 7'. You may prefer to plant it in a dry spot, where it won't be as vigorous as it would be in moist soil. I know of one keen gardener who pondered for months over whether a large clump of rather weedy-looking foliage with coarse leaves up to 2' long and 6" wide was something she had planted or was simply a weed out of control. Fortunately, she followed the dictum: "If in doubt, don't pull it out." In late autumn she was rewarded with clusters of lavender-blue daisies with yellow centers.*

WHEN TO PLANT
Plant in early spring or fall. Easy to propagate by division, clumps can be divided every few years.

WHERE TO PLANT
Plant this aster at the back of the perennial border where it can lean over flowers that bloom earlier in the season. You may plant in a moist spot, but planting it in dry soil will help to keep this fast grower in bounds.

HOW TO PLANT
There is no need to amend the soil for this aster. Plant it in full sun or part shade. As is true of most perennials, you can expect better flowering if you plant in a full-sun location. For an eye-catching

combination of purples, try planting *Callicarpa americana* in the same area. The purple fruit of the callicarpa and the lavender daisies make a striking display in the fall garden.

CARE AND MAINTENANCE

Divide clumps every few years if the aster becomes too aggressive. There is no need to fertilize this fast grower.

ADDITIONAL ADVICE FOR CARE

There are over 600 species of aster. Although many are considered roadside weeds, there are hundreds of desirable kinds to select, many of which are native to Georgia. Great for late-summer or fall blooms, they are attractive when planted in combination with Joe-Pye weed and goldenrod, especially *Solidago* 'Fireworks,' which blooms for weeks.

ADDITIONAL CULTIVARS AND SPECIES

Many other gardenworthy asters bloom in late summer and in the fall. One favorite: *A. novae-angliae*, 'Harrington's Pink,' which grows 3' to 5' tall and has salmon-pink flowers. *A.* 'Hella Lacy' has violet-blue daisies on 4' to 5' plants. For colorful foliage, try *A. lateriflorus* 'Prince.' It has deep purple foliage and tiny white daisies.

Baptisia australis

Wild Indigo

False Indigo

Height: 3'–5' or taller
Flowers: blue Blooms: spring

An adaptable native with handsome blue-green foliage and beautiful indigo-blue flowers, this is a plant for gardeners who claim they "can't grow anything." Wild indigo is slow to become established in the garden, but after a few years it should become a large clump. Left alone, it will thrive with little or no care. Like many members of the pea family, this legume adapts to poor soils and grows in shade or sun. The inch-long, pea-like flowers bloom on 10"–12" tall stems for close to 4 weeks in the spring. This is an easy-to-grow plant that offers attractive foliage, beautiful flowers, and decorative seed pods. Shaking the dry pods makes a sound like a child's rattle. Even without the sound effects, this hardy ornamental makes a fine specimen plant in sunny borders or along the edge of a woodland. After the plant blooms, the foliage provides a good foil for other summer-blooming perennials. Provided it gets plenty of sun, you shouldn't need to stake wild indigo. The genus name Baptisia *comes from the Greek* bapto, *to dye. In ancient times, several species of* Baptisia *were used to make dyes.*

WHEN TO PLANT

Plant *baptisia* in spring or fall. Root divisions should be taken in the late fall to early spring.

WHERE TO PLANT

Baptisia australis will tolerate poor soils with low fertility, but it will thrive in full sun in soils that are moist and rich. Plants grown in the shade may need to be staked. Site this plant at the middle or back of the flower border, so its foliage can serve as a backdrop for other perennials.

ZONE
6,7,8

HOW TO PLANT

It is desirable to prepare the soil so that it is rich and moist, but it is not mandatory. Allow room to grow, as a clump will eventually be 2'–3' across. Plant wild indigo in full sun or partial shade.

CARE AND MAINTENANCE

Wild indigo will need to be staked only if it is planted in a very shady location. No special fertilizer or pruning is required. Leave seed pods to dry on the plant for winter decorations, or collect them to use in dried bouquets and arrangements.

ADDITIONAL ADVICE FOR CARE

Wild indigo may take several years to produce many blooms, but once it is established in the garden, it will thrive for years with little or no care.

ADDITIONAL CULTIVARS AND SPECIES

B. alba has white flowers in late spring. It is not as stately in the garden as *B. australis*. *B. tinctoria* has yellow flowers and blooms in the summer.

Begonia grandis (evansiana)

Hardy Begonia

Height: 18"–24"
Flowers: pink Blooms: late summer to fall

The elegant hardy begonia is like Cinderella waiting to be discovered, while the gaudy stepsisters, wax begonias, get all the attention—wax begonias are planted in huge numbers every year in Georgia gardens. A true patrician, hardy begonia waits until late in the season to put on a show, whether in the woodland garden or in the shady corner of a flower border. The waxy leaves look fresh all season, especially when late afternoon light hits the red undersides from behind. Airy sprays of pink flowers rise above the foliage and bloom for weeks. Then the seed capsules dry on the plant, providing additional ornamental interest that lasts into the winter. Easy to grow, hardy begonia spreads by little bubils that take root where they touch the ground, maturing into plants of flowering size in one season. This plant can grow in acid or alkaline soils. The best soil is one that is reasonably fertile and well-drained, but hardy begonias have been known to do well even in clay soil.

When to Plant

Plant hardy begonias in the spring or fall. Propagate by seed, by the bubils which form in the leaf axils, by stem cuttings, or by divisions taken in late summer.

Where to Plant

A woodland garden where the soil is cool, moist, and well drained offers perfect conditions. Plant as a groundcover under spring-blooming shrubs, among other shade-loving perennials, or anywhere you want to have a touch of color from the end of the summer into early fall. Hardy begonia grow best in dappled sunlight. If you plant it in a site with too much sun, the leaves take on a bleached-out look.

ZONE
6,7,8

How to Plant

Plant container-grown begonias in the spring. Sow seed in the early spring, and take divisions in late summer. Because it self-sows, look for seedlings in late spring that can be transplanted to other parts of the garden. Plant this begonia in a moderately fertile soil that is well-drained.

Care and Maintenance

Unlike many begonias, hardy begonias require no staking or pruning. Let the seeds ripen on the plant. Sow them in early spring if you want flowers that same year. If plants become leggy, cut them back in late spring so that they will be bushy by fall when they begin to bloom.

Additional Advice for Care

It's a good idea to draw a map of where you plant this perennial since it comes up so late in the season. It grows happily in combination with evergreen ferns like the autumn fern and Christmas fern.

Additional Cultivars and Species

B. grandis 'Alba' is a selection with white flowers.

Belamcanda chinensis

Blackberry Lily

Leopard Flower

Height: 3'–4'
Flowers: orange, red spotted Blooms: summer

Occasionally the common name of a plant suits it perfectly. In the fall, blackberry lily forms shiny, round black seeds that look like clusters of blackberries inside their open pods. This plant is a prolific seeder, one that will provide you with plenty to share with friends and family. It grows everywhere and has a habit of moving around the garden and appearing wherever it pleases. It is as easy to control as it is to grow. Just pull out the young plants you don't want. It is also called the leopard flower, for its orange flowers marked with red spots. Its star-shaped flowers, about 2" across, last for about 2 weeks, but its iris-like foliage and showy seed pods make this plant a worthy candidate for the perennial garden. Plant in full sun or light shade in an average soil. If the soil is rich and moist, plants will grow taller and more robust. Originally from China, this transplant has adapted well to Southern gardens.

WHEN TO PLANT

Plant in the spring or early fall. Transplant young seedlings that come up in early spring. Plant blackberry lily in full sun. If the soil is dry and has low fertility, plants will not grow as tall. Planted in a rich, moist soil, they will grow as tall as 4' and may require staking.

WHERE TO PLANT

Plant this perennial in the middle or back of the border next to other summer bloomers like daylilies or next to foliage perennials like lamb's ears. Avoid areas where the soil stays wet in the winter months.

HOW TO PLANT

Amend the soil before you plant. Use $1/3$ equal parts of coarse sand, organic matter, and the existing soil. In shadier sites, plant blackberry lily so that it is supported by other perennials. 'Powis Castle' artemisia may be used as a sort of living trellis that the blackberry lily can grow up through.

CARE AND MAINTENANCE

Cut fresh flowers hold up well. Harvest seed pods before they open completely for dried flower decorations.

ADDITIONAL ADVICE FOR CARE

With its iris-like foliage, blackberry lily provides a strong vertical accent in the flower garden.

ADDITIONAL CULTIVARS AND SPECIES

B. flabellata, often sold as 'Hello Yellow,' is shorter and has unspotted yellow flowers.

Boltonia

Height: 3'–4'
Flowers: white daisies Blooms: late summer to fall

It's curious that this native American perennial, considered "weedy" by some, is named in honor of the English botanist James Bolton. The cultivar 'Snowbank' is better behaved as an ornamental in the garden than is the species, growing 3'–4' tall instead of 5'–6' and rarely requiring staking. Small, inch-wide white daisies with yellow centers cover the plant and look graceful against the gray-green linear foliage. Often the first blooms appear in August and continue well into September. The flower display is impressive in the fall garden when this aster relative blooms alongside other asters, salvias, sedums, goldenrods, Joe-Pye weed, and shrubs like butterfly bush. To avoid staking, site 'Snowbank' in full sun in a rich, moist, well-drained soil. It should be noted that this native will survive periods of drought and soil conditions that are less than ideal. The flowers also hold up well in fresh arrangements.

WHEN TO PLANT
Plant divisions or new plants of *Boltonia* 'Snowbank' in the spring or fall. The cultivar 'Snowbank' will not come true from seed.

WHERE TO PLANT
Plant 'Snowbank' toward the middle or back of a flower border in combination with asters or other fall-blooming perennials. Site it in a rich, moist soil in full sun.

HOW TO PLANT
Amend the soil using equal thirds of organic matter, coarse sand, and existing soil. Water well.

ZONE 6,7,8

CARE AND MAINTENANCE

Topdress in the spring and fall with a good organic mulch. Fertilize in the first spring. Divide every 2 or 3 years as needed when clumps become large and start to split open. This plant should do well during periods of drought, especially if the soil has been amended.

ADDITIONAL ADVICE FOR CARE

Boltonia is also a candidate for naturalized areas, planted in combination with other wildflowers like swamp sunflowers, ironweed, butterfly weed, bee balm, and black-eyed susan.

ADDITIONAL CULTIVARS AND SPECIES

There is a pink flowering cultivar called *B.* 'Pink Beauty.'

PERENNIALS AND HERBS

Threadleaf Coreopsis

Height: 2'–3'
Flowers: pale yellow to bright yellow Blooms: late spring to
late summer

*Many different types of coreopsis, both annual and perennial, grow in the
wild. They brighten the spring and summer landscape with their yellow-
orange flowers as they bloom along roadsides, in meadows, in open
woodlands, and on dry slopes. One of the best perennials for the garden is*
Coreopsis verticillata. *The common name, threadleaf coreopsis, describes
its foliage texture: finely cut leaves that give the plant a whorled look. The
scientific name,* Coreopsis, *comes from the Greek* koris, *meaning bug, and*
opsis, *indicating the resemblance of the seeds to ticks. One of the most
popular cultivars, 'Moonbeam,' grows 18"–24" and has pale-yellow, daisy-
like flowers from June to October. A well-drained soil in a sunny spot is
recommended, but given our intense summer heat, filtered sun during
the hottest part of the day will keep plants from burning. For larger and
louder blooms, try 'Golden Showers' with its 2½" golden-yellow flowers.
'Zagreb' is more compact and displays flowers that are deeper yellow. It
grows to 18".*

WHEN TO PLANT
Plant threadleaf coreopsis in spring or fall. Propagate by division.

WHERE TO PLANT
Plant threadleaf coreopsis in a sunny location. In too much shade,
'Golden Showers' will develop an open habit and require staking.
For contrast, plant next to perennials with bold foliage like lamb's
ears and coneflowers, or spiky flowers like salvias and loosestrife.
When planting the cultivar 'Moonbeam,' avoid locations that bake
in the hot afternoon sun.

ZONE
6,7,8

HOW TO PLANT

Plant in a moderately fertile, well-drained soil. A sandy soil is fine as well. When the flowers have stopped blooming, cut back the flowering stems to encourage a new crop of leaves and more blooms.

CARE AND MAINTENANCE

Fertilize the first spring after planting. For best blooming, water during periods of drought. Deadhead the flowers to prolong flowering.

ADDITIONAL ADVICE FOR CARE

Coreopsis verticillata 'Moonbeam' looks good when planted in combination with the electric-blue flowers of hardy plumbago, *Ceratostigma plumbaginoides*. In the hottest parts of the state, *C.* 'Moonbeam' is not the best choice. The flowers are short-lived and the plants never look happy.

ADDITIONAL CULTIVARS AND SPECIES

Coreopsis rosea is a pink-flowered form that is similar to 'Moonbeam,' but in the warmest parts of Georgia it can become an invasive weed.

Bath's Pink

(Cheddar Pinks)

Height: 9"–12"
Flowers: soft pink Blooms: April–May

This delightful dianthus was discovered in Georgia by Jane Bath of Stone Mountain. It was named in her honor by the owners of Goodness Grows, a wonderful nursery in Lexington, Georgia, that specializes in perennials. In early spring, usually in April when some of the early tulips begin to open, masses of clove-scented, pink-fringed flowers create a blanket of bloom atop mounds of blue-gray, needle-like foliage. The quick-spreading handsome foliage forms a tightly woven carpet that looks good all year. This dianthus is especially heat-tolerant and does not melt during our hot summers. Ideal for edging in front of the flower border, as a groundcover creeping over a wall, or planted in the rock garden with other small treasures, this may be the perfect perennial for Georgia gardens. After two or three years, large clumps may begin to open up, losing fullness in the center. This is a good time to start new plants using divisions or cuttings that are easy to root.

WHEN TO PLANT

Plant dianthus in early spring or fall. Propagate by divisions or tip cuttings taken in summer.

WHERE TO PLANT

Plant 'Bath's Pink' in full sun in a soil that is well drained. Use it for edging a flower border or in a rock garden. 'Bath's Pink' is a good weaver to fill in gaps between perennials.

HOW TO PLANT

Plant a little high if drainage is a concern. A moderately fertile soil is fine as long as it's well drained.

ZONE
6,7,8

CARE AND MAINTENANCE

To prolong the flowering, remove spent flowers before they set seed. After the plants have bloomed, shear them back to tidy mounds. Divide clumps every 2 or 3 years, when they begin to open up in the middle. No special fertilization is required. Water during periods of drought.

ADDITIONAL ADVICE FOR CARE

Cuttings root easily in wet sand.

ADDITIONAL CULTIVARS AND SPECIES

There are many different species and cultivars of dianthus, a plant that many of our grandmothers grew. *Dianthus* 'Itsaul White' is another fragrant white-flowered selection made by Saul Nurseries in Atlanta, Georgia.

Echinacea purpurea

Purple Coneflower

Height: 4'
Flowers: purple rays and orange-brown cones Blooms: summer

If you've ever touched the cones of the purple coneflower, it will come as no surprise that Echinacea *comes from the Greek* echinos, *meaning hedgehog. This tactile plant is much friendlier than it looks and is a tough native that performs well for Georgia gardeners. Blooming for a long period in the summer, it resembles black-eyed susan except for its purple petals. A perennial favorite of butterflies for its nectar and of flower arrangers for its flowers and dried cone heads, purple coneflower is an easy-care flower that can go in the sunny border or meadow garden. The hairy, dark-green leaves that are up to 8" in length, the stiff branching stems, and the drooping ray petals all contribute to its coarse texture. Planted next to butterfly bushes and coreopsis, they will quickly transform your garden into a haven for butterflies. Coneflowers like full sun and a well-drained soil, and they are a good choice for areas that are subject to drought. If the soil is too rich, or if there is too much shade, you may need to stake them.*

WHEN TO PLANT

Divide clumps and plant divisions in the spring. Plant container-grown plants in the spring or fall. Plants will benefit from being divided once every 4 years. Seeds take 2 or more years to flower, and cultivars will not come true from seed.

WHERE TO PLANT

Plant coneflower in full sun in a well-drained soil. Plant them in the middle or back of a border next to finer-textured perennials and annuals to soften their coarse look. *Artemisia* 'Powis Castle' is a good gray, soft-textured perennial to plant in combination with coneflowers.

How to Plant

There is no need to amend the soil. Just make sure it is well drained, adding sand if necessary. Avoid soils that are overly rich in organic matter.

Care and Maintenance

If you want to make a dried arrangement, cut flowers early when the coneheads are still tight. No special fertilization or pruning is required. Coneflowers are susceptible to some leaf spot and to Japanese beetles. Check with your local Extension Service to learn about recommended controls.

Additional Advice for Care

Some people take *Echinacea* for health reasons. Health food stores sell it in the form of capsules, tinctures, and tea.

Additional Cultivars and Species

E. 'Bright Star' has bright, rose-red flowers with maroon centers that grow to 2″–3″. White selections include 'White Lustre,' a good bloomer even in dry areas, and 'White Swan,' a good cut flower.

PERENNIALS AND HERBS

Eupatorium coelestinum

Hardy Ageratum

Blue Mistflower

Height: 24"
Flowers: bluish purple Blooms: midsummer to frost

Late September brings the appearance of the carpets of blue mistflower that seem to be everywhere. Their color is not a true blue, but the lavender-blue flowers are easy to use in combination with other perennials and annuals like perennial sunflowers or hardy chrysanthemums. Blue mistflowers look like clusters of tiny powder puffs. If you don't plant them in your garden, they may just show up like uninvited guests. The much-admired Southern garden writer Elizabeth Lawrence wrote about her attempt to eradicate this plant from her garden because of its weedy nature and its tendency to be killed back by a disease, but later she wrote about its ability to outgrow the disease and to endure in poor soil and partial shade. Mistflower is quick to spread and its shallow roots are easy to keep in bounds, making it the perfect companion for summer and fall bulbs like Lycoris *and* Crocus. *This adaptable plant has been in Southern gardens for years, offering maximum blooms for little care.*

WHEN TO PLANT

Take divisions of mistflower clumps in the spring. Tip cuttings in early spring also provide a viable means for propagating this plant.

WHERE TO PLANT

It is best to plant blue mistflower in a moist soil in a sunny spot, although it will tolerate dry soils. Use it as a filler in the flower border where late summer and fall color is needed. It can also be naturalized in meadows or near ponds.

ZONE
6,7,8

HOW TO PLANT

There is no need to amend the soil. In fact, this stoloniferous perennial has a habit of moving around the garden without much encouragement. To keep it from spreading too much, plant it in an area where its shallow roots can be easily contained.

CARE AND MAINTENANCE

Cutting back plants 2 or 3 times during the growing season will help keep them full. No special fertilizer is needed. Dividing clumps regularly will help prevent this aggressive perennial from taking over your garden.

ADDITIONAL ADVICE FOR CARE

The tough blue mistflower is lovely in fall bouquets and adds welcome color to the garden in late summer and fall. If it develops powdery mildew, just cut back the diseased leaves and it will quickly put out a flush of new growth.

ADDITIONAL CULTIVARS AND SPECIES

There is a selection with white flowers that is equally aggressive.

Eupatorium purpureum

Joe-Pye Weed

Height: 5'–7'
Flowers: purple Blooms: fall

A classic American native, Joe-Pye weed grows along roadsides, in meadows, and in fields as far north as Maine and as far south as Georgia. Like many of our unsung natives, Joe-Pye weed receives greater appreciation from English gardeners, who haven't grown up with it. A perfect choice for a bold architectural statement in the perennial border, joe-pye can grow 5'–7' tall and 3'–4' wide. The 8"–12" long leaves are whorled, usually with 3 to 5 leaves at each node. Strong, hollow, cane-like green stems are often marked with purple where the leaves attach. The huge purple flower heads, up to 18" in diameter, are showy for weeks beginning in early fall. Joe-pye weed is effective for naturalized areas and responds well to lots of moisture. For best performance, plant Joe-Pye weed in full sun in a moist soil. Cutting it back a few feet early in the season, no later than June, can help keep this giant from getting so tall. A dramatic plant, Joe-Pye weed can be a focal point in the fall garden, attracting butterflies and eliciting admiring comments as its big masses of flowers sway in the breeze.

When to Plant

Plant Joe-Pye weed in the spring or early fall so it will have plenty of time to establish a good root system. Divide clumps every 2–3 years.

Where to Plant

This garden giant is not for the small garden, but it works well in a flower border as a bold background accent, or in naturalized plantings like meadows along streams. Full sun and a moist soil are ideal, but Joe-Pye weed will grow in shadier gardens too.

ZONE
6,7,8

How to Plant

Plant Joe-Pye weed behind smaller and earlier-flowering perennials. A moderately fertile soil is best, but this perennial does not need fertilization.

Care and Maintenance

If joe-pye weed is planted in a very dry soil in full sun, it will become scorched and wilted during the heat of Georgia summers. Keep it well watered. Cut the stalks back early in the summer to achieve a more compact plant.

Additional Advice for Care

Other large perennials for late summer and autumn are the cardinal flower, swamp sunflowers, iron weed, and the Tartarian aster.

Additional Cultivars and Species

E. maculatum 'Gateway' is a smaller cultivar that grows 5'–6'. It has large, mauve-pink flowers atop reddish stems.

Perennials and Herbs

Gaillardia x *grandiflora*

Blanket Flower

Height: 2'–3'
Flowers: red and yellow Blooms: summer to fall

In her book Southern Gardening, *Elizabeth Lawrence writes: "Gardens can still be gay in dry summers if one is satisfied with coarse perennials such as the false sunflower of the eastern states and some of the gaillardias." Other than deadheading (removing spent flowers), the blanket flower requires no special care and blooms from early summer until frost. In coastal areas of Georgia where soils are sandy, plants may bloom more profusely but may not grow as tall as they do in a more compact soil. In heavy clay soils, the blanket flower is a short-lived perennial, but it reseeds itself freely, so don't worry if plants don't overwinter. While it is true that plants grown from seed will not be as uniform as cultivars, plants grown from seed do produce some interesting color variations. Cutting back leggy growth in late summer will encourage a flush of fall blooms. These colorful daisy-type flowers offer a mix of reds and yellow. Blanket flowers make good cut flowers and are happy when left to mingle with other perennials and annuals in the garden.*

WHEN TO PLANT

Divide and transplant blanket flower in the spring. Unlike many perennials which take 2 or more years to develop into blooming-size plants, gaillardia plants grown from seed will flower the first year. Seeds started indoors in early spring should be ready to transplant into the garden in 6 to 8 weeks.

WHERE TO PLANT

Plant blanket flower in full sun in a well-drained soil. In hard, compact soils, it may become a short-lived perennial. In sandy soils, plants will have more blooms and be more compact. *Gaillardia* provides almost constant bloom in the flower border from early summer to fall.

ZONE 6,7,8

HOW TO PLANT

Dig a hole as large as the blanket flower's container. Firm the soil around the root ball, water it, and watch the blanket flower grow. Transplant new growth that appears from the old crown. Take root cuttings in early spring.

CARE AND MAINTENANCE

No special care is needed for this tough heat-lover, but a soil that is well drained and moderately fertile is best. Remove spent flowers to encourage longer blooming. Cutting plants back in late summer will encourage a flush of growth and blooms in the fall.

ADDITIONAL ADVICE FOR CARE

By letting blanket flower set seed in the fall, you may get some wonderful color variations the following year.

ADDITIONAL CULTIVARS AND SPECIES

A popular dwarf cultivar, 'Goblin' has large dark-red flowers with wide, irregular yellow borders. G. 'Baby Cole,' another dwarf culti-var, grows 6"–8" high. G. 'Red Plume' has double bright-red flowers on a dense mound growing 12"–14" tall.

Geranium macrorrhizum

Bigroot Geranium

Height: 15"–18"
Flowers: magenta Blooms: in spring

True geraniums are a diverse group of hardy perennials that belong to the genus Geranium. *They should not be confused with the common house-plant geranium, genus* Pelargonium, *that has been grown for years in colors ranging from electric red to shocking pink. Of the garden-variety geraniums, bigroot is one of the easiest to grow. It holds up well in the Georgia heat even during periods of drought, especially if it is planted in partial shade. Its vigorous root system spreads quickly and makes a dense groundcover that few weeds can penetrate. With its thick, fleshy rhizome,* G. macrorrhizum *is easy to propagate by division. One way to identify this geranium is by the distinctive fruit-like scent the leaves give off when bruised or crushed. 6"–8" wide, they are divided into 7 blunt, lobed segments. Although not evergreen, the leaves hang on late into the season, and during late summer to fall they take on tinges of red and maroon. The flowers, 1" in diameter, are held above the foliage in clusters of pink, magenta, or white.*

WHEN TO PLANT
Plant bigroot geranium in early spring or fall so that it has time to develop a strong root system before hot or cold weather sets in.

WHERE TO PLANT
For best success, plant bigroot geranium in partial shade in a moist, well-drained soil. Although the geranium will adapt to various soil types, soil rich in organic matter is best, especially if plants are planted in full sun. Hardy geraniums make a good groundcover under summer-flowering shrubs like butterfly bushes and roses. You can also plant hardy geraniums in the flower garden or on the edge of a woodland garden with ferns, hostas, and small bulbs.

ZONE 6,7,8

How to Plant

The thick, fleshy roots make division the easiest method of propagation. Rosettes of new growth at points along the stem can also be treated as cuttings and are easy to root. Bigroot geranium can also spread by self-seeding. Be sure plants are well watered after transplanting divisions or cuttings.

Care and Maintenance

No special care is required for these easy-care perennials. Dead leaves removed from the center of plants will quickly be replaced by new growth. For the best growth, make sure the soil is rich in organic matter. A topdressing applied once in the spring and then in the fall will replace depleted organic matter.

Additional Advice for Care

Hardy geraniums are little-known versatile perennials that many gardeners have not discovered. Their flowers come in a range of colors, with foliage that varies from delicate to coarse in texture. In the flower garden they act like weavers, combining well with other plants or creating colorful statements, lacy groundcovers, thick mounds, or handsome specimens.

Additional Cultivars and Species

'Album' is a white-flowered selection. A hybrid that does well in Georgia gardens is G. 'Biokovo.' It has white flowers flushed with pink at the center. Another hybrid that is a proven survivor in our heat is G. 'Johnson's Blue.' It has a sprawling habit, violet-blue flowers, and a long blooming season.

Helleborus orientalis

Lenten Rose

Height: 15"–18"
Flowers: white, purple, maroon Blooms: early spring

An aristocrat of the garden, the hellebores bridge the gap from winter to spring. Elegant evergreens, hellebores have shiny, leathery 12"–16" wide leaves that are divided into 7 to 9 segments. One of the gems of the winter garden, the Lenten rose looks good all year. Its colorful nodding flowers, ranging in color from pure white to dark maroon and sometimes speckled or splotched with green or purple, appear as early as February and may produce flowers over a period of 8–10 weeks. Both the leaves and flowers on this hellebore are stemless and arise directly from the root stock. This long-lived perennial is perfect for the shade garden and grows happily alongside ferns and next to hostas. The Lenten rose makes an effective groundcover to plant with daffodils, showing off their flowers in spring and masking their ugly foliage in summer. Once it becomes established in the garden, the Lenten rose will thrive, even in a dry shade situation. If planted in a sunny location, it needs a moist, well-drained soil rich in organic matter.

WHEN TO PLANT

For best success, plant in the spring or early fall using hellebores that have been grown in containers. Once established in the garden, usually in 2–3 years, the Lenten rose will often produce masses of seedlings around the base of the mother plant which can be easily dug as clumps and transplanted in spring.

WHERE TO PLANT

Plant hellebores in partial to full shade in soil that is rich in organic matter and well drained. If hellebores are planted in full sun, growth will not be as vigorous and plants will lose their elegant look. A small clump will enhance a woodland garden, especially during the dark days of winter. You can grow hellebores in containers provided they have good drainage.

HOW TO PLANT

Hellebores resent having their root system disturbed, and you will have bigger and better clumps if you don't divide them. But because the Lenten rose seeds freely, you can transplant seedlings easily in spring or fall. Just dig up a big clump with as much soil as possible and plant in a shady spot where you would like evergreen foliage and early flowers. Another bonus that comes from growing hellebores is the wide range of colors that occur from seedling-grown plants.

CARE AND MAINTENANCE

Fertilize hellebores after planting the first spring, using a 10–10–10 to give them a boost. Once established, they should require little care except for some watering during periods of drought. If any of the leaves suffer from winter burn, cut them off and they will be quickly replaced by new ones.

ADDITIONAL ADVICE FOR CARE

Helleborus leaves and roots are poisonous. This is probably why animals tend to leave it alone in the garden.

ADDITIONAL CULTIVARS AND SPECIES

There are many different types of hellebores and more varieties being offered every year for gardeners. Try *H. foetidus*, the stinking hellebore with pale green flowers edged in maroon, and *H. argutifolius*, which has a coarse, holly-like texture and chartreuse flowers streaked with purple.

Alumroot

Coralbells

Height: 12"–24"
Flowers: tiny on 18" sprays Blooms: August to September

Alumroots are tough and durable plants that are well suited for Georgia gardens. It is its evergreen foliage that steals the show, not its flowers. H. americana has marbled leaves in combinations of green with silver or white. H. 'Palace Purple' has purple-bronze foliage. Both provide instant and long-season color in the flower garden or at the edge of a woodland. The foliage of these two clump-like alumroots stands out when other perennials are looking tired and faded. The first frost of the fall enhances the colors, and the leaves will seem to glisten in the sunlight. H. americana makes a good groundcover and will tolerate fairly dry soils in sun or shade. The marbled, heart-shaped leaves provide a contrast to bright flowers or complement foliage like ferns, iris, liriope, and blue-leaved hostas. A striking selection, 'Pewter Veil' has copper-pink leaves in spring that fade to a metallic color with purple undersides as the summer progresses. H. 'Palace Purple' has ivy- shaped leaves that start out a purple-bronze in spring and become more green with the heat of summer.

WHEN TO PLANT

Plant alumroot or *Heucheras* in the spring or fall. Propagate them by division of the clumps, by stem and leaf cuttings, or by seed.

WHERE TO PLANT

Although they will tolerate full sun in cooler parts of the state, alumroots tend to be shade-lovers in Georgia, making them best suited for the woodland garden. For a dramatic effect, plant in groups with four or more plants per group.

ZONE
6,7,8

HOW TO PLANT

Alumroots like a moist, well-drained soil that is rich in organic matter. Topdressing once or twice a year helps keep the crowns of the plants looking good and postpones the need for division.

CARE AND MAINTENANCE

Heucheras are shallow-rooted. To keep plants from heaving during the winter or drying out in summer, plant the crowns 1" below the soil level and topdress with organic matter once or twice a year.

ADDITIONAL ADVICE FOR CARE

Heucheras look good when planted with other native perennials like the foamflower (*Tiarella cordifolia*) or the dwarf crested iris.

ADDITIONAL CULTIVARS AND SPECIES

There have been many different selections made of the native *H. americana*. 'Garnet' has garnet-colored foliage in spring and in winter. Many alumroots are grown for their flowers, but the flowering kinds are not as tough or durable in the garden.

Fragrant Hosta

Height: 2'–3'
Flowers: white, fragrant Blooms: late summer

When it comes to shade gardening, hostas are indispensable. While many are heat-resistant, few can tolerate full sun like 'Royal Standard.' This adaptable hybrid of the old-fashioned favorite H. plantaginea grows happily in shade or sun, forming large mounds up to 3' across of bold, yellow-green, deeply veined foliage. With large heart-shaped leaves 8" long and 5" wide, even one plant makes a bold statement in the garden. Worth growing for the handsome foliage alone, this hosta also rewards us with sweetly scented flowers in late summer at a time when few other perennials are blooming. Although hostas can survive in most soils, including heavy clay, to reach their full potential they need a rich, moist, well-drained soil. 'Royal Standard' makes a good border on the edge of a deciduous woodland where it gets plenty of sun and moisture. This perennial is effective as a groundcover or when planted with other shade-loving perennials and with spring bulbs. When their new leaves emerge in late spring, hostas provide the perfect foil for the withering foliage of early spring-blooming bulbs like daffodils.

WHEN TO PLANT

Plant hostas in early spring or fall. Divide and transplant clumps early in the spring just as the leaves are emerging and the crowns are visible.

WHERE TO PLANT

Plant 'Royal Standard' along the sunny edge of a woodland, along a path, or in a flower border that gets shade during the hottest part of the day. Plant hostas as groundcovers for early bulbs. While it is true that 'Royal Standard' will grow in sun or shade, it does not really thrive in deep shade. With its fragrant white flowers, 'Royal Standard' is a good plant to include in the moonlight garden.

ZONE
6,7,8

How to Plant

Plant hostas in a rich, moist, well-drained soil. If the soil is compact or too dry, plants will be stunted and leaves will be discolored. Site 'Royal Standard' near pathways where you can appreciate the fragrant flowers in late summer.

Care and Maintenance

For the most part, hostas are free of pests and diseases, but they do suffer from slugs that can turn leaves into an ugly mess of holes. Check with your local Extension Service for recommended controls. Water hostas during periods of drought.

Additional Advice for Care

Remove unsightly flower stalks as soon as hostas finish blooming and before they set seed. If the foliage becomes unsightly early in the season, shear plants back to encourage a flush of new growth. While early spring is the best time to divide hostas, division can be done at almost any time of year provided plants are watered well and replanted quickly.

Additional Cultivars and Species

There are hundreds of varieties of hostas available to gardeners today, including types with interesting foliage in shades of blue and chartreuse. They range in size from a few inches tall like *H. venusta* with its 1"–2" leaves to those like *H. ' Sum and Substance'* whose mature plants grow up to 6' wide. This chartreuse-foliaged selection tolerates sun and adds interesting color and texture to the garden.

Iris tectorum

Japanese Roof Iris

Height: 12"–18"
Flowers: lilac or white Blooms: summer

*Georgia gardeners, particularly iris lovers, may be pleasantly surprised
to learn that the ideal climate for growing Japanese roof iris is one of hot
summers and moderately cold winters. The species name* tectorum *means
"growing on roofs." These flowers were grown on thatched roofs in Japan.
While this iris does not grow on roofs in our climate, it is a vigorous and
adaptable perennial that grows happily in full sun or partial shade. In
climates with cool summers, flowering may be inhibited, but in coastal
areas this beardless rhizomatous iris grows like a weed, thriving in light,
sandy soils. The lilac flowers look almost star-shaped and are marked with
dark-blue or black blotches. The pale green foliage grows in a fan-like
fashion, making it well-suited for the front of a border or for a rock garden.
The rhizomes grow close to the surface and tend to push themselves out of
the ground. The roof iris benefits from spring and fall mulching. Divide
clumps or break off small pieces with roots as soon as plants stop flowering.*

WHEN TO PLANT

The best time to divide Japanese roof iris is right after they finish
flowering, but as long as the plants are watered, they may actually
be transplanted anytime during the growing season.

WHERE TO PLANT

Plant Japanese roof iris in the front of the flower border in a moderately fertile, well-drained soil. The plants respond well to light,
sandy soils. The Japanese roof iris may not produce many blooms in
a shady garden, but its light-green, fan-like foliage will add a touch
of elegance.

ZONE
6,7,8

HOW TO PLANT

Plant Japanese roof iris with rhizomes covered in a light, well-drained soil in full sun or partial shade. A layer of mulch in the spring and fall will help prevent plants from heaving out of the ground. Plants may be grown from seed, but division is much easier and has faster results.

CARE AND MAINTENANCE

There is some debate over whether Japanese roof iris should be fertilized or not. If the soil is moderately fertile and a topdressing of organic mulch is applied in spring and then again in fall, plants should thrive. Be sure to keep mulch away from the crown of the plant. If foliage looks tattered after going through the winter, cut it back to a few inches in early spring and new leaves will quickly replace the old.

ADDITIONAL ADVICE FOR CARE

There are many types of iris for Georgia gardens. A type that does well in our climate is the native dwarf crested iris, *Iris cristata*, which is like a miniature version of the Japanese roof iris. This tiny gem grows in woodlands and adapts well to the shade garden.

ADDITIONAL CULTIVARS AND SPECIES

Equally elegant in the garden is the white-flowered form called *Iris tectorum* 'Album.'

Lantana camara 'Miss Huff'

Hardy Lantana

Height: 3'–6'
Flowers: yellow, orange, red Blooms: summer to frost

Lantana has long been a favorite of Southern gardeners, not only because it's easy to grow, but because it blooms all summer and attracts hordes of butterflies. Fairly drought-resistant, 'Miss Huff' is supposed to be hardier than many of the other lantanas. Clusters of yellow, orange, and red flowers cover plants for months, thriving in our hot, humid weather. While deadheading will encourage maximum flower production, even the the lazy gardener who does not deadhead will have plenty of flowers. Grow lantana in the flower garden with annuals and perennials, in containers, or in hanging baskets. Plants will sometimes layer themselves, providing additional instant plants to share with others who will be happy to have them. Some books recommend cutting back lantana in the fall and mulching it. We have found that it is better to mulch the plants, but not to cut them back until the spring just before new growth starts. This practice seems to help plants make it through the winter. It's a good idea to avoid planting in areas where the soil will stay wet during the winter.

WHEN TO PLANT

Plant lantana in the spring. It is really a tender perennial. You can grow lantana from seed, but young plants are inexpensive and much quicker to provide satisfaction. Propagate it from cuttings in the summer.

WHERE TO PLANT

Plant lantana in full sun, the hotter the better. If you plant it in containers, it will need regular watering. In the ground it will require much less care. Plant it in combination with annuals and perennials or on a sunny slope in a big mass.

ZONE
8

HOW TO PLANT

Lantana requires no special care, just an average garden soil and
some water during times of drought. Avoid soils that stay wet or
don't drain well. For best success at overwintering, don't prune back
plants at the end of the growing season. Instead, mulch them using
pine straw or a lightweight mulch, and cut them back in early
spring just before new growth begins.

CARE AND MAINTENANCE

Though lantana requires no special care, if you want to give plants a
jump start, fertilize them with a liquid fertilizer like 10–10–10 after
you plant them in the spring. Plants in containers will benefit from
regular fertilizer once a month during the growing season, but this
is not required for them to grow and bloom.

ADDITIONAL ADVICE FOR CARE

Lantana is good for summer color in the garden, especially in hot
and dry spots. Few perennials require so little care and bloom over
such a long period of time. There are many annual types of lantana,
including dwarf and trailing types that are also easy and rewarding
to grow. Lantana can be trained to grow as a standard with a single
trunk. Plants grown in this way should be protected in the winter.

ADDITIONAL CULTIVARS AND SPECIES

Annual types of lantana come in many different colors and forms.
Popular varieties include 'Irene,' with rose-and-yellow flowers,
'New Gold,' with gold flowers, 'Lemon Drop,' with light yellow
flowers, and two trailing varieties, one with lavender flowers and
one with white flowers.

Liatris spicata

Blazing Star

Gayfeather

Height: 3'
Flowers: purple or white Blooms: summer

In summer, the colorful wands of blazing star, a native wildflower, attract butterflies and dazzle gardeners. A good choice for the flower border, meadow, or naturalistic garden, blazing star is also an outstanding cut flower, both fresh and dried. The vertical spikes are made of small flower heads which, unlike those of most flowers, open from the top down. The bright flowers and the linear foliage provide a bold vertical accent in the garden. This native that is tolerant of heat and drought is ideal for Georgia gardens. While it tolerates soggy soils during the growing season, it resents wet feet in winter. A tough perennial, blazing star looks good when planted in combination with black-eyed susan and coneflowers. Site blazing star in a moist, well-drained soil in full sun or partial shade. It will provide you with weeks of colorful blooms from mid- to late summer.

WHEN TO PLANT

Plants grown from seed take two years to flower. Divisions can be taken in the spring. Containerized plants can be planted in the spring or fall.

WHERE TO PLANT

Plant blazing star in a flower border, cut-flower garden, meadow, or wildflower garden. Although it adapts well to heat and drought, it will tolerate wet soils during the growing season. You may place it near a stream or pond as long as the area is dry in winter.

HOW TO PLANT

For best results, plant blazing star in a moderately fertile, moist, well-drained soil in full sun or partial shade. After the first year, plants may need staking.

ZONE
6,7,8

CARE AND MAINTENANCE

Make sure that blazing star has "dry feet" in winter. No special pruning or fertilization is required for this native perennial to thrive in the garden.

ADDITIONAL ADVICE FOR CARE

Plants should be divided every 4 years and cultivars should be asexually propagated.

ADDITIONAL CULTIVARS AND SPECIES

L. spicata 'Kobold' is a compact cultivar. 18"–30" and with dark purple flowers, it is one of the best selections for cut flowers and the border. 'Floristan White' is 3' tall with creamy-white flowers.

PERENNIALS AND HERBS

Lythrum virgatum 'Morden Pink'

Loosestrife

Height: 3'–5'
Flowers: pink Blooms: mid- to late summer

Sometimes there can be too much of a good thing in a garden. Although it may be pretty when it's in flower, lythrum has become a noxious weed in many parts of the country, taking over wetland areas. Some suggest this plant should not even be recommended, but some good selections have been developed for gardens. One that is well-known is L. 'Morden Pink,' a pink-flowered selection of Lythrum virgatum. *It is one of a number of cultivars that are not likely to produce seed and become invasive. L. 'Morden Pink' is an easy-care perennial that offers tall spikes of pink flowers in a sunny flower border or in more naturalized areas. Cutting back flowers after they finish blooming will sometimes encourage a second flush of blooms. This perennial tolerates average garden soil, wet or dry, making it equally suitable for growing along a pond or in a more formal garden. Planted with other summer-blooming perennials or next to gray foliage plants like artemisias and lamb's ears, this lythrum adds a spiky texture to the garden. It combines well with purple coneflowers and gayfeather.*

WHEN TO PLANT

Plant plants in the spring or fall. Propagate plants by divisions or stem cuttings. Plants grown from seed will vary greatly.

WHERE TO PLANT

Use loosestrife in naturalized areas like meadows, along streams or ponds, or in the flower garden. Full sun is best, but it will tolerate a wide range of soil types from wet to dry. If the soil is too rich, plants may need staking. Plant it toward the middle or back of the border where the spikes will add height to the garden.

HOW TO PLANT

Any average garden soil is fine. Be sure to give it room to spread out up to 2'.

CARE AND MAINTENANCE

Japanese beetles can be a problem. Consult your local Extension Service for recommended controls. No special fertilization is required. Cutting back flowers after they finish blooming may encourage more blooms.

ADDITIONAL ADVICE FOR CARE

While the species of *L. salicaria* is known to be an invasive weed, this is not true of the ornamental *L.* 'Morden Pink.' This is a good reason to know both scientific names of a plant, so that you can be sure of what you are getting.

ADDITIONAL CULTIVARS AND SPECIES

Do not plant *L. salicaria*. Look for selections of *L. virgatum*, which is very similar in appearance but not a weedy pest. Other gardenworthy hybrids include 'Dropmore Purple' with its deep purple flowers and 'Happy,' a selection for smaller gardens. 'Happy' grows only 15"–18" tall and has dark pink flowers.

Monarda didyma

Bee Balm

Oswego Tea, Bergamot

Height: 2'–4' tall
Flowers: scarlet red, pink, violet, white Blooms: summer

Bergamot has long been popular not only as a garden flower but as a substitute for tea: its common name is Oswego tea. Bergamot is a key ingredient of the commercially produced Earl Grey tea, enjoyed by many for its distinctive flavor and aroma. Bees and hummingbirds are attracted to the scent of bergamot. Just brush against a leaf and it will release a strong mint aroma. Quick to spread, especially in shady places, this native bee balm can be invasive, which makes it ideal for naturalizing in a meadow or along a stream. Other distinctive features of bee balm are its square stems and large flower heads. Deadheading can prolong the bloom period, and moist soils may help cut down on powdery mildew. If clumps become too large, they are easy to divide and separate. Wild bergamot, Monarda fistulosa, *is a common summer sight throughout Georgia and across the country. Its pale lavender flowers bloom along roadsides, in meadows, and in fields. It is tolerant of dry conditions and is not susceptible to powdery mildew.*

WHEN TO PLANT

Bee balm can be started from seeds or divisions in the spring. It can also be propagated from softwood cuttings in early summer.

WHERE TO PLANT

Plant bee balm in a naturalized area, in the flower garden with other summer-blooming perennials, or at the edge of a woodland garden next to hostas.

ZONE
6,7,8

HOW TO PLANT

M. didyma is not tolerant of drought. It is less susceptible to powdery mildew if planted in a moist soil and allowed some shade and good air circulation. A moist, well-drained soil is ideal.

CARE AND MAINTENANCE

Deadheading will prolong the blooming period, but the dry seed heads add ornamental interest to the garden. If the foliage gets covered with powdery mildew, shear it back in late summer for a new flush of growth. Keep plants watered during periods of drought.

ADDITIONAL ADVICE FOR CARE

Divide this plant about every 3 years to keep it from taking over the flower border. The dried seed heads are good for decorative arrangements.

ADDITIONAL CULTIVARS AND SPECIES

There are many selections of *M. didyma* that do well in Georgia gardens. A recent introduction that was selected and named in Georgia is *M.* 'Jacob Cline.' It has intense red flowers. 'Croftway Pink' has pink flowers all summer long, and 'Cambridge Scarlet' grows 4'–5' tall and exhibits scarlet-red flowers.

Ocimum basilicum

Sweet Basil

Height: 6"–2'
Flowers: white Blooms: summer

An annual herb, basil comes in a wide range of flavors, colors, and sizes. The one used in classic Italian-style tomato sauce and pesto is called sweet basil. Its bright-green lustrous leaves are soft and succulent, and just one strongly flavored leaf (part clove, part mint) will enhance a serving of eggs, mushrooms, tomatoes, or fish. Generally the names of scented basils indicate a particular flavor such as cinnamon, lemon, chocolate, or licorice. These easy-to-grow fragrant herbs add not only fragrance but color to the garden. 'Red Rubin' has deep purple leaves edged in bright green. A variety favored by gardeners for its dramatic dark-purple leaves, 'Dark Opal,' is also used by cooks to flavor vinegars and oils. Whether you have a large herb garden or just enough room for a few pots, there are basils both big and small. A small variety, 'Dwarf Bush,' grows only 12" high and 18" wide, making it an ideal choice for pots in a sunny kitchen window. If space is unlimited, 'Mammoth' basil will produce foliage the size of lettuce leaves, and it has a delicious flavor!

WHEN TO PLANT

Basil resents cold weather. Start seeds indoors in March and set seedlings out once night temperatures have climbed well into the forties. After the weather turns warm, sow additional seedlings directly into your garden, and continue sowing them throughout the summer. Thin seedlings as needed and enjoy!

WHERE TO PLANT

Plant basil in the flower garden, in the herb garden, in pots, or in the vegetable garden in full sun in a well-drained soil. The smaller varieties like 'Piccolo' and 'Green Bush' are perfect for growing in pots. Use the small-leafed basils to edge the flower garden or create a knot garden using a combination of different herbs.

How to Plant

Basils like full sun and a moist, well-drained soil. Be sure to let plants dry out between thorough waterings. Space plants about 8" or more apart, depending on the variety you choose to grow. Varieties like 'Purple Ruffles' are not only edible but highly ornamental. Use a liquid fertilizer like 10–10–10 once every few weeks during the summer.

Care and Maintenance

To keep basil plants bushy and producing, pinch them back early in the summer, and don't let them flower and set seed. As you harvest individual leaves throughout the season, continue to pinch the plants back. Water plants during dry spells. At the end of the growing season before frost, you can harvest entire plants to dry or freeze and use over the winter.

Additional Advice for Care

In addition to its ornamental appeal in the garden and its many culinary uses, basil adds unusual fragrance and brightness to floral bouquets. Try growing at least 3 or 4 different varieties of these delightful plants. If you have a sunny kitchen window, overwinter a pot inside the house for a constant supply of this delightful herb.

Additional Cultivars and Species

'Valentino' has large leaves with an old-fashioned Italian basil flavor. There are many different types of basil. Each offers its own rewards.

Origanum vulgare

Common Oregano

Height: 24"
Flowers: white or pinkish-purple Blooms: mid- to late summer

*Oregano is a favorite herb for Italian cooking. Its culinary popularity
extends to Greece, Brazil, Mexico, and Spain. As an ornamental plant,
it is often grown with other perennials and annuals in the flower garden or
herb garden, or in containers with other herbs and combinations of herbs
and annuals. Naturalized throughout much of the eastern United States,
common oregano grows in full sun in a well-drained soil. A member of
the mint family, oregano has distinctive square stems, a wiry habit, and
rounded or heart-shaped leaves. The small whorled flowers are borne on
slender spikes at the ends of the branches. To keep plants bushy, cut them
back before they flower. There are several lower-growing selections which
make good accents in the garden. These include golden oregano with its
golden-yellow leaves and gold variegated oregano, which has green leaves
marbled with gold. This adaptable and edible herb adds a welcome spot of
color in the garden and looks good from spring until frost.*

WHEN TO PLANT

Oregano can be grown from seed, but propagation by cuttings is the
best way to insure that your plants will be as flavorful and colorful
as the variety you want to grow. Cuttings and divisions should be
taken in the spring.

WHERE TO PLANT

There are a few oreganoes that are known more for their ornamental
appeal than for their use in cooking, and these are best suited for the
flower garden. One of them is *O. laevigatum* 'Herrenhausen,' which
has dark-green leaves with tinges of purple and red-violet flowers.
Plants can grow up to 2' tall. Plant oregano in the flower garden, in
the herb garden, in containers, or between stepping stones.

ZONE
6,7,8

HOW TO PLANT

Plant oregano in full sun in a well-drained soil. The golden oregano and the variegated selection need some light shade to prevent their leaves from scorching. Plant them where you will have easy access to the leaves for cooking.

CARE AND MAINTENANCE

Oreganoes are easy-care perennials that benefit from regular shearing, at least once every 2 years, if the foliage is not killed back in the winter. They require no special fertilization program. Water them during periods of drought.

ADDITIONAL ADVICE FOR CARE

The low-mounding oreganoes with golden and variegated foliage can be grown under shrubs where they will get some shade and at the same time brighten up the garden. For contrast, plant them next to dark foliage perennials like *Heuchera* 'Palace Purple' or *Penstemon* 'Husker Red.'

ADDITIONAL CULTIVARS AND SPECIES

O. vulgare 'Aureum,' the golden oregano, grows 8"–12" tall and creates a striking accent in the garden. *O. vulgare* 'Variegatum,' the gold variegated oregano, is not as hardy as some of the other oreganoes, but it makes an effective groundcover or container plant.

Petroselinum crispum

Parsley

Height: 6"–12" tall
Flowers: insignificant

Most people associate parsley with the sprigs that accompany the main course at a restaurant, but this edible ornamental has many uses both in the garden and the kitchen. In Georgia, parsley is a good plant to grow for winter color, especially when planted in combination with pansies, violas, and red mustard greens. If plants become frosted or are sheared for cooking, they quickly recover and send out new flushes of growth. Easy to grow in pots or in the ground, parsley is also a good plant to use for edging in a flower or herb garden. The bright green foliage, especially the curly variety, looks good in flower arrangements. Parsley is a plant that is recommended for butterfly gardens as a source of food for the swallowtail larvae. This finely textured herb is popular as a garnish in soups and sauces. For the effect of a breath mint, chew on a few sprigs. Plant parsley in full sun or partial shade in a soil that is moist and well drained. The broad-leaf Italian parsley has a stronger flavor and is better for drying.

WHEN TO PLANT

Start new plants every year by seed or from young plants. Plants can be started in early spring and then again in fall. Seeds need to be covered and the temperature should be 65–70 degrees F. for germination. Seeds may germinate more quickly if they are soaked in cold water (34 degrees F.) for 24 hours. Although parsley is a biennial, it is best grown as an annual.

WHERE TO PLANT

Plant parsley in containers with other plants, in an herb garden, or in a flower garden. Use it as an edger or in masses to contrast with flowering plants like pansies and violas. It also looks good in combination with other herbs such as basil, thyme, and alliums.

HOW TO PLANT

Parsley likes full sun to partial shade in a moist, well-drained soil. Shearing back mature plants to use for cooking will encourage a flush of new growth. Parsley grows easily in the ground or in containers. If it is planted in too much shade, the plants will be open in the center and the leaves will turn yellow.

CARE AND MAINTENANCE

Fertilize parsley with a liquid fertilizer like 10–10–10 once a month during the growing season. For the best growth, shear back plants rather then cutting off small pieces for cooking. Both the stems and leaves may be used for cooking.

ADDITIONAL ADVICE FOR CARE

Parsley is often included in lists of plants to put in a garden designed to attract butterflies. It is a good source of larval food for swallowtails. Bronze fennel is another larval food for butterflies.

ADDITIONAL CULTIVARS AND SPECIES

The variety *neopolitanum*, the broad-leaf Italian parsley, has a stronger flavor than the curly parsley and is better for drying. The variety *tuberosum*, the turnip-rooted parsley, forms an 8"–10"-long root.

Phlox subulata

Moss Phlox

Thrift, Moss Pink

Height: 3"–6"
Flowers: red-purple, violet-purple, pink or white Blooms: early to mid-spring

Moss phlox is just the plant for gardeners who want bright, bold colors. Forget about those subtle pastels, and bring on the moss phlox! This is the phlox that jumps out at us with its bright flowers in early spring as we drive by a garden at 50 mph. Quickly forming a dense mound, moss phlox is a familiar flower in many old country gardens where it may cover a steep bank or drainage ditch or creep over an old stone wall next to a farmhouse. Wherever it grows, moss phlox does not go unnoticed. Easy to grow, it likes full sun and a well-drained soil, especially soils that are somewhat sandy or gritty. A slightly alkaline soil is fine, too. Moss phlox makes an effective evergreen groundcover or edging plant for a rock wall. It will also grow in the crevices of rock walls if it has some soil to grab onto. To keep the foliage looking its best, shear plants back after they bloom. If you really want to create a bold statement, plant some of each different color.

WHEN TO PLANT

Propagate plants by layering or division in summer or fall. Cuttings taken in the fall should be overwintered in a greenhouse or cold-frame. Plants have shallow root systems, so cut back the foliage before transplanting divisions.

WHERE TO PLANT

Plant moss phlox in a rock garden, in a flower garden, or on a steep, sunny slope. If you have a rock wall, let plants cascade over the wall. This phlox is a good choice for bright color when few other plants are blooming.

How to Plant

Plant moss phlox in full sun in a well-drained soil. Make sure it has some sharp sand (builder's sand, not play sand) or gritty material to help with drainage. If you plant divisions, cut back the foliage. Water plants during the hot summer months to keep foliage looking good.

Care and Maintenance

These plants benefit from watering during periods of drought. Prune the foliage back after it blooms. No special fertilization is required; just make sure the soil is well drained.

Additional Advice for Care

Moss phlox would be a good groundcover in which to plant early-blooming bulbs like lavender crocus or small varieties of pale-colored daffodils.

Additional Cultivars and Species

There are numerous cultivars of moss phlox available, including some whose flowers come in colors softer than those of the species. *P. subulata* 'Oakington Blue' has sky-blue flowers, and 'White Delight' has large white flowers. A good creeping phlox for shade gardens is *Phlox stolonifera*. It bears flowers in a range of colors including white, pink, violet, and blue.

Perennials and Herbs

Rosmarinus officinalis

Rosemary

Height: 3′–5′ tall
Flowers: pale blue Blooms: early to midsummer

A popular culinary herb, rosemary can be a beautiful evergreen ornamental in the flower garden as well. The linear foliage, ⅛″ wide and ¾″–1″ long, is closely spaced on the stem. If you don't have enough room in your garden to accommodate this small shrub, it is a choice plant to grow in a decorative pot. Rosemary needs full sun (at least 6 hours) and a well-drained soil. If you grow it in a pot, it will probably need more water than if it is planted in the ground. This herb looks great in an informal garden as a backdrop for blooming perennials, and also looks good pruned into a short hedge in more formal gardens. It can be used in bouquets or potpourri. The pale blue flowers are an unexpected bonus when they appear in clusters among the leaves in summer. Cooks use rosemary as a seasoning for chicken, potatoes, and vegetables, and the long branches can be used as skewers on which to grill vegetables. Believed to be a symbol of remembrance, friendship, and love, rosemary adds elegance to the garden and provides a source of fresh herbs for the kitchen.

WHEN TO PLANT
Rosemary should be planted in early spring. Stem cuttings (about 3″ in length) taken in spring should root in 2 to 3 weeks. When rooting cuttings, be sure to strip off the lower leaves and use a rooting hormone.

WHERE TO PLANT
Plant rosemary in the flower garden, in a herb garden, or in a large container in full sun. If you grow rosemary in a container, you may need to move it indoors for the winter in the northern parts of Georgia or protect it by covering plants during periods of extreme temperatures in winter. There are prostrate forms that can be used to cascade over walls or sprawl along the ground.

HOW TO PLANT

Rosemary tolerates a wide range of soil pH but for best success, the soil should be moisture-retentive and well-drained and should be amended with organic matter. The plants like full sun, but growth may be acceptable with 4 hours of midday sun. Rosemary responds to pruning and can be trained to grow into geometric shapes over wire forms, as hedges or into wreaths.

CARE AND MAINTENANCE

Plants in containers should be fertilized regularly using a liquid fertilizer like 10–10–10, and the soil should be amended with organic matter. Prune rosemary as you need to for cooking or to make potpourri; otherwise, it requires no regular pruning. If plants are declining due to weather and becoming leggy, prune them back in early spring to encourage a flush of growth. Keep plants well watered, especially if they are grown in pots.

ADDITIONAL ADVICE FOR CARE

Rosemary is a beautiful small shrub that offers intensely fragrant foliage, texture, and pale blue flowers in early to midsummer. Rosemary oil is used to add a pine-like scent to soaps, creams, and perfumes. It can also be used as a tea or an infusion for a refreshing bath or facial.

ADDITIONAL CULTIVARS AND SPECIES

R. officinalis 'Arp' has a sprawling habit, growing wider than it does tall. It has gray-green leaves. *R. officinalis* 'Prostratus' makes a good groundcover with its arching habit and trailing stems to 2' tall. Not as hardy as the species is 'Tuscan Blue,' a cultivar with short, glossy leaves on erect stems.

Rudbeckia fulgida 'Goldsturm'

Black-eyed Susan

Height: 2'–3'
Flowers: golden-yellow black-eyed daisy Blooms: summer to fall

Even the most inexperienced gardener can probably identify black-eyed susan. These flowers bloom for weeks in summer along roadsides and in meadows and fields throughout the southern and eastern United States. There are a number of different gardenworthy species of this native wildflower and its hybrids, including annuals, perennials, and biennials. The familiar annual black-eyed susan, R. hirta, blooms for up to 3 months in Georgia gardens. R. 'Indian Summer' is one selection that is outstanding in our climate. It grows 3'–4' tall and blooms for weeks, with gloriosa daisy-type flowers that are 6"–9" across. It is best treated as an annual. A perennial favorite that shows up in formal landscapes and small cottage gardens, R. 'Goldsturm' blooms for weeks. Quick to colonize by underground roots, it is easy to control in the garden. Unlike the annual black-eyed susan which tolerates hot, dry soils, R. 'Goldsturm' prefers a moist well-drained soil. Once established in the garden it is a long-lived, easy-care perennial.

WHEN TO PLANT

Plant black-eyed susan in the spring or fall. Annual types are easy to grow from seed, but perennial selections like 'Goldsturm' will not come true from seed and must be propagated by cuttings or divisions. Plants are easy to divide and transplant in spring or fall.

WHERE TO PLANT

Annual black-eyed susan will tolerate drier conditions than will the perennial R. 'Goldsturm,' but a moderate, well-drained soil is best for all types. All black-eyed susan are happiest if grown in full sun. Black-eyed susan are ideal for naturalized plantings such as meadows and are wonderful in the flower garden with other annuals and perennials.

ZONE
6,7,8

How to Plant

Plant black-eyed susans divisions in a soil that is moderately fertile and well-drained. If you plant them in a meadow, sow the seed in the fall. Tilling the area first will result in better germination and plants will come into bloom more quickly.

Care and Maintenance

Cutting off spent flowers of the annual types will prolong the bloom period. With perennial varieties like 'Goldsturm,' leaving the dried seed heads (coneflowers) will add interest to the fall and winter garden. Fertilize the annual types if you grow them in a formal flower garden. Use a liquid fertilizer like 10–10–10 once or twice during the growing season. For perennial varieties, just make sure the soil is moderately fertile and apply a layer of mulch in the spring and again in the fall. If plants spread too quickly, divide clumps to keep them inbound.

Additional Advice for Care

Black-eyed susans look good in combination with ornamental grasses and plants such as *Sedum* 'Autumn Joy.' The annual types make great cut flowers and both types can be dried for use in dried flower arrangements.

Additional Cultivars and Species

These cheerful flowers are welcome wherever they grow. There are numerous selections. A tall, upright perennial growing up to 7' tall, *R. nitida* 'Herbstonne' has large single yellow flowers with green ray flowers. It is a great addition to the fall garden. *R.* 'Goldquelle' grows 2'–3' tall with double yellow flowers in late summer.

Sedum 'Autumn Joy'

Autumn Joy Sedum

Height: 12"–24"
Flowers: pink Blooms: late summer, fall

This is a great plant for those timid gardeners who claim they "don't have a green thumb." Nearly indestructible, all it needs to thrive is sun or light shade and any soil that is well drained. Unlike many perennials that are suited to either hot or cold climates, S. 'Autumn Joy' performs equally well in Northern and Southern gardens. In early spring, it sends up gray-green buds. In midsummer, the flat-topped flower heads, 6" in diameter, look like broccoli. As the summer progresses, the flower buds turn from a whitish shade to a pink and finally a deep rose color. The flowers are showy late into the fall. They dry on their stems, turning to a rust color as they age. Perfect for creating interest in the winter garden, the dried flower stalks last until spring. Planted in combination with ornamental grasses and other perennials like black-eyed susans, S. 'Autumn Joy' provides months of interest in the flower garden. Left undisturbed, plants will grow and bloom for years without any special care, but they can also be easily propagated by division.

WHEN TO PLANT

Divide and transplant clumps of S. 'Autumn Joy' in the spring. Propagate by leaf cuttings in the summer. Container-grown plants may be planted in spring or fall.

WHERE TO PLANT

Plant this sedum in the flower border with other perennials in full sun or light shade in a well-drained soil. Tough plants, sedums will grow in planting beds surrounded by pavement (they don't seem bothered by reflected heat), on sandy slopes, or in containers. If they are in too much shade, cut back the flower stalks in late June to about 12" to keep plants bushy and full.

How to Plant

Plant sedums in a well-drained soil. This is one perennial that does not need a rich fertile soil. If the fertility is too high, plants will become open in the center and the long flower stalks will flop over.

Care and Maintenance

Sedums do not need fertilizer or soil amendments. Sometimes, if they are grown in too much shade or the soil is very fertile, sedums will become big clumps, open at the center and unsightly. Dividing and transplanting clumps like this will help rejuvenate them. Leave the dried flower stalks on the plants for winter interest and cut them back in early spring just as buds are swelling.

Additional Advice for Care

Larger sedums like S. 'Autumn Joy' look good in combination with other sedums including groundcover types: S. *kamtschaticum* grows 4" to 6" and has yellow flowers in summer, and S. *ternatum* grows 2" to 6" high with white flowers in spring. A native sedum, S. *ternatum* tolerates more shade than most species.

Additional Cultivars and Species

Sedum sieboldii grows 6"–8" tall with blue-green leaves and pink flowers in late summer to early autumn. *Sedum kamtschaticum*, with foliage about 4" tall, makes a good groundcover and produces masses of tiny yellow flowers in summer.

Perennials and Herbs

Thymus vulgaris,

Garden Thyme

Height: 12"
Flowers: lilac to pink Blooms: summer

Native from the western Mediterranean to southeastern Italy, garden thyme has been a favorite herb of cooks for centuries. In Georgia gardens, it also makes a beautiful evergreen groundcover. Plant it between stepping stones and along steps or walks, or let it creep over the edge of a wall. It also makes a good edging plant for the front of the flower garden. Now you can literally walk on thyme. The tiny leaves release their aromatic scent when they are bruised or crushed. Low-growing mounds reach 12" high and 12" wide, and when in flower, thyme draws bees from all around. A vigorous perennial, thyme prefers full sun and a light, airy soil, but it will also grow happily in poorer soils. In too much shade and soils that are not well drained, thyme becomes open and woody and may develop fungal diseases. Cut back plants in the early spring if they get too leggy and repropagate them with cuttings taken in the spring. All parts of the plant are aromatic, and the leaves and flowering stems are used in sachets. The oil of "Thymol" is used in pharmaceuticals.

WHEN TO PLANT

Plant in the spring, and propagate by division or cuttings in the spring. 3-inch long tip cuttings taken from the new growth should root in about 2 weeks. Seed will germinate in 3–4 weeks.

WHERE TO PLANT

Plant thyme where it will be in full sun or partial shade. It is a perfect plant to use as a creeping groundcover between stepping stones and rocks, and in a rock garden with other herbs. Thyme also makes a good border plant in the flower garden or may be combined in containers with other herbs.

How to Plant

Plant thyme in a moist, well-drained soil. If the soil is too rich or holds moisture, plants will become open and leggy. Adding some coarse sand will make the soil lighter. This Mediterranean native likes full sun, but will tolerate some light shade. If you grow thyme in containers, make sure the soil mix is light and doesn't hold too much moisture.

Care and Maintenance

Provided it is planted in the right location, garden thyme requires very little maintenance. If plants become open and woody after a few years, cut them back in early spring and fertilize with 10–10–10. Once plants are established, they shouldn't need watering except during periods of drought or if they are grown in containers.

Additional Advice for Care

Garden thyme would make a good groundcover to plant under shrub roses (make sure the roses are varieties you won't be spraying with insecticides that would get on the thyme as well) or with other fragrant plants like rosemary. By planting different types of thymes together, you can create a tapestry of scented groundcovers. Thymes come in a range of leaf colors and vary greatly in scent.

Additional Cultivars and Species

A silver-leaf selection of garden thyme is *T. vulgaris* 'Argenteus. *T. x citriodorus*, lemon thyme, has a fragrant lemon odor. A yellow variegated form of lemon thyme called 'Aureus' makes a good contrast when planted with other thymes in the garden. A thyme with fuzzy gray foliage that seems to do particularly well in Georgia is *T. glabrescens* 'Long-Leaf-Grey.'

'Homestead Purple' Verbena

Height: 10"
Flowers: purple Blooms: summer into fall

This verbena was discovered growing in a patch of weeds on the side of a road in Georgia by Dr. Michael Dirr and Dr. Allan Armitage, two well-known plantsmen and professors at the University of Georgia. The large clusters of velvety rich purple flowers bloom on and off from May until frost and the mildew-resistant foliage, dark green above and gray-green below, looks good all season. V. 'Homestead Purple' is evergreen and peren-nial except in the very coldest parts of the state. Even if its foliage is killed back, its roots will overwinter and put up new growth in the spring. To make sure it survives the winter, it is best not to prune back in the fall, or the center may die out as new plants take root all along the long, sprawling stems. Great as a groundcover, it quickly forms a dense carpet. 'Homestead Purple' is ideal for hanging baskets, containers, and the flower garden. For the best blooming, plant this verbena in full sun in a well-drained soil. Because it is a rapid grower, it is a good idea to propagate new plants every few years. Dig up divisions that have taken root and transplant them to a desired spot.

WHEN TO PLANT

Plant 'Homestead Purple' in the spring or early fall so roots will have plenty of time to get established.

WHERE TO PLANT

Plant 'Homestead Purple' in a rock garden or flower garden where it will get full sun and can creep around at will. This adaptable perennial is a good plant for hanging baskets or containers, especially when placed in combination with foliage plants like the purple sweet potato vine.

How to Plant

Like all verbenas, 'Homestead Purple' needs a well-drained, moderately fertile soil. Too much fertility will result in a lot of foliage and few blooms. Divisions can be taken and transplanted during the growing season as long as they are kept well watered.

Care and Maintenance

This is a perennial that you should not cut back in the fall, as it seems to better survive the winter if there is more leaf surface. It is a good idea to apply a light coating of mulch in the fall, making sure you avoid the crown of the plant. Be sure, too, that the soil doesn't stay wet in the winter. Once new growth has started in early spring, plants can be cut back hard to encourage bushy growth.

Additional Advice for Care

This vigorous verbena adds welcome color to a flower garden and looks good with artemisias, lamb's ears, salvias, coneflowers, and daisies. It also makes a good carpet to plant over early spring-flowering bulbs such as crocus.

Additional Cultivars and Species

Like 'Homestead Purple,' *Verbena tenuisecta* has a habit of creeping along the ground, but its lacy foliage displays a much more graceful texture. This tropical verbena, hardy from Zone 8 to 10, thrives in sandy, well-drained soils, thus is better for coastal gardens.

PERENNIALS AND HERBS

The Georgia Gardener's Guide

Photographic gallery of featured plants

Florida Maple
Acer barbatum

Paperbark Maple
Acer griseum

Japanese Maple
Acer palmatum

Red Maple
Acer rubrum

Striped Sweet Flag
Acorus calamus 'Variegatus'

Northern Maidenhair Fern
Adiantum pedatum

Bottlebrush Buckeye
Aesculus parviflora

Fiveleaf Akebia
Akebia quinata

Chives
Allium schoenoprasum

Drumstick Allium
Allium sphaerocephalum

Arkansas Blue Star
Amsonia hubrichtii

Japanese Anemone
Anemone x hybrida
'Honorine Jobert'

Snapdragon
Antirrhinum majus

Columbine
Aquilegia canadensis

Powis Castle Artemisia
Artemisia 'Powis Castle'

Wild Ginger
Asarum spp

Butterfly Weed
Asclepias tuberosa

Tartarian Daisy
Aster tartaricus

Southern Lady Fern
Athyrium filix-femina

Japanese Painted Fern
Athyrium nipponicum 'Pictum'

Wild Indigo or False Indigo
Baptisia australis

Hardy Begonia
Begonia grandis (evansiana)

Wax Begonia
Begonia semperflorens

Blackberry Lily, Leopard Flower
Belamcanda chinensis

River Birch
Betula nigra

Cross Vine
Bignonia capreolata
(Anisostichus capreolata)

Boltonia
Boltonia asteroides
'Snowbank'

Butterfly Bush
Buddleia davidii

Caladium
Caladium bicolor

Feather Reed Grass
Calamagrostis spp.

Purple Beautyberry
Callicarpa dichotoma

Sweetshrub, Carolina
Allspice, Sweet Bubby
Calycanthus floridus

Camellia
Camellia spp.

Trumpetcreeper
Campsis x Tagliabuana
'Madame Galen'

Canna
Canna x generalis

Eastern Redbud
Cercis canadensis

Pink Turtlehead
Chelone lyonii

Fringe Tree,
Grancy Gray-Beard
Chionanthus virginicus

Armand Clematis
Clematis armandii

Sweetautumn Clematis
Clematis maximowicziana

Clematis
Clematis sp.

Spider Flower, Cat's Whiskers,
Needle and Thread
Cleome hassleriana

Summersweet
Clethra alnifolia

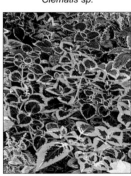

Coleus
Coleus x hybridus

Threadleaf Coreopsis
Coreopsis verticillata

Flowering Dogwood
Cornus florida

Korean Dogwood
Cornus kousa

Pampas Grass
Cortaderia selloana

Yellow Cosmos
Cosmos sulphureus

Smokebush
Cotinus coggygria

Crinum
Crinum bulbispermum

Tommies
Crocus tommasinianus

Japanese Cryptomeria
Cryptomeria japonica
'Yoshino'

Japanese Holly Fern
Cyrtomium falcatum

Daphne
Daphne odora

Bath's Pink
Dianthus gratianopolitanus
'Bath's Pink'

Hyacinth Bean Vine
Dolichos lablab
(Dipogon lablab)

Log Fern
Dryopteris celsa

Autumn Fern
Dryopteris erythrosora

Purple Coneflower
Echinacea purpurea

Elaeagnus
Elaeagnus pungens

Hardy Ageratum,
Blue Mistflower
Eupatorium coelestinum

Joe-Pye Weed
Eupatorium purpureum

Forsythia, Yellow Bells
Forsythia x intermedia

Dwarf Fothergilla
Fothergilla gardenii

Pink Panda Strawberry
Fragaria frel 'Pink Panda'

Blanket Flower
Gaillardia x grandiflora

Gardenia, Cape Jasmine
Gardenia jasminoides

Carolina Jessamine
Gelsemium sempervirens

Bigroot Geranium
Geranium macrorrhizum

Ginkgo, Maidenhair Tree
Ginkgo biloba

Globe Amaranth
Gomphrena globosa

Witchhazel
Hamamelis x intermedia

English Ivy
Hedera helix

Variegated English Ivy
Hedera helix

Common Sunflower
Helianthus annus

Lenten Rose
Helleborus orientalis

Coralbells
Heuchera micrantha
'Palace Purple'

Scarlet Rose Mallow
Hibiscus coccineus

Rose-of-Sharon, Shrub Althea
Hibiscus syriacus

Fragrant Hosta
Hosta x 'Royal Standard'

Spanish Bluebell or Wood Hyacinth
Hyacinthoides hispanica
(Scilla campanulata)

Climbing Hydrangea
Hydrangea anomala
subsp. Petiolaris

'Annabelle' Hydrangea,
Hills-of-Snow Hydrangea
Hydrangea arborescens 'Annabelle'

Common Hydrangea,
French Hydrangea
Hydrangea macrophylla

Oakleaf Hydrangea
Hydrangea quercifolia

Chinese Holly
Ilex cornuta

Japanese Holly
Ilex crenata

Winterberry
Ilex verticillata

Yaupon Holly
Ilex vomitoria

Anise, Anise-Tree
Illicium spp.

Impatiens, Sultana, Busy Lizzie
Impatiens wallerana

Japanese Blood Grass
Imperata cylindrica
'Red Baron'

Moonflower
Ipomoea alba

Cypress Vine
Ipomoea quamoclit

Yellow Flag
Iris pseudacorus

Japanese Roof Iris
(White Form)
Iris tectorum

Juniper
Juniperus spp.

Goldenraintree
Koelreuteria paniculata

Crapemyrtle
Lagerstroemia indica

Hardy Lantana
Lantana camara 'Miss Huff'

Summer Snowflake
Leucojum aestivum

Blazing Star, Gayfeather
Liatris spicata

Sweetgum
Liquidambar styraciflua
'Rotundiloba'

Monkey Grass, Liriope
Liriope spp.

Cardinal Flower
Lobelia cardinalis

Loropetalum,
Chinese Fringeflower
Loropetalum chinense

Spider Lily, Surprise Lily
Lycoris radiata

Loosestrife
Lythrum virgatum
'Morden Pink'

Southern Magnolia
Magnolia grandiflora

Saucer Magnolia
Magnolia x soulangiana

Flowering Crabapple
Malus spp.

Dawn Redwood
Metasequoia glyptostroboides

Maiden Grass
Miscanthus sinensis

Bee Balm, Oswego Tea,
Bergamot
Monarda didyma

Nandina, Heavenly Bamboo
Nandina domestica

Daffodils
Narcissus spp. and cultivars

Sweet Basil (Annual Herb)
Ocimum basilicum

Mondo Grass
Ophiopogon japonicus

Common Oregano
Origanum vulgare

Royal Fern
Osmunda regalis

Fountain Grass
Pennisetum spp.

Parsley
Petroselinum crispum

Petunia
Petunia x hybrida

Moss Phlox, Thrift, Moss Pink
Phlox subulata

Red Tip Photinia
Photinia x fraseri

Pine
Pinus spp.

Christmas Fern
Polystichum acrostichoides

Moss Rose
Portulaca grandiflora

Kwanzan Cherry
Prunus 'Sekiyama'

Cherrylaurel
Prunus caroliniana

Yoshino Cherry
Prunus x yedoensis

Bradford Pear
Pyrus calleryana 'Bradford'

Oak
Quercus spp.

Plumleaf Azalea
Rhododendron prunifolium

Rhododendron
Rhododendron spp.

Spring Flowering Azalea
Rhododendron spp.

The Sweetheart Rose
Rosa 'Cecile Brunner'

Mister Lincoln Rose
Rosa 'Mister Lincoln'

New Dawn Rose
Rosa 'New Dawn'

Sun Flare Rose
Rosa 'Sun Flare'

The Fairy Rose
Rosa 'The Fairy'

Lady Banks Rose
Rosa banksiae var. Alba plena

Yellow Lady Banks Rose
Rosa banksiae

Rosemary
Rosmarinus officinalis

Black-eyed Susan
Rudbeckia fulgida 'Goldsturm'

Fan Flower
Scaevola 'Blue Wonder'

Autumn Joy Sedum
Sedum 'Autumn Joy'

Purple Heart
Setcreasea pallida
'Purple Heart'

Bumald Spirea
Spiraea x bumalda

Lilac
Syringa spp.

Southern Shield Fern
Thelypteris kunthii

Garden Thyme
Thymus vulgaris

Thyme
Thymus spp.

Wishbone Flower,
Clown Flower
Torenia fournieri

Canadian Hemlock
Tsuga canadensis

Chinese Elm, Lacebark Elm
Ulmus parvifolia

Homestead Purple Verbena
Verbena 'Homestead Purple'

Doublefile Viburnum
*Viburnum plicatum
var. tomentosum*

Prague Viburnum
Viburnum x pragense

Periwinkle, Myrtle, Vinca
Vinca minor

Pansies
Viola x wittrockiana

Chastetree
Vitex agnus-castus

Leyland Cypress
X Cupressocyparis leylandii

Rain Lily
Zephyranthes candida

Zinnia
Zinnia linearis (angustifolia)

Cherokee Rose
Rosa laevigata

CHAPTER SIX

Roses

*T*HAVE ALWAYS HAD A PASSION *for fragrant flowers, and I still remember the time I fell in love with the intoxicating scent of Rosa 'Chapeau de Napoleon.' It was growing in the rose garden at Swarthmore College in Pennsylvania. Not only did the flowers smell heavenly, but I found that by lightly touching the crested buds and stems I could take some of their perfume with me. But as the summer progressed, the plant looked "the worse for wear." What this meant for me was that I would not include this rose in my own garden. I adhere to this same guideline when choosing roses for my garden in Georgia today. Not only must they be able to survive and provide fragrant flowers without a lot of fuss, but they must look good most of the time. These requirements narrow my choices. My favorites include R. 'New Dawn,' a great climber; the butterfly rose, a colorful shrub rose; and R. Perle d'Or, a deliciously scented rose. All three resist pests and disease, bloom repeatedly, and offer at least some type of fragrance.—E.L.G.*

Roses have been revered by gardeners and non-gardeners alike for centuries. With the vast numbers of new selections offered each year, there are now roses to suit almost every type of garden from the very formal to the old-fashioned rambling cottage garden. We may envy gardeners in Portland and California whose climate is better for growing the classic hybrid teas, but the resurgence of interest in old garden roses has resulted in the availability of a large number of roses that will live and bloom happily in Georgia gardens without being decimated by blackspot and powdery mildew. Prior to this development, many of these "old roses" had only been grown by "little old ladies" (and men), who kept them in cultivation by passing cuttings from one generation to the next. Today one of the large suppliers of old-fashioned or heirloom roses, *The Antique Rose Emporium,* has a retail location in Dahlonega, Georgia. Here gardeners have the opportunity to view display gardens and purchase roses. For a small fee they can also purchase a catalogue which serves as a valuable reference.

ROSE CLASSIFICATION

With hundreds of roses to choose from, it's a good idea to have a basic understanding of how roses are classified. When it comes to nomenclature, *Modern Roses 10* is the standard for rose breeders. But for gardeners, it's only important to know which types do what and which roses will perform best in your garden. What follows is a brief description of some of the major classes of outdoor roses.

Species Roses: Species roses usually have single petals and some have edible fruits. Easy to care for, disease-resistant, and adaptable, many have contributed to crosses with other roses, resulting in improved hybrids. This is a good place to talk about the Georgia state flower: the Cherokee rose, *Rosa laevigata*. While this species is not native to Georgia, it was introduced into cultivation from Asia early in American history and has naturalized throughout much of the South. It is a sight to behold when in full bloom with its pure white flowers and glossy golden-green foliage. A word of caution: this rose is the definition of vigorous and the thorns are wicked! If you plant it, make sure it has lots of room to grow. Keep your gloves close by for pruning.

Hybrid Teas: One of the most popular roses, they feature attractive buds and large flowers. They grow from two-and-a-half to five feet tall. Most are fragrant, and are popular both in the garden and as cut flowers. Usually double, the flowers have twenty to fifty or more petals. If you are determined to grow hybrid teas in Georgia, be prepared to spray your roses once every seven to ten days for clean plants free of insects and disease. Check with your local Extension Service or Rose Society for specific recommendations.

Grandifloras: These tall and vigorous plants come in many colors. They are good for the background and for cutting.

Floribundas: These roses are known for the clusters of flowers they produce throughout the growing season. Look for selections that have been made for Southern gardens.

Polyanthas: Free-flowering and low-growing, these roses combine well with perennials and annuals and grow well in containers.

Heritage Roses: Georgia gardeners have a large number of heritage roses to choose from. While they may not be disease-free, they are mostly disease-resistant and require little or no spraying. Unlike some of the more modern hybrids, which may have no fragrance, they offer a whole range of different scents from a light "tea scent" to a heavy musk-like scent.

Climbing Roses: Climbing roses, both the old-fashioned types and the more modern selections, offer the gardener with a tiny yard a chance to train roses up a wall or structure. Some climbers bloom only once, but many are repeat bloomers.

Rosa banksiae var. *alba plena* and *R. banksiae* var. *lutea*
(Species Rose)

Lady Banks Rose

Yellow Lady Banks Rose

Height: 15'–20' or more
Flowers: 1/2"–2" pompons, white or yellow

Lady banks, a vigorous climber, is outstanding among the roses that thrive in Georgia with little or no care except in the very coldest parts of the state. One of the first roses to bloom in spring, its scent, especially that of the white form, has been compared to the scent of violets. When in bloom, it looks like a blanket of flowers that covers the plant for up to 6 weeks. It was introduced to our country in 1807. Chances are that if your grandmother grew this rose, it is still thriving in the same spot today. The long-lived and vigorous large plants may threaten to pull down buildings when the trunks get as big around as small trees! Lady banks does not suffer from any serious pest or disease problems, but a late freeze can kill flower buds. Even without blooms, the willow-like foliage looks good year round. This rose is a good one to train up a tree or over a high wall where the foliage can cascade down. It is also a good climber on which to train annual vines like the purple hyacinth bean. The yellow form of lady banks is slightly more hardy than the white form.

WHEN TO PLANT

Plant bare root plants as soon as you receive them during the dormant season. Container-grown plants should be planted in early spring or early fall so that they have plenty of time to establish healthy root systems.

WHERE TO PLANT

Because it is a long-lived fast grower, it is best to plant lady banks where it will have lots of room. Its habit of producing long shoots makes it easy to train up a structure. Lady banks should be planted where it gets at least 4 to 5 hours of direct sunlight per day. It will grow in shady gardens but will not produce as many blooms.

ZONE
8

How to Plant

The best time to amend your soil is well before you actually plant. Roses are heavy feeders, and they benefit from a well-drained soil that is rich in organic matter. Hand dig, or use a tiller for large areas, and combine 1/3 coarse sand, 1/3 organic matter (compost, manure, or composted pinebark), and 1/3 clay. For bare root roses, dig a hole large enough so you can place the roots over a small mound of soil to allow them to spread out in all directions. The depth of the hole should be measured from the line that divides the top growth from the soil. Prune all damaged roots, and remember: root pruning should be balanced by an equal amount of pruning of top growth.

Care and Maintenance

A topdressing of mulch applied 2 or 3 times a year provides additional organic matter and helps keep roots cool and moist. Most shrubs, roses in particular, benefit from deep watering once a week instead of daily surface sprinkling. Placing a hose on slow trickle at the base of a plant for an hour each week encourages strong roots and a healthy plant, which means there will be more blooms. Many chemical and organic rose fertilizers are commercially available, and regular applications of one of these during the growing season will help keep plants vigorous. Be sure to follow the recommendations on the product label.

Additional Advice for Care

Use a good commercial potting mix if you plant in containers. Remember, roses grown in containers need more fertilizer. When you plant lady banks rose, be patient. It will be a few years before you see good blooms. Prune every other year. This rose flowers on second- and third-year wood. Prune carefully, removing only old wood.

Additional Cultivars and Species

A good rose for hedging, *R*. 'Balleriana' produces masses of small, single pink flowers with white eyes. It can be pruned as a shrub or trained as a climber, reaching up to 10'. It also produces tiny, bright orange-red hips in the fall.

The Sweetheart Rose

Height: 3'–4' tall

Flowers: 2"–3", multi-petaled cream pink with salmon centers

It's hard to believe that this delightful, well-behaved rose is related to the invasive Rosa multiflora *that is considered to be a noxious weed in most states. Perhaps 'Cecile Brunner's' other parent, the tea rose, contributed its everblooming, compact habit to this little beauty. The buds are like those of hybrid teas, but the sweetheart rose does not have the problems that hybrid teas do. 'Cecile Brunner' (named after a woman) was introduced in 1881, and it often shows up in old, well-established gardens where it thrives with little or no care. A delightful rose, it is disease-resistant and it tolerates poor soil and partial shade. From mid-spring until frost time, sprays of up to twelve flowers appear above the foliage, perfuming the air with a heady scent. The plant is long-lived and healthy, and the foliage looks good even without spraying. 'Cecile Brunner's' relatively few thorns make it a favorite in many parts of Georgia. It is a perfect complement to perennials and annuals, yielding maximum bloom from a minimum-sized plant.*

When to Plant

Plant your bare root roses during the dormant season as soon as you receive them. *R.* 'Cecile Brunner' is often sold in a container, and you can plant it any time the ground is not frozen. However, for best results, plant container-grown roses in the early spring or early fall so that each rose will have plenty of time to establish a healthy root system.

Where to Plant

Most roses require a minimum of 6 hours of direct sunlight, but the sweetheart rose grows happily with only 3 to 4 hours of sun per day. Although it tolerates poor soil, it will thrive in a soil that is rich in organic matter. Good air circulation will reduce the threat of diseases such as powdery mildew and black spot.

How to Plant

The best time to amend your soil is well before you actually plant. Roses are heavy feeders, and they benefit from a well-drained soil that is rich in organic matter. Hand dig, or use a tiller for large areas, and combine 1/3 coarse sand, 1/3 organic matter (compost, manure, or composted pinebark), and 1/3 clay. For bare root roses, dig a hole large enough so you can place the roots over a small mound of soil to allow them to spread out in all directions. The depth of the hole should be measured from the line that divides the top growth from the soil. Prune all damaged roots, and remember: root pruning should be balanced by an equal amount of pruning of top growth.

Care and Maintenance

A topdressing of mulch applied 2 or 3 times a year provides additional organic matter and helps keep roots cool and moist. Most shrubs, roses in particular, benefit from deep watering once a week instead of daily surface sprinkling. Placing a hose on slow trickle at the base of a plant for an hour each week encourages strong roots and a healthy plant—and that means more blooms! Many chemical and organic rose fertilizers are commercially available. Be sure to follow the recommendations on the product label.

Additional Advice for Care

Although many modern roses require regular pruning, old-fashioned roses do not. The only pruning the sweetheart rose requires is the removal of dead and damaged wood and a light pruning of tips in order to shape the plant. You can restrict your pruning to cutting flowers!

Additional Cultivars and Species

A climbing form of 'Cecile Brunner' is also available, but it is a much larger plant, and it grows from 15' to 20' tall. It is not a repeat bloomer like the shrub variety.

Rosa chinensis var. *mutabilis* (China)

Butterfly Rose

Height: 4'–6' or taller
Flowers: yellow, orange, pink, and crimson

The butterfly rose is not what most people think of as a classic rose. The silky, single-petaled blooms open as a soft yellow, but instead of fading with age as most roses do, the flowers later darken and become more intense, turning shades of orange, pink, and crimson. When this rose is in bloom and different colors flicker in the breeze, it looks as if a host of butterflies had taken up residence on the plant. A twiggy shrub with an upright spreading habit, the plant can become quite large, and it makes a dramatic statement when planted in groups. It produces a flower at the end of almost every new growth, so it is either in bud or in flower from early summer until the first hard frost. Although it is not evergreen, the foliage starts out a bronze color and persists late into the fall, providing another ornamental effect that we don't expect from most roses. The butterfly rose is usually grown on its own roots; therefore, if it is killed back to the ground during a severe winter, it will come back and recover. Highly disease-resistant, this rose should thrive in your garden for years without any special care.

WHEN TO PLANT

Plant bare root plants during the dormant season as soon as you receive them. Plant containerized plants in early spring or in early fall so that they have plenty of time to establish healthy root systems.

WHERE TO PLANT

Plant the butterfly rose where it will receive at least 6 hours of direct sunlight. If you plant it with annuals and perennials, allow it plenty of space to grow. A mass of butterfly roses on a bank or in a shrub border makes a beautiful display.

How to Plant

The best time to amend your soil is well before you actually plant. Roses are heavy feeders, and they benefit from a well-drained soil that is rich in organic matter. Hand dig, or use a tiller for large areas, and combine 1/3 coarse sand, 1/3 organic matter (compost, manure, or composted pinebark), and 1/3 clay. For bare root roses, dig a hole large enough so you can place the roots over a small mound of soil to allow them to spread out in all directions. The depth of the hole should be measured from the line that divides the top growth from the soil. Prune all damaged roots, and remember: root pruning should be balanced by an equal amount of pruning of top growth.

Care and Maintenance

A topdressing of mulch applied 2 or 3 times a year provides additional organic matter and helps keep roots cool and moist. Most shrubs, roses in particular, benefit from deep watering once a week instead of daily surface sprinkling. Placing a hose on slow trickle at the base of a plant for an hour each week encourages strong roots and a healthy plant, which means there will be more blooms. Many chemical and organic rose fertilizers are commercially available, and regular applications of one of these during the growing season will help keep plants vigorous. Be sure to follow the recommendations on the product label.

Additional Advice for Care

The butterfly rose needs little or no pruning except to remove any dead or diseased wood.

Additional Cultivars and Species

All China roses are disease-resistant, everblooming, and long-lived. Other good Chinas to try are 'Old Blush,' 'Archduke Charles,' and 'Ducher.'

Mister Lincoln Rose

Height: 5' tall
Flowers: red

Despite the fact that hybrid tea roses grown in Georgia can require spraying every 7 to 10 days along with frequent fertilizing and deadheading, growing them can be rewarding. Because of their sturdy stems, large open flowers held high above the foliage, and long blooming season, it's understandable that these high-maintenance plants are still popular, especially among beginning rose growers. This flower's strong stems, urn-shaped buds, and large cupped flowers that contain up to thirty-five petals make it ideal for cutting and using in arrangements or bouquets. This hybrid tea represents the classic red rose. Its dark, leathery foliage and vigorous habit make it one of the better hybrid teas for Georgia gardens, in which powdery mildew and black spot can wreak havoc. It was introduced in 1964, and even after all these years has a big following among rose lovers.

WHEN TO PLANT

Plant bare root plants as soon as you receive them during the dormant season. Container-grown plants should be planted in early spring or early fall so that they have plenty of time to establish healthy root systems.

WHERE TO PLANT

Plant 'Mister Lincoln' where it will receive at least 6 hours of direct sunlight per day. Use low-growing perennials like hardy geraniums or groundcovers to help hide the "ugly knees" that so many hybrid teas develop.

HOW TO PLANT

The best time to amend your soil is well before you actually plant. Roses are heavy feeders, and they benefit from a well-drained soil that is rich in organic matter. Hand dig, or use a tiller for large areas,

and combine 1/3 coarse sand, 1/3 organic matter (compost, manure, or composted pinebark), and 1/3 clay. For bare root roses, dig a hole large enough so you can place the roots over a small mound of soil to allow them to spread out in all directions. The depth of the hole should be measured from the line that divides the top growth from the soil. Prune all damaged roots, and remember: root pruning should be balanced by an equal amount of pruning of top growth.

CARE AND MAINTENANCE

A topdressing of mulch applied 2 or 3 times a year provides additional organic matter and helps keep roots cool and moist. Most shrubs, roses in particular, benefit from deep watering once a week instead of daily surface sprinkling. Placing a hose on slow trickle at the base of a plant for an hour each week encourages strong roots and a healthy plant, which means there will be more blooms. Many chemical and organic rose fertilizers are commercially available, and regular applications of one of these during the growing season will help keep plants vigorous. Be sure to follow the recommendations on the product label.

ADDITIONAL ADVICE FOR CARE

Growing hybrid tea roses in Georgia requires a spray program that applies a combination fungicide-insecticide every 7 to 10 days during the growing season. Prune canes in early spring to a height of 4 to 6 buds from the base of the previous year's growth.

ADDITIONAL CULTIVARS AND SPECIES

Other hybrid teas to try in Georgia are R. 'Dolly Parton,' noted for its fragrant orange and orange-red flowers that measure 6 to 7 inches across, and R. 'New Zealand,' a bushy, disease-resistant selection with pink-orange flowers. Introduced in 1867, 'La France,' with its silvery pink double flowers, is still considered a choice hybrid tea.

Rosa 'New Dawn' (Climbing Rose)

New Dawn Rose

Height: a climbing rose of 20' or more
Flowers: double soft pink, fragrant

Both climbing and rambling roses are appealing for their flowers and for their growth habits, which add vertical elements even to the smallest garden. One drawback of many old-fashioned ramblers is that they bloom only once; however, it is a spectacular display that lasts for weeks. This everblooming hybrid is a sport of the favorite one-time bloomer 'Dr. W. Van Fleet.' Popular since it was first introduced in 1930, 'New Dawn' can be seen covering a log cabin or rambling over an arbor in a long-forgotten garden when you drive the back country roads in Georgia. The flowers hold up well even in the rain, another reason for its popularity. Producing canes that can grow to 10' tall or more in a single season, it can easily cover an arbor or trellis or, in some cases, an entire house! 'New Dawn' is a good rose for covering an ugly chain link fence. Just weave its new shoots in and out of the links. Give this rose lots of room and plenty of sun. Although it is disease-resistant, it is susceptible to black spot.

When to Plant

Plant bare root plants during the dormant season as soon as you receive them. If your 'New Dawn' rose is grafted rather than grown on its own roots, be sure to plant it so that the bud union is at ground level. Container-grown plants should be planted in early spring or early fall so that they have plenty of time to establish healthy root systems.

Where to Plant

Plant 'New Dawn' so it can be trained to climb over a structure, or place it against a building or bank where it has lots of room to spread. Choose a location that gets plenty of direct sunlight: 6 hours or more per day is ideal. This is not a plant for a small garden unless you can train it to grow vertically.

How to Plant

The best time to amend your soil is well before you actually plant.
Roses are heavy feeders, and they benefit from a well-drained soil
that is rich in organic matter. Hand dig, or use a tiller for large areas,
and combine 1/3 coarse sand, 1/3 organic matter (compost, manure,
or composted pinebark), and 1/3 clay. For bare root roses, dig a hole
large enough so you can place the roots over a small mound of soil
to allow them to spread out in all directions. The depth of the hole
should be measured from the line that divides the top growth from
the soil. Prune all damaged roots, and remember: root pruning
should be balanced by an equal amount of pruning of top growth.

Care and Maintenance

A topdressing of mulch applied 2 or 3 times a year provides additional organic matter and helps keep roots cool and moist. Most
shrubs, roses in particular, benefit from deep watering once a week
instead of daily surface sprinkling. Placing a hose on slow trickle at
the base of a plant for an hour each week encourages strong roots
and a healthy plant—and that means more blooms! Many chemical
and organic rose fertilizers are commercially available. Be sure to
follow the recommendations on the product label.

Additional Advice for Care

Using twine or stretch ties that expand, train the canes to grow in a
fan-like fashion. Do not use wire, as it will girdle the plant.
Horizontal rose canes produce more flowers than do vertical ones.
Climbing roses require less vigorous pruning than hybrid tea roses.
In early spring, when the buds are swelling, prune older and dis-
eased canes.

Additional Cultivars and Species

R. 'White Dawn' is very similar to 'New Dawn,' but it displays
white flowers.

Rosa 'Sun Flare' (Floribunda)

Sun Flare Rose

Height: 3'–4'
Flowers: double, yellow, 2"–3"

Next to red roses, yellow roses offer the most popular rose color choice for gardens. 'Sun Flare' has clusters of delicately scented blooms that start out golden yellow and fade as they open. This delightful rose provides a good transition in the flower garden between bright colors like pinks, reds, and oranges. It can extend the blooming season in the shrub border, offering flowers long after the traditional spring bloomers have come and gone. Although it does not have the long stem that we associate with traditional roses like hybrid teas, it more than makes up for this shortcoming with a profusion of blooms, 3 to 12 per cluster, from spring until frost time. Other qualities that make this rose a good choice for Georgia gardens are its resistance to disease and its shiny green foliage which starts out with tinges of red. It is difficult to find roses that don't require an aggressive spray program to keep them looking good throughout the growing season in our hot, humid climate. An exception is 'Sun Flare,' a yellow rose with prolific blooms and handsome foliage that does not require spraying on a regular basis.

WHEN TO PLANT

Plant bare root roses during the dormant season as soon as you receive them. Plant containerized plants in the early spring or in early fall so they have plenty of time to establish healthy root systems.

WHERE TO PLANT

Plant 'Sun Flare' in a shrub border or in a flower garden with perennials and annuals. Choose a location where it will receive 6 hours or more of direct sunlight per day.

ZONE 6,7,8

How to Plant

The best time to amend your soil is well before you actually plant. Roses are heavy feeders, and they benefit from a well-drained soil that is rich in organic matter. Hand dig, or use a tiller for large areas, and combine 1/3 coarse sand, 1/3 organic matter (compost, manure, or composted pinebark), and 1/3 clay. For bare root roses, dig a hole large enough so you can place the roots over a small mound of soil to allow them to spread out in all directions. The depth of the hole should be measured from the line that divides the top growth from the soil. Prune all damaged roots, and remember: root pruning should be balanced by an equal amount of pruning of top growth.

Care and Maintenance

A topdressing of mulch applied 2 or 3 times a year provides additional organic matter and helps keep roots cool and moist. Most shrubs, roses in particular, benefit from deep watering once a week instead of daily surface sprinkling. Placing a hose on slow trickle at the base of a plant for an hour each week encourages strong roots and a healthy plant, which means there will be more blooms. Many chemical and organic rose fertilizers are commercially available. Be sure to follow the recommendations on the product label.

Additional Advice for Care

'Sun Flare'is a Floribunda rose. It should be pruned in early spring just as buds are swelling. Prune back to 5 or 7 buds from the base, and remove any damaged or dead wood.

Additional Cultivars and Species

Try R. 'Betty Prior,' a Floribunda rose which displays bright pink single flowers and is a good repeat bloomer.

Rosa 'The Fairy' (Polyantha)

The Fairy Rose

Height: 3'–4'
Flowers: pink, 1"–2" double

'The Fairy' is the ideal choice for a limited space, especially for growing in containers or at the front of a flower border. Just make sure it is not planted too close to aggressive perennials such as Artemisia *'Powis Castle,' which can quickly consume it. Although they are small, the clusters of slightly fragrant flowers put on a good show. Its flowers stand out against its tiny, glossy, light-green foliage as 'The Fairy' blooms throughout the summer and into the fall. The sprays of blooms hold up well as cut flowers. Cut these roses before they are fully open and have begun to fade. Flowers are the perfect size to use for making nosegays, or one may be worn in a single buttonhole. Unlike many short-lived miniature roses that can be magnets for pests and diseases, 'The Fairy' is a tough survivor and has persisted in Georgia gardens for years. It was introduced in 1932 and it is still a popular choice today. This rose is sometimes sold as a standard, a plant grown and pruned to resemble a small tree.*

WHEN TO PLANT
Plant bare root plants as soon as you receive them during the dormant season. Container-grown plants should be planted in early spring or early fall so that they have plenty of time to establish healthy root systems.

WHERE TO PLANT
Plant 'The Fairy Rose' where it will get at least 6 hours of direct sunlight. Its small size and flowers make it best suited for the front of the border or for containers placed where they can be viewed up close.

How to Plant

The best time to amend your soil is well before you actually plant. Roses are heavy feeders, and they benefit from a well-drained soil that is rich in organic matter. Hand dig, or use a tiller for large areas, and combine 1/3 coarse sand, 1/3 organic matter (compost, manure, or composted pinebark), and 1/3 clay. For bare root roses, dig a hole large enough so you can place the roots over a small mound of soil to allow them to spread out in all directions. The depth of the hole should be measured from the line that divides the top growth from the soil. Prune all damaged roots, and remember: root pruning should be balanced by an equal amount of pruning of top growth.

Care and Maintenance

A topdressing of mulch applied 2 or 3 times a year provides additional organic matter and helps keep roots cool and moist. Most shrubs, roses in particular, benefit from deep watering once a week instead of daily surface sprinkling. Placing a hose on slow trickle at the base of a plant for an hour each week encourages strong roots and a healthy plant, which means there will be more blooms. Many chemical and organic rose fertilizers are commercially available, and regular applications of one of these during the growing season will help keep plants vigorous. Be sure to follow the recommendations on the product label.

Additional Advice for Care

After the first year, polyantha roses benefit from a pruning in early spring just as the buds are swelling before they begin to leaf out. Cut back plants to about 1 to 2 feet, depending on the vigor of each plant. This will encourage lots of new growth and blooms.

Additional Cultivars and Species

Other polyantha roses to try are R. 'Perle d'Or,' R. 'La Marne,'and R. 'Marie Pavie.'

CHAPTER SEVEN

Shrubs

*I*F TREES ARE THE WALLS AND ceiling of our outdoor landscape rooms, shrubs are the furniture. Their flowers are like a colorful upholstery over a soft but solid frame. They are placed against the walls just as we would place a sofa or bookcase. Shrubs are planted in the center of an outdoor room to give it texture, color, and depth, just like an easy chair or coffee table. Around shrubs we plant wide beds of flowers—the end tables and lamps of our outdoor living room.

Shrubs in Georgia come in a wide range of sizes, from ground-hugging junipers to tree-formed hollies. Their flowers range from the purest white of a doublefile viburnum to the deepest blue of a French hydrangea. If your taste runs to the bold statement rather than the subdued pastel, the flowers of a loropetalum or a native azalea will satisfy your needs.

Shrubs serve dual functions in a landscape. They are a solid green background for perennial and annual flowers. Many shrubs add their own flowers and berries to the riot of color that erupts each year. The shrubs we have chosen to describe in this chapter are the best of the best for Georgia. Most can grow well from the seashore to the mountains. We have also indicated the superior selections and variations of individual shrubs. Those who have a penchant for variegated leaves will find several to choose from. For those who enjoy fragrance, we have described the ones which smell the sweetest. The descriptions explain how to plant and grow shrubs properly.

As is true of indoor decorating, sometimes the urge may strike to move the furniture around or replace the fabric. Let's take a moment to learn how to do these exercises properly with shrubbery.

TRANSPLANTING

Most shrubs should be transplanted when the demand for water is least, in late fall or winter. Since many roots will inevitably be lost, they need many weeks to regenerate themselves before the hot, dry blasts of summer arrive. If fate dictates that your favorite rose must be moved in July because you are adding onto your garage, transplanting can still be successful with a little more care. Follow these steps to make the move a success:

The perfect time to transplant is on a cool November afternoon, a few days after a good rainfall. Small-sized shrubs are easier to transplant than large ones. You might need to prune away several branches to make your plant small enough to easily handle.

Plunge a shovel straight down into the soil in a circle around the plant, 12" from the trunk on all sides. You'll be forming a root ball 24" across as you proceed, severing underground roots as you thrust the shovel.

Just outside the slit you've made in the soil, begin digging a trench completely around the root ball. The trench should be 8" deep. When you have finished digging the trench, place the point of the shovel at the bottom and push it underneath the root ball. A flat spade or a long-tongued plumber's shovel is helpful for this task.

When you have thrust underneath the shrub from all sides, get a friend to tilt the plant to one side while you slide an old shower curtain or a threadbare bedsheet underneath the root ball. With a bit of huffing and puffing and root clipping, the cloth or plastic can be slid under the entire plant. Wrap it tightly around the roots to keep the soil in place, and go inspect the new planting spot.

Assuming the new site is well dug, carry or slide the shrub to its new home. Plant it at the same level as it was growing before and water thoroughly. When springtime comes, your shrub won't have the faintest memory of being in its old spot!

PRUNING

While trees may never need pruning after they acquire a mature shape, many shrubs need regular pruning. Pruning can serve one or more of three functions: to give a shrub the proper size or shape, to help it produce more flowers, or to rejuvenate a weary old plant into youthful vigor. Here are some examples and tips.

Proper size: We've all seen shrubs pruned into topiary animals. That's not what normal pruning is about. In your landscape, you may simply need an upright oval shape between two windows rather than a wide ball that obscures them both. The best time to achieve this shaping is from February through early March. You can clip then to your heart's content, secure in the knowledge that the shrub will produce new leaves in a few weeks to hide any stubs or mistakes. A fast-growing shrub like Leyland cypress or Burford holly may achieve its needed size rapidly, then surpass it! You'll need to prune shrubs like these yearly to keep them in bounds.

Attempt to make every pruning cut just beyond a healthy bud or small branch you would like to preserve on the plant. One of the pleasures of pruning is doing the job with a sharp pair of by-pass (not anvil) hand pruners. When larger limbs need to be cut, a long-handled lopper makes the job a breeze. An electric hedge trimmer is a seductive tool, but the problems it can cause usually outweigh its benefits. Clippers and trimmers will tempt you to form "green meatballs" in your yard. In addition, the resulting dense shell of green leaves on the outside of the shrub will cause the inside to be dark, dead and lifeless. You will achieve a much more natural shape by using hand tools.

More flowers: Some shrubs make more flowers if they are pruned severely each spring. Smokebush and summersweet make their summer flowers on branches that have grown since spring. A light "nipping and tipping" all over these shrubs in March will reward you with a thick covering of flowers. Butterfly bush will bloom moderately on old branches, but new branches make more of the honey-scented blossoms. The bush should be cut back to 12" to 24" tall in March.

Most gardeners know that the best time to prune azaleas is during the month after they finish flowering. Why? Because azaleas, camellias, rhododendrons, and many other spring-flowering shrubs make blooms on branches that grew the previous year. If you prune any of these in winter, you'll remove the flower buds for next spring!

Rejuvenation: Occasionally a shrub will just look old. Ancient azaleas, floppy hydrangeas, and bare-legged hollies are simply not attractive. If the shrub seems healthy otherwise, it can be rejuvenated by massive pruning in late February. Massive pruning means just that: remove all of the limbs down to 6" to 12" from the ground.

Though it may seem drastic, severe pruning can force the plant to send out new shoots at a height that is more appropriate. If your holly has bare limbs for the first three feet from the ground, no amount of pruning above that height will cause it to make new limbs and leaves near the ground. Broadleafed shrubs have plenty of dormant buds near the soil which will cover the trunk with growth in just a couple of months.

Bottlebrush Buckeye

Height: 8'–10' Width: 8'–12'
Deciduous flowering shrub

What other plant has a common name that describes the two features you're sure to remember? Spectacular white bottlebrush flowers cover a bottlebrush buckeye in June. In October, the small brown nuts that resemble a deer's eye fall from the branch tips, ready for a passing child to collect a pocketful and marvel. Bottlebrush buckeye has been overlooked for no apparent reason. If you plant one, you will certainly be the first in your neighborhood to do so, but then everyone else will want one, too. It is quite adaptable in the landscape. Bottlebrush buckeye can be grown as a specimen shrub surrounded by pansies, or as a background for a perennial flower bed. Prepare to be surprised by its fall leaf color: it is almost the same yellow that makes ginkgo trees so bright at the same time. There are other summer-flowering shrubs, but few can compare with this dramatic plant.

WHEN TO PLANT

Plant your bottlebrush buckeye in very early spring, before it has leaves if possible. Large specimens are sold balled and burlapped, but it is common to find container-grown plants for sale at nurseries.

WHERE TO PLANT

A bottlebrush buckeye can tolerate full sunshine without difficulty, but it seems to be happier in dappled shade. In the flatlands of south Georgia, tall pine trees offer the perfect amount of shade. In any situation, be sure to give this shrub plenty of room to spread. It sends up suckers near the trunk, and if a branch touches the ground, it will usually root. A years-old massed planting is a stunning sight.

HOW TO PLANT

Bottlebrush buckeye is a woodland native. It appreciates any attempt to approximate woodland conditions. Dig a hole 5 times as wide as the root ball, and add 2 cubic feet of soil conditioner or compost to the soil removed from the hole. If the roots seem to be growing densely in the pot, unwind the longest ones and spread them in the hole before shoveling soil back in place. Pack the earth back around the roots. Water occasionally for the first month. Spread a layer of pine straw mulch or wood chips under your buckeye to conserve moisture.

CARE AND MAINTENANCE

Bottlebrush buckeye can grow well with little fertilizer. Apply 1 tablespoon of 10–10–10 fertilizer per foot of height in April and again in midsummer. Do not allow the soil to dry out beneath the plant until it is well established; mulch will be your best ally in summer. After a few years, an annual reapplication of shredded leaves will be all the care that is needed. Pruning is not required on a regular basis, but sprouts can be pulled up and discarded if they pop up where you don't want them.

ADDITIONAL ADVICE FOR CARE

Other species of buckeye have problems with diseases and insects, but no pests seem to affect bottlebrush buckeye. If you want to pass along this gem to friends, transplant the sprouts in early spring or try collecting seed. Plant the seeds immediately after they fall; they are viable for only a few days.

ADDITIONAL CULTIVARS AND SPECIES

Aesculus parviflora 'Rogers' has flower clusters that are more slender but longer than those of other bottlebrush buckeyes. The leaves are also a bit more droopy, but not in an unpleasant way.

Buddleia davidii

Butterfly Bush

Height: 5'–8' Width: 5'–8'
Deciduous flowering shrub

Butterfly bush is a garden mainstay with flowers that last all summer. The combination of scent and flower shape will attract butterflies to your yard from all over the neighborhood. The shrub will occasionally be in motion from the movements of dozens of butterflies as they flutter from flower to flower. If you like the thought of hosting butterflies throughout the summer, your butterfly bush should be only one of several plants chosen to make them feel at home. A butterfly garden should include bronze fennel (Foeniculum vulgare), *parsley* (Petroselinum crispum), *and yarrow* (Achillea spp.) *to feed the caterpillars. Good nectar plants include purple coneflower* (Echinacea purpurea), *lantana* (Lantana camara), *and common zinnia* (Zinnia elegans). *Place a birdbath near the butterfly plants. Fill the birdbath with pebbles, and cover the pebbles with water. You'll appreciate the butterflies' iridescent beauty as they bask and drink.*

WHEN TO PLANT
Winter can be hard on a butterfly bush, so spring planting is best. As long as the bush is watered during the first summer, establishment will proceed without problems.

WHERE TO PLANT
"More sun equals more flowers" is the motto for a butterfly bush. In the shade it will grow lanky and sport few, if any, blooms. Other tall, flowering plants which attract butterflies make good companions to butterfly bush. They include tall verbena (*Verbena bonariensis*), Mexican sage (*Salvia leucantha*), and joe-pye weed (*Eupatorium maculatum*).

How to Plant

Dig a hole 3 times as wide as the root ball of the plant. There is no need to add soil amendments as long as the soil is thoroughly broken up. When the butterfly bush is out of its pot, gently untangle some of the larger roots and spread them in the hole before filling it with earth. Water immediately after planting, then spread mulch under the plant. Attempt to keep the soil evenly moist for at least 4 weeks. If planted in sandy soil and/or in full sun, drought stress may occur during the first summer if the plant is not watered regularly.

Care and Maintenance

Apply 1 tablespoon of 10–10–10 fertilizer per foot of height in March, June, and August. Plan on watering during the heat of summer for the first two years. Unless your butterfly bush is on a hot, dry site, watering will not be needed after this. The blooms will appear on branches that have grown since spring. This means that every March you should severely prune your bush down to 12" to 24". You'll also have more flowers for a longer period if you regularly snip off the blooms when they begin to turn brown.

Additional Advice for Care

Spider mites can become a problem in a hot, dry site. Twisting, mottled yellow leaves that are drying up usually mean spider mites. It is much easier to control the mites early in the season with horticultural oil or neem insecticide than to wait until August, when only a miticide will help. Call your local Extension office for more advice.

Additional Cultivars and Species

Buddleia davidii 'Black Knight' has dark purple flowers. *B. davidii* 'Snowbank' has pure-white flowers. The *B. davidii* 'Nanho' colored varieties are more compact than the normal butterfly bush, growing only 3' to 5' high in most gardens.

Callicarpa dichotoma

Purple Beautyberry

Height: 4'–5' Width: 4'–5'
Deciduous berrying shrub

*Holly berries . . . Nandina berries . . . Most of us recognize the red
berries that appear on common landscape shrubs. But would you be able to
identify a shrub that loses its drab yellow leaves in September to reveal
"screamingly purple" berries? This is the purple beautyberry. It is eye-
catching in fall, all the more so because it is nondescript during the rest of
the year. The tiny pink flowers are hidden by the leaves in summer. The
individual berries that follow are only 1/4" in diameter, but they grow in
1" clusters up and down multiple gray stems. Mockingbirds and brown
thrashers love the fruits and will consume most of them by late fall. Try
collecting a few branches of beautyberry to include with fall wildflowers for
autumn table decorations. The native beautyberry,* Callicarpa americana,
*grows in old fields and woodland edges from the Tennessee state line down
to Florida. It has rather coarse leaves and is not as attractive as purple
beautyberry.*

WHEN TO PLANT

Plant in fall or in early spring. Fall planting is better for the shrub's
establishment, but occasionally the branch tips may be frozen by a
severe winter. If this occurs and the plant was healthy at the start,
plenty of sprouts will emerge below the damage during the following spring.

WHERE TO PLANT

Beautyberry does best in full sun but is adaptable to partial shade.
It can tolerate most soil types but a moist, well-drained soil is preferred. Place your beautyberry in front of evergreen shrubs that will
provide a backdrop to the berries in fall. A dwarf Burford holly,
Japanese camellia (*Camellia japonica*), or English laurel (*Prunus
laurocerasus* 'Otto Luyken') are all good choices for backup.

How to Plant

Dig a hole 3 times as large as the root ball of your beautyberry. It will do well without adding soil conditioner as long as the earth is completely broken up. Untangle the roots if necessary and spread them in the hole before filling it with soil. Make sure the root ball is planted at the same level it was growing in the container. Pack the soil in place and water thoroughly. Add more soil if the earth settles around the roots. Mulch with pine straw.

Care and Maintenance

A beautyberry has several stems and grows loosely upright. The flowers and berries grow on the current year's branches, so a yearly pruning will produce more berries. Prune in early March to a height equal to half the height to which you want the shrub to grow. Fertilize in April and August with 1 tablespoon of 10–10–10 per foot of plant height. After a beautyberry has become established, it rarely needs watering.

Additional Advice for Care

If you have room, try to duplicate the natural growth arrangement of a beautyberry in a row or large mass at the base of taller trees. Tall pine trees make just enough shade to protect a beautyberry from the sun. This protection will allow the growth of the most beautiful berries.

Additional Cultivars and Species

Callicarpa dichotoma var. *albifructus* has white berries instead of purple. Shrubs with these differently colored berries can be combined to make an interesting display in the fall.

Calycanthus floridus

Sweetshrub

Carolina Allspice, Sweet Bubby

Height: 5'–8' Width: 5'–8'
Deciduous flowering shrub

This native plant is found from Virginia to Florida. It grows well in all but the sandiest, driest parts of Georgia. One of the best "passalong plants," sweetshrub is universally easy to grow and transplant. The reddish-maroon flowers appear in May. The smell is variously described as "pleasantly fruity" and "a combination of banana, strawberry, and pineapple." One reason sweetshrub is passed along so solicitously may be that the strength of the fragrance definitely varies between plants. The sweetshrub in your mother's backyard may have smelled heavenly, but the one you discover in the woods may have no scent at all. Another "passalong" property is the sweetshrub's vigorous sprouting energy. Plant one and in a few years you'll have three or four beside it. A single plant can become a dense colony in a decade.

WHEN TO PLANT

Plant or transplant in late spring while the sweetshrub is flowering. In this way you'll know if you have a "smeller" or not.

WHERE TO PLANT

Sweetshrub tolerates sun or shade and most types of soil. Give it a moist, organic soil, and it will thrive in most sites. The main reason for planting a sweetshrub is to enjoy its fragrance, so put one near your driveway or patio for an early summer treat. While the leaves of a summersweet are pleasantly green, use other plants around it, behind it and under it to avoid a visual hole in the landscape.

ZONE 6,7,8

How to Plant

A sweetshrub sprout can be simply jerked out of the ground and handed to a friend who wants one to plant. Even with minimal roots, sweetshrub seems to be able to withstand any transplanting. Planting a container-grown sweetshrub is especially easy. Dig a hole 3 times as wide as the root ball. No soil conditioner is necessary as long as the earth is broken up. If a sprout has emerged in the pot, use a sharp knife to divide it out along with its roots. Plant the sprout a few feet away as a bonus plant.

Care and Maintenance

Its foliage will be more dense if sweetshrub is pruned each year after flowering. If pruning is neglected, the shrub will grow to look wild and "scraggly." Little fertilizer is needed unless you want the plant to spread more rapidly. In that case, apply 1 tablespoon of 10–10–10 fertilizer per foot of height in spring and again in mid-summer. Water in the heat of summer if the leaves become droopy.

Additional Advice for Care

Sweetshrub has no major pests. Occasionally beetles or caterpillars chew on the leaves, but the damage is never major.

Additional Cultivars and Species

Calycanthus floridus 'Athens' has yellow flowers and a powerful fragrance that can permeate a neighborhood.

Camellia spp.

Camellia

Height: 6'–8' Width: 4'–6'
Evergreen flowering shrub

Gardeners familiar with camellias that grow 6' to 8' tall are surprised to find that in their native China, these shrubs can reach more than 20' in height and are often trained as small trees. Camellias have dark-green, leathery leaves, making them excellent background shrubs for flowering plants. During the camellia's blooming season, however, few plants can match the camellia's own firepower. Its flowers range in color from white through yellow, pink, red, even blue! The color variations of the flowers make endless combinations possible. Camellia sasanqua *begins blooming in late fall, with some varieties blooming in mid-December. Many sasanquas are fragrant. The blooms are smaller than* Camellia japonica. Camellia japonica *takes over in late December and may have blooms until April.* Camellia japonica *was the earliest camellia to be cultivated in America, but* Camellia sinensis, *the tea camellia, was not far behind. Seeds were sent to the Savannah Trust Gardens in 1744. It is fitting that Georgians love both camellias and iced tea!*

WHEN TO PLANT

Camellias are usually purchased in the spring while the plant is in bloom. This is an appropriate time for planting, but planting in fall is even better so the roots will have time to grow. Whether bought in containers or balled and burlapped, camellias are easy to plant. If one of yours needs to be moved, try to transplant in mid-fall.

WHERE TO PLANT

In their native lands, camellias grow in the shade of taller trees. Try planting them in the dappled shade under tall pine trees. As it is most important to limit the amount of exposure to warm sunshine in winter, the north or east side of a structure is a good spot. Protection from drying winds can be provided by placing camellias in the shelter of evergreen shrubbery.

HOW TO PLANT

Moist, well-drained soil is essential for good growth. Dig a planting
hole 5 times as wide as the root ball of your plant. Since camellias
are shallow-rooted, the hole need not be more than 12" deep. If the
area is lower than the surrounding landscape, add 2 to 3 bags of
compost or soil conditioner to the soil removed from the hole. The
resulting mound will keep the camellia roots above standing water.
If the camellia is container-grown, try to untangle the circling roots
and spread them in the hole before filling it with soil.

CARE AND MAINTENANCE

If you want the shrub to grow large, fertilize 3 times each year, in
spring, summer, and fall. Spread 1 tablespoon of 10–10–10 fertilizer
for every foot of plant height. Once your camellia is grown, fertilize
only in spring and summer with the same amount of fertilizer. No
lime is needed at planting or afterwards, for camellias thrive in acid
soil. Pruning is rarely needed. If an unruly limb appears, it can be
shortened back to a bud or small branch. If your camellia needs to
be cut back considerably, prune it just after its flowering ceases.

ADDITIONAL ADVICE FOR CARE

Growers of camellia flowers live in fear of a sudden cold snap. If
your camellia needs protection from the cold, cover it with an old
bedsheet. Make sure the sheet goes completely down to the ground
on all sides and is held down by stones or heavy limbs. If a camellia
is regularly damaged by cold, consider moving it to a more sheltered site.

ADDITIONAL CULTIVARS AND SPECIES

More than 200 species of camellia have been identified. There are
more than 20,000 varieties of *Camellia japonica* alone. Cuttings are
easy to root. You may not find your favorite flower color at a nursery but at the house of a neighbor, who can propagate the plant
for you.

Clethra alnifolia

Summersweet

Height: 4'–8' Width: 4'–6'
Deciduous flowering shrub

*If you like the flower shape and scent of fothergilla (Fothergilla gardenii)
in April, you will appreciate the blooms and accompanying spicy scent of
summersweet in July. Summersweet is prized for its white summer blooms
that appear at a time when only perennial flowers seem brave enough to
face the heat. The individual flowers are small, but hundreds of them line
each flower stem, making it look like a bottlebrush. A shrub will be covered
with multitudes of these 6" flower spikes when it blooms. The sweet odor
spreads throughout a garden and attracts butterflies and bees. To attract
more pollinating insects, plant lantana (Lantana camara 'Miss Huff') and
Mexican heather (Cuphea hyssopifolia) nearby. Although common summersweet can grow up to 8' tall, in most gardens it will stay closer to 4' to
5' in height. The leaves are deciduous, turning from a deep green in spring
to a vivid yellow in autumn.*

WHEN TO PLANT

Transplant from a container when small, or purchase balled and
burlapped if a larger specimen is needed. Fall planting works best,
but spring planting can succeed if watering is done regularly
throughout the summer. Because it can tolerate moist soils, it should
be one of the first plants to consider for the adornment of a landscape pond.

WHERE TO PLANT

Summersweet will produce a tremendous number of flowers if
planted in full sun. It will also thrive, with fewer blooms, in deep
shade. In fact, deep shade and moist conditions are where it seems
most adapted. On the shady side of a house where nothing seems to
grow well, summersweet can be combined with evergreen azaleas
for two seasons of bloom.

ZONE 6,7,8

HOW TO PLANT

Dig a hole 3 times as wide as the root ball and mix at least 1 cubic foot of soil conditioner with the soil removed from the hole. Summersweet thrives in swamps and on stream banks, so you should try to approximate those conditions. Watering will be a regular chore for the first year; a soaker hose laid under your summersweet and adjacent shrubs will make the job easier. Plant the root ball 1/2" deeper than it was grown in the nursery. Cover the top of the root ball with soil so moisture will be constant. Mulch heavily with pine straw, but be sure to pull the mulch back 3" from the stem on all sides.

CARE AND MAINTENANCE

Fertilize lightly for the year after planting by spreading 1 tablespoon of 10–10–10 fertilizer per foot of shrub height in March, June, and August. Afterwards, apply the same amount of fertilizer once a year in April. Pruning is usually not necessary except when an older shrub has grown too large. In that case, lightly clip it back for several years, each time in early spring.

ADDITIONAL ADVICE FOR CARE

Your neighbors will probably remark on the beauty of your summersweet. It is an easy task to root cuttings so you can share. Cut 6"-long branch tips in July and stick them 3" deep in pots filled with coarse sand. Dust rooting hormone on the cut tips to speed root formation. Cover the pots with a clear plastic bag and place them in a shady spot outdoors. You'll have gifts for friends in October.

ADDITIONAL CULTIVARS AND SPECIES

Clethra alnifolia 'Hummingbird' was selected by Fred Galle, the azalea expert, from the shore of Hummingbird Lake at Callaway Gardens. He noticed that it had large flowers that virtually covered the shrub. *Clethra alnifolia* 'Rosea' has pink flowers. The mature size of both plants is 4' tall and 4' wide.

SHRUBS

Cotinus coggygria

Smokebush

Height: 8'–12' Width: 8'–12'
Deciduous flowering shrub

*Imagine a shrub that looks as if it is surrounded by hazy smoke in the late afternoon June sunshine. This is the visual effect of smokebush. The source of the "smoke" is difficult to identify until you walk up close. On examination, you'll see that each branch has sent out fine stems that were recently covered with small flowers. When the flowers fell off, the flower stems, covered in silky hair, were left. It is that hair that gives this shrub a smoky look from June until September. Purple-leafed forms of smokebush have become more available than green-leafed varieties in recent years. Some have leaves which fade to green as the summer progresses, but a few keep their purple leaves until fall. If you use a purple smokebush as a specimen plant, try surrounding it with three or four artemisias (*Artemisia x 'Powis Castle'*). The gray leaves of an artemisia make a wonderful contrast with the purple smokebrush leaves.*

WHEN TO PLANT

Smokebush is hardy throughout Georgia, although it may suffer from the heat in the extreme south of the state. It can be planted in fall or in spring.

WHERE TO PLANT

Full sunshine develops both good leaf color and more flowers for a strong smoky effect. Although the plant may be placed anywhere, try to find a spot where the low sunshine of early morning or late afternoon can shine through the branches. A mature smokebush makes a good specimen shrub, or it may be used in a mixed shrub border.

HOW TO PLANT

Dig a hole 3 times as wide as the root ball. If the plant has been in the pot for a while, the roots will be densely wound around inside.

ZONE 6,7,8

Use a sharp knife to make two slits on opposite sides of the root ball, starting halfway down and continuing down to the base. Using two hands, spread apart the roots as you put the plant in its hole. Keep the roots spread in the hole while you put the soil back in place. Make sure the main stem of the smokebush is not buried more deeply in the earth than it grew in the pot. Pack the soil around the roots by hand, then water well. Mulch with pine straw or pine chips under the new plant to help conserve moisture.

CARE AND MAINTENANCE

Apply 1 tablespoon of 10–10–10 per foot of height to a newly planted smokebush in March, June, and August. After the first year, fertilize in April and June. If left to grow in an open spot, smokebush grows tall and wide by sending up a multitude of stems. If you prune it once, you'll have to prune each year after that, for it sends up vigorous stems from each pruning cut. Some gardeners cut back their purple smokebush every year to emphasize the bright foliage in spring. If you have the space, it is best to let a smokebush find its own natural shape.

ADDITIONAL ADVICE FOR CARE

Occasionally examine the stems and undersides of the leaves for small white scale insects. Each scale covers itself with wax and does not move. The waxy covering makes them difficult to kill. If you find them, call your local Extension office to learn about effective controls.

ADDITIONAL CULTIVARS AND SPECIES

Cotinus coggygria 'Royal Purple' is the most common purple-foliaged cultivar. Its "smoke" is a purple-red color. *Cotinus coggygria* 'Daydream' has dense branches, green leaves, and pink "smoke."

Daphne odora

Daphne

Height: 2'–4' Width: 2'–4'
Evergreen flowering shrub

*"What is it that smells so good?" The aisles at the Southeastern Flower
Show in Atlanta were crowded. The many people streaming by made the
diminutive shrub in the three-gallon pot hard to see. But everyone knew by
the fragrance that something delicious was near. Those that found it had to
have one. The next year, Atlanta nurseries sold triple their usual number of
daphne plants. Daphne is not a "stick it in the ground and leave it" plant.
It demands very well-drained soil, just the right amount of sun, and careful
removal of diseased leaves. But oh, that smell! On a cold February day
when you are wondering if anything is still living in your perennial flower
bed, a single bloom of daphne is enough to remind you that spring will
come again. According to legend, the young Daphne was pursued by the
god Apollo. She did not welcome his advances, and she appealed to the
other gods for help. Since they could not stop Apollo, the gods turned
Daphne into a sweet-smelling shrub.*

When to Plant
Plant in early spring as soon as your garden center offers daphne
for sale.

Where to Plant
Think carefully when you decide on a site for your daphne. Is
there a chance the site will become more sunny or more shady?
Will you be able to reach the daphne to pluck the blooms in
February? Is it close enough to the door so you can smell it when
you arrive home? Would it be better to keep it in a large pot by your
entrance and move the pot somewhere else for the summer? With
good initial decisions you won't have to face the problems of transplanting a daphne.

HOW TO PLANT

Few plants require so much attention to soil drainage as does a daphne. Start by digging a hole 5' wide and 12" deep. Place the top 4" of the soil in a wheelbarrow and discard the rest. Pulverize the soil in the wheelbarrow and mix in one 40-pound bag of children's play sand and one 50-pound bag of pea gravel. With two bags of composted pine bark nearby, shovel alternately from the wheelbarrow and from the bags until the hole is filled. Mix the hole's contents with a shovel, then add more material until a mound is formed. Plant the daphne in the center, spreading the roots slightly into the surrounding soil. Water thoroughly. Make sure the root ball does not become uncovered after a few weeks.

CARE AND MAINTENANCE

Daphne seems to become more susceptible to disease with an excess of fertilizer. Apply 1 tablespoon of 10–10–10 fertilizer per foot of height in spring and again in midsummer. Pruning is rarely needed. Mulch is vital; a 2" layer of shredded leaves over the mound is good. Pull the mulch 3" back from the stem to prevent stem rot. If you decide to plant a daphne in a pot, use a container at least 16" wide. The potting soil should be light and porous. If it seems too "mucky," holding too much water, mix the soil 1:1 with perlite, then fill the pot with the mixture.

ADDITIONAL ADVICE FOR CARE

Float some of the rosy pink blooms in a shallow blue bowl on the dining room table for a scented February pick-me-up. Because the flowers are small, you might try combining them in the bowl with red Japanese camellia blossoms.

ADDITIONAL CULTIVARS AND SPECIES

A bit less fragrant but a lot less demanding is *Daphne x burkwoodii* 'Carol Mackie.' This daphne has green-and-white striped foliage and large clusters of pinkish-white flowers in May. *Daphne odora* 'Aureomarginata' has a white margin around each leaf.

Elaeagnus pungens

Elaeagnus

Height: 6'–15' Width: 8'–20'
Evergreen shrub

Many landscapers laughingly refer to elaeagnus as "Ugly Agnes," but this shrub has enough worthy characteristics to defy their scorn. The landscaper's complaint, that elaeagnus just doesn't know when to stop growing, is a useful characteristic in certain landscape situations. Elaeagnus can literally stop traffic: it is widely used on highway medians to stop the occasional misdirected Buick. It also stops foot traffic at Barnsley Gardens, near Adairsville, where it grows on both sides of an arbor-covered path. Visitors appear comical in October when they halt abruptly, noses in the air, trying to determine from what plant the delicious scent is coming. They are puzzled because no flowers are evident; the flowers are hidden under the silvery-backed elaeagnus foliage. If you would like a screening hedge to block the view of your neighbor's parked motor home, the lowly "Ugly Agnes" may provide just what you need.

WHEN TO PLANT

Plant an elaeagnus any time from September 1 through August 31 of the following year. It has very sharp thorns: transplanting a large elaeagnus can be accomplished in fall by the foolhardy who have had a recent tetanus shot.

WHERE TO PLANT

Elaeagnus is not particularly decorative. Its green foliage does have a silvery cast because of the white backsides of its leaves, but that's about the only thing ornamental about this shrub. It could provide a green background for a large flowering plant, but the flowering shrub should be planted well in front of the elaeagnus. One little-noticed talent of elaeagnus is that it can grow in fairly dense shade.

246

How to Plant

Any planting method seems to be successful. You could even use a posthole digger and drop the root ball in the hole like a cork! For fastest growth, dig a hole 3 times as large as the root ball and place the plant in the center of the hole. Pack soil around the roots and water thoroughly. If you have the room to make a screening hedge, you can use two staggered rows of elaeagnus, leaving 10' between each shrub.

Care and Maintenance

No amount of pruning seems to be able to make a silk purse out of this sow's ear. Pruning itself is so painful, because of the thorns on each stem, that "Prune the Elaeagnus" will probably be at the bottom of your gardening "to do" list each year. This is one plant for which electric hedge trimmers were invented. It is possible to train the plant over an arbor, as can be seen at Barnsley Gardens. Growth can be accelerated by applying 1 tablespoon of 10–10–10 per foot of plant height in April, June, and August each year. Watering is needed only at establishment.

Additional Advice for Care

Elaeagnus tolerates salt spray and therefore makes a good, tough windscreen for beach homes along the coast.

Additional Cultivars and Species

Elaeagnus pungens 'Maculata' is occasionally found at garden centers. Each leaf has a yellow-gold splotch in the center.

Forsythia x intermedia

Forsythia

Yellow Bells

Height: 4′–8′ Width: 6′–10′

A familiar harbinger of spring, this yellow-flowered deciduous shrub quickly grows large from a small plant. Its slender stems arch constantly outward, so forsythia is always wider than it is tall. Due to its rather unruly appearance, it is usually pruned to 5′, but if left unpruned, it will become a very graceful shrub. The bell-shaped flowers appear before the leaves, usually in early February. Forsythia is a shrub that everyone can identify in Georgia. Although common, it is a fairly recent introduction to the American landscape. Our forsythia is a hybrid that was discovered in Germany in 1878. Its parents, Forsythia suspensa *and* Forsythia viridissima, *were growing near each other in a city botanical garden. The plant resulting from their crossbreeding was noticed by a visiting botanist who admired its yellow flowers and vigorous growth. Though forsythia fades into the landscape for most of the year, its yellow flowers are our first true sign that spring is on the way.*

WHEN TO PLANT

Plant in fall while the soil is still warm. If your forsythia has been treated well in the nursery, it will bloom the following spring. If you need to move a forsythia from one spot to another, wait until just after it has finished flowering before the leaves appear. Prune it back severely to make the shrub easier to dig and handle.

WHERE TO PLANT

In full sun, a forsythia will have the most flowers, but it can tolerate some shade as well. Only in dense and complete shade will a forsythia refuse to flower. Forsythia can be used as a groundcover on steep banks. It rivals juniper for its ability to thrive under tough conditions. As a single shrub, it is best positioned in a group of other plants that have flowers at other times of the year.

HOW TO PLANT

Dig a hole 3 times as large as the root ball of the shrub. No soil conditioner needs to be added as long as the soil is broken up and is not clumpy. If the roots seem to be growing densely in the pot, unwind the longest ones and spread them in the hole before shoveling soil back in place. Pack the earth back around the plant and water occasionally for the first month. Spreading mulch under a forsythia is useful while it is becoming established, but as the shrub matures, its arching limbs will cover the ground and make further mulching unnecessary.

CARE AND MAINTENANCE

A forsythia will grow vigorously in all directions. It is a good idea to plant a solitary specimen with plenty of space on all sides; otherwise, you'll be forced to prune it drastically each year. If pruning becomes necessary, do it just after flowering. Try each year to remove the oldest branches from the bush since most of the flowers emerge on 2- to 3-year-old branches. Apply 1 tablespoon of 10–10–10 fertilizer per foot of height in spring and again in midsummer. Watering is rarely needed.

ADDITIONAL ADVICE FOR CARE

Forsythia branches can be forced to bloom earlier than normal in the spring. Watch the bloom buds in January; when they are swollen, cut branches 18" to 24" long and bring them indoors to a warm room. Arrange the branches in a vase of water and the buds will begin to open almost overnight.

ADDITIONAL CULTIVARS AND SPECIES

The parents of our forsythia interbreed easily, and several introductions have been made since 1885. *Forsythia x intermedia* 'Lynwood Gold' is common. *Forsythia x intermedia* 'Arnold's Dwarf' does not make many flowers, but it can form a useful groundcover. *Forsythia x intermedia* 'Karl Sax' has very large, deep-yellow flowers.

Fothergilla gardenii

Dwarf Fothergilla

Height: 3′ Width: 3′
Deciduous flowering shrub

Not many flowers remind you of the scent of honey, but the scent of fothergilla is enough to start you buzzing! The flowers are distinctive (they look like white bottlebrushes), but the most memorable characteristic of a fothergilla may be its fall leaf color. A group of 3 to 5 shrubs in a corner of your landscape can make a dazzling yellow, red, and orange kaleidoscope in October. You might find Fothergilla major *at some of the larger nurseries. It grows 10′ tall, too large perhaps for a suburban landscape. Because dwarf fothergilla remains small, it can be an attractive addition to a perennial border. Try planting blue asters (*Aster novae-angliae*) in front and a blue baptisia (*Baptisia australis*) on each side for good color contrast. Fothergilla can also be combined with azaleas, as they grow in the same types of soil.*

WHEN TO PLANT

Plant a fothergilla in fall or spring. If you plant in fall, you'll be able to enjoy the flowers in April. Dr. Michael Dirr, who selected the 'Mt. Airy' fothergilla described below, notes that fothergilla cuttings can be collected in mid-June and then easily rooted. He has found that the cuttings must be transplanted while they are actively growing.

WHERE TO PLANT

Fothergilla can tolerate full sun, but leaves on a shrub grown in full sun may not be as brightly colored in the fall. A better location is under high pine trees or in a slightly shady spot on the west side of your lawn. When placed in a long border or in a mass planting, fothergilla is an arresting sight twice a year. Between spring flowering and fall color, the foliage is a pleasant green but not very interesting.

ZONE
6,7,8

HOW TO PLANT

Dig a hole 3 times as big as the root ball. A fothergilla is not very particular about the soil it grows in, but do pulverize the earth before packing it around the roots. Fothergilla can tolerate a boggy site if the shrub is planted on a 3'-wide mound of soil. Summer drought can cause fall foliage to be less than fiery. Spread a 2" to 3" layer of mulch around the fothergilla. Plan on watering it in the summer if you notice the plant becoming parched.

CARE AND MAINTENANCE

Fothergilla does not demand a lot of fertilization. Apply 1 table-spoon of 10–10–10 per foot of plant height in April, June, and August each year. Little pruning is needed except for an occasional nip here and there to keep the shape attractive. Clipping some of the flowers for indoor fragrance in spring will probably accomplish all of the pruning that is needed. You may find volunteer sprouts underneath your fothergilla. These root "suckers" can be carefully dug up and transplanted to another spot. If the suckers are left, the shrub will gradually grow wider over the years.

ADDITIONAL ADVICE FOR CARE

Fothergilla can be easily propagated in mid-June. Take 6" cuttings that are stiff, not limber. Dust some rooting hormone on the cut end of each cutting and bury it 3" deep in a small pot filled with moist sand. Cover each cutting with a glass jar and move all to a shady place for the summer. The cuttings will root in 6 weeks if you keep the sand constantly moist.

ADDITIONAL CULTIVARS AND SPECIES

Both *Fothergilla gardenii* and *Fothergilla major* are considered native shrubs, but *F. gardenii* is a little less hardy in winter. Dr. Michael Dirr, Professor of Horticulture at the University of Georgia, has selected a particularly good-looking small fothergilla: 'Mt. Airy.' It is available at garden centers and should be your first choice for an outstanding plant.

Gardenia

Cape Jasmine

Height: 4'–6' Width: 4'–6'
Evergreen flowering shrub

For some Georgians, the smell of gardenia flowers on a warm June after-noon is the emblem of summer. Though a gardenia's glossy green foliage is handsome, its flowers and their scent are what most people love about this shrub. A gardenia is marginally hardy north of Atlanta; from mid-Georgia southward, it makes a reliable specimen shrub or component of a mass planting. Several gardenias together can supply fragrance to a whole neighborhood. Indoors, a little scent goes a long way. A bowlful of blooms indoors can be almost sickeningly sweet. Gardenias were once commonly grown in greenhouses and forced to bloom during the winter to provide cut flowers in the Northern states. Gardenia was named for Alexander Garden, a resident of Charleston, South Carolina.

WHEN TO PLANT

Because Georgia winters are fickle, plant a gardenia in spring when the soil is warm. Spring is also a good time to transplant this shrub from another location.

WHERE TO PLANT

Certainly the best place to plant a gardenia is where the scent can be experienced. If planted next to a patio or sidewalk, visitors can enjoy this singular summer treat. Do not plant where winter wind rushes or where the plant will be very warm in January. A shrub next to a south-facing brick wall is almost guaranteed to be frozen to the ground each winter. An eastern or northern exposure is a better choice.

How to Plant

Dig a hole 3 times as large as the root ball of the shrub. No soil conditioner needs to be added as long as the soil is broken up and not clumpy. If the roots seem to be growing densely in the pot, unwind the longest ones and spread them in the hole before shoveling soil back in place. Pack the earth back around the roots. Water occasionally for the first month. Spread a layer of pine straw mulch under your gardenia to conserve moisture.

Care and Maintenance

Apply 1 tablespoon of 10–10–10 fertilizer per foot of height in spring and again in midsummer. A severe winter may freeze a gardenia shrub to the ground, but it will usually sprout back within a few months. If extreme cold threatens, drape an old bedsheet over the shrub. Make sure the sheet goes down to the ground on all sides and is held down by stones or heavy limbs. If your gardenia grows in the shade, lower limbs may fall off, leaving a bare trunk. Even though you'll sacrifice flowers, prune the whole shrub back to 12" tall in late March and let it resprout.

Additional Advice for Care

Whiteflies are common gardenia pests. They suck sap from the leaves and excrete a sticky "honeydew" that covers the lower leaves. These leaves turn black when sooty mold covers the honeydew. You can manage whiteflies by spraying for them in the spring. Check with your local Extension office for an effective insecticide.

Additional Cultivars and Species

Because cold weather is such a threat, breeders working on improving the species usually work with cold-hardy selections. *G. jasminoides* 'Klein's Hardy' is cold-resistant; *G. jasminoides* 'Michael' is reputed to have resistance to cold *and* to whiteflies. *G. j.* var. *radicans* is a dwarf form, more a groundcover than a shrub, and much less resistant to cold.

Hamamelis x intermedia

Witchhazel

Height: 5'–10' Width: 4'–8'
Deciduous flowering shrub

Few are the shrubs which flower in February. Witchhazel is one plant which not only flowers in late winter but has a pleasant scent and intensely colored fall foliage as well. The flowers consist of 4 narrow, twisting petals approximately 1" long. They occur in clusters up and down the branches, virtually covering the upper 2/3 of the plant. Flower color on the different cultivars ranges from yellow to orange to red. Since the flowers appear when the shrub is leafless, their effect is dramatic, even in the gloom of a February evening. The effect is best if your witchhazel is placed in front of large evergreen shrubs like Burford holly. Another nice spot is at the sunny edge of a shady spot that stays dark in winter. Most of the ommonly available witchhazels are hybrids, the off-spring of Chinese witchhazel (Hamamelis mollis) *and* Japanese witchhazel (Hamamelis japonica). *The hybrids are usually referred io as* Hamamelis x intermedia.

WHEN TO PLANT

Plant your witchhazel in fall so you can enjoy the flowers in February. The first year's blooms will likely be heavy, as the plant will have grown vigorously in its nursery container. Don't expect this number of blooms again until the third spring, when the shrub has become established in its new site.

WHERE TO PLANT

Look out your kitchen or living room window and imagine that you have not seen the sun for days. Imagine a gray sky with only drab green-and-brown foliage in your landscape. Anywhere within that field of your vision is a good place for a witchhazel. If the spot is sunny, you'll have bright color in both spring and fall.

ZONE 6,7,8

SHRUBS

How to Plant

Dig a hole 3 times as large as the root ball of your witchhazel. The shrub will do well without adding soil conditioner as long as the earth is completely pulverized and broken up. Untangle the roots if necessary and spread them in the hole before filling it with soil. Pack the soil in place and water thoroughly. Add more soil if the earth settles around the roots. Mulch the entire planting area with pine straw.

Care and Maintenance

One of the advantages of a witchhazel is its almost complete disdain for special care. You can fertilize lightly each year by applying 1 tablespoon of 10–10–10 per foot of height in March, June, and August. A good layer of slowly decaying mulch underneath can provide most of the nutrients needed. Left to grow as Mother Nature dictates, a witchhazel will have a wide, vase-shaped form. You can prune it to a more rounded shape by removing the top third of its central stems in late March.

Additional Advice for Care

Witchhazel attracts virtually no pests. Occasionally chewing insects will make a meal of a few leaves, but this problem is not serious enough to treat with pesticides.

Additional Cultivars and Species

Hamamelis x intermedia 'Diane' is the best red-flowering variety. *Hamamelis x intermedia* 'Primavera' has bright yellow flowers. If you like a witchhazel's appearance, you will also like fothergilla (*Fothergilla gardenii*) and loropetalum (*Loropetalum chinense*).

Rose-of-Sharon

Shrub Althea

Height: 5'–12' Width: 5'–8'
Deciduous flowering shrub

*Four species of hibiscus are commonly grown in Georgia gardens. Along
the coast, tropical hibiscus (Hibiscus rosa-sinensis) brings dazzling color
to the shady streets of Savannah. Near the Okefenokee swamp, swamp
mallow (Hibiscus moscheutos) makes huge red blooms. In Macon,
Confederate rose (Hibiscus mutabilis) blooms every September. In
Atlanta, rose-of-sharon (Hibiscus syriacus) grows like a weed beside
garden sheds and along property lines. Rose-of-Sharon is one of those
"passalong plants" that some believe has passed itself along a little too
often. The shrub is legendarily prolific, rivaling privet with its ability to
seed and grow on unused land. The growth is unkempt no matter how you
prune, and the winter seed capsules are not attractive. But the multitudes
of summer flowers that appear on this tough plant will cause all the gardener's negative thoughts about it to vanish. The white, red, or lavender
blooms appear freely for even the beginning gardener—who will have at
least one flowering shrub to point to with pride!*

WHEN TO PLANT

You can plant in fall or spring or the middle of summer. Rare is the
Rose-of-Sharon that cannot survive even the most inappropriate of
planting times.

WHERE TO PLANT

Rose-of-Sharon will not grow in swampy or extremely dry sites. All
other spots are fair game. In order to enjoy the plant without the
labor of weeding its progeny, put it where it has little room to
"escape." If it is surrounded by turf, regular mowing will eliminate
seedlings. Against a garage, the shrub will hide the bare wall and
provide beauty during the summer.

ZONE
6,7,8

SHRUBS

How to Plant

Dig a hole 3 times as wide as the root ball of the plant. There is no
need to add soil amendments as long as the soil is thoroughly broken up. When the shrub is out of its pot, gently untangle some of
the larger roots and spread them in the hole before filling it with
earth. Water immediately after planting and spread mulch under the
plant. Attempt to keep the soil evenly moist for at least 4 weeks. A
plant in sandy soil or in full sun may experience drought stress during the first summer if it is not watered regularly.

Care and Maintenance

Once a Rose-of-Sharon is established, it will grow for decades without any problems. Apply 1 tablespoon of 10–10–10 fertilizer per foot
of height in spring and again in midsummer. To keep it smaller than
8' tall, prune it severely each winter. Water is rarely needed except
once a week for a month after the shrub has been planted.

Additional Advice for Care

Japanese beetles find Rose-of-Sharon almost as delicious as they
do garden roses, resulting in tattered leaves and blooms. Check
with your local Extension office to learn about measures to control
this pest.

Additional Cultivars and Species

Hibiscus syriacus 'Diana' has solid white blooms. Because it is a
hybrid, the seeds are not fertile, and you will not have to weed
hibiscus seedlings each summer. This should be your first choice
for a Rose-of-Sharon. *Hibiscus syriacus* 'Cedar Lane' is occasionally
found in nurseries near Athens. It has white blossoms, each with a
red center.

'Annabelle' Hydrangea

Hills-of-Snow Hydrangea

Height: 4'–6' Width: 5'–8'
Deciduous flowering shrub

Almost everyone recognizes the common French hydrangea. Its blue blooms are unmistakable. Most gardeners recognize the oakleaf hydrangea as well. Its distinctive leaf shape and white, cone-shaped blooms are dead give-aways. But would you be able to identify a hydrangea that has leaves that look like those on a French hydrangea and huge, round, white blooms? The blooms on an 'Annabelle' are truly astounding—nearly 12" across! That the stems can hold the weight of the blossoms, even after a rain, is a tribute to the vigor of the shrub. On closer inspection, the leaves of an 'Annabelle' are revealed to be much softer than those of the other hydrangeas, a quality that is the source of another common name: Smooth Hydrangea. We call the collection of individual flowers at the end of a hydrangea branch a "bloom," but the broad blue, pink, or white single flowers are actually male blossoms. Look carefully inside the round flowerhead to find blooms with tiny petals. These are the real flowers; like most plants, they have both the male and the female parts.

WHEN TO PLANT
Plant in spring after the last frost. Otherwise, a late freeze may damage new foliage.

WHERE TO PLANT
'Annabelle' hydrangea can survive in more sunshine than most other hydrangeas. It will also grow well, though it will not flower, in deepest shade. It does best planted with other plants that can draw attention away from it while it is not flowering. Try Virginia sweetspire (*Itea virginica*), lantana (*Lantana camara* 'Miss Huff'), or purple fountain grass (*Pennisetum setaceum* 'Rubrum) as sunny companions.

ZONE
6,7,8

How to Plant

Dig a hole 5 times as wide as the root ball of the shrub. In a wheel-barrow, mix the soil taken from the hole 1:1 with soil conditioner or compost. Put the plant's roots in the hole and shovel the amended soil back in place. Pack it down by hand, then water thoroughly. Check back in an hour. If the soil has settled around the roots and exposed the top surface, add more soil to cover. If you plant it in full sun, it is important to plan for regular summer irrigation.

Care and Maintenance

Little fertilizer is needed by an 'Annabelle' hydrangea. Apply 1 tablespoon of 10–10–10 per foot of height to a newly planted shrub in March, June, and August. After the first year, fertilize in March and June with the same amount of 10–10–10. Irrigation is a key to the establishment and long-term good health of your hydrangea. The shrub shows its need for water with wilting leaves. Water immediately and deeply if the leaves get droopy. 'Annabelle' pro-duces flowers on new growth. For this reason, the whole plant can be cut nearly to the ground in February and the vigorous regrowth will make blooms in late June.

Additional Advice for Care

Though the flowers emerge a bright white, they gradually fade to light green and then to brown by fall. You can cut off the flower branches when they begin to fade and hang them upside down indoors to dry. The large bloom is very sturdy and can be used in dried arrangements for the winter.

Additional Cultivars and Species

Hydrangea arborescens 'Annabelle' was discovered by two gardeners near Anna, Illinois. It was named by the University of Illinois for the two *belles* who admired its large blooms. *H. arborescens* 'Grandiflora' is commonly available. It is showy, but its blooms are not quite as large as 'Annabelle.'

Hydrangea macrophylla

Common Hydrangea

French Hydrangea

Height: 2'–6' Width: 2'–8'
Deciduous flowering shrub

French hydrangeas are commonplace in Georgia gardens. Most have blue blossoms in June. Adventurous gardeners may add lime to the soil every year to make the blooms turn pink. Some have suggested that hydrangeas are all so similar that only a beginning gardener would want to grow more than a few. The members of the American Hydrangea Society based in Atlanta roll their eyes skyward when this suggestion is offered. "What about the new varieties with deep maroon blooms?" they ask. "What about the ones with variegated leaves? What about all the different sizes and shapes of flowers? You could collect dozens of hydrangeas and still not exhaust all their possibilities!" Indeed, the common hydrangea offers many possibilities for color, foliage, and bloom time in your garden. Nowadays there is much interest in the different bloom forms. "Hortensia" blooms are the familiar globe shapes we all recognize. "Lace-cap" blooms are flat and much daintier; they can break the monotony of a hydrangea hedge.

WHEN TO PLANT

In south Georgia, where winter is not a threat, plant hydrangeas in the fall. In Atlanta and northward, plant in the spring after April 15. This later planting time means you will avoid the possibility of a late frost which could freeze all of the foliage and rob you of blooms.

WHERE TO PLANT

Hydrangeas like a moist, well-drained, organic soil. They do best in partial shade. Full sunshine in the morning will not cause problems as long as there is shade during the afternoon. Hydrangeas do well in combination with camellias, rhododendrons, and azaleas. They can also provide a nice backdrop for astilbe (*Astilbe x arendsii*) and bleeding heart (*Dicentra spectabilis*).

ZONE
6,7,8

How to Plant

Dig a hole 5 times as wide as the root ball of the plant. Because hydrangeas grow best in shade, you will probably have to contend with the roots of trees in the vicinity. Dig down past the tree roots, trying not to damage them. Damaged roots make vigorous sprouts which will compete with your hydrangea for moisture in the summer. In a wheelbarrow, mix the soil taken from the hole 1:1 with soil conditioner or compost. Put the plant's roots in the hole and shovel the amended soil back in place. Pack it down by hand, then water thoroughly. Check back in an hour. If the soil has settled around the root ball and exposed its top surface, add more soil to cover.

Care and Maintenance

Little fertilizer is needed by a hydrangea. Apply 1 tablespoon of 10–10–10 per foot of height to a newly planted shrub in March, June, and August. After the first year, fertilize with the same amount in March and June. Irrigation is important to the establishment and long-term good health of a hydrangea. The shrub shows its need for water with wilting leaves. Water immediately and deeply if the leaves get droopy. If pruning is needed, do it in late June, immediately after the flowers have faded. The pruning will stimulate new growth which might produce more flowers in October.

Additional Advice for Care

Hydrangeas are easy to propagate. Dig a shallow hole 18" from the plant, and bend a limb down so that part of it rests in the hole and 10" extends beyond the hole. Scrape the portion of the limb in the hole with a dull knife and dust this portion with rooting hormone. Bury the wounded portion with soil and place a brick on top to hold it down. It will root in three months.

Additional Cultivars and Species

Hydrangea macrophylla 'Nikko Blue' is a standard with deep-blue flowers. *H. macrophylla* 'Ami Pasquier' produces pink blooms even in acid soil. *H. m.* 'Lanarth White' has white lace-cap blooms. *H. m.* 'Pia' is pink dwarf. *H. m.* spp. *serrata* 'Preziosa' has white blooms that gradually fade to a long-lasting maroon by August.

Hydrangea quercifolia

Oakleaf Hydrangea

Height: 4'–6' Width: 5'–8'
Deciduous flowering shrub

On a late, gray October afternoon, the last rays of the sun may reveal what seems to be a huge campfire burning at the edge of a meadow. On closer examination, we see this is poison ivy climbing a tall pine tree, giving it a fiery golden trunk. At the pine's base, a brilliant red mass of oakleaf hydrangea foliage crackles and pops in the wind. Gardeners may exclaim over the large white blooms of an oakleaf hydrangea in June, but they often forget its leaf color that rivals the maples in autumn. They might also forget that underneath the green leaves are thick branches that are striking in winter because of their peeling bark. A single oakleaf hydrangea can be attractive in a small landscape, but the coarseness of the leaves makes it difficult to blend with other plants. When room is available, it is better used in a shrub border or in a mass planting. You might place a small sign at the base of your blooming oakleaf hydrangea that reads: "If you like me now, just wait a few months!"

WHEN TO PLANT

Plant in spring after the last frost; otherwise, a late freeze may damage new foliage and potential blooms.

WHERE TO PLANT

An oakleaf hydrangea can tolerate more sunshine than a common French hydrangea, but do not tempt fate by placing it in direct afternoon sun. It does best as an "edge plant" placed under a deciduous tree so that it gets sun in the morning and shade in the afternoon. It is useful as a screening plant.

How to Plant

Dig a hole 5 times as wide as the root ball of the plant. In a wheel-barrow, mix the soil taken from the hole 1:1 with soil conditioner or compost. Place the plant's roots in the hole and shovel the amended soil back in place. Pack it down by hand, then water thoroughly. Check back in an hour. If the soil has settled around the roots and exposed the top surface, add more soil to cover it. The roots prefer a moist but well-drained soil. An oakleaf hydrangea will get root rot if it is planted where water pools frequently.

Care and Maintenance

Little fertilizer is needed by an oakleaf hydrangea. Apply 1 table-spoon of 10–10–10 per foot of height to a newly planted shrub in March, June, and August. After the first year, fertilize in March and June. Irrigation is important to the establishment and long-term good health of a hydrangea. The shrub shows its need for water with wilting leaves. Water immediately and deeply if the leaves get droopy. If pruning is needed, do it in late June immediately after the flowering. Every year, remove the oldest, woody stems. The flowers may be left on the plant to dry or they may be removed when they begin to fade.

Additional Advice for Care

The white flower heads fade from white to purple and then to brown by September. Though they are attractive when dry, mischie-vous gardeners have been known to spray-paint them so they will have color throughout the winter!

Additional Cultivars and Species

Hydrangea quercifolia 'Snow Queen' has huge, dense white flowers that are held erect above its foliage.

Ilex cornuta

Chinese Holly

Height: 8'–20' Width: 8'–15'
Evergreen shrub

It is said that the word holly *derives from the use of holly branches in early English* holy *celebrations. It is documented that the ancient Romans used holly branches and berries to celebrate the solstice feast of Saturnalia. Chinese hollies have various mature heights in the landscape.* Ilex cornuta *'Rotunda' stops growing at 4', but a mature* Ilex cornuta *'Burfordii' might grow anywhere from 4' and 25' tall. All of the Chinese hollies have sharp, needle-like spines on each leaf. Chinese hollies can be either male or female; the female holly is the one with the berries. The bright red berries make great Christmas decorations. Fortunately, the popular 'Burford' holly will produce berries without pollination. Although* I. crenata. *'Rotunda' and* I. crenata *'Carissa' rarely have berries, the glossy green foliage of these plants makes up for the lack of bright color.*

WHEN TO PLANT

Chinese hollies are easy to plant, when newly purchased or when transplanted from another spot in the landscape. Fall planting is better in theory, but this holly seems to do as well when planted in spring.

WHERE TO PLANT

The smaller varieties make fine foundation shrubs. If more height is needed, a 'Burford' holly can be used. A small holly in a gallon pot may grow surprisingly large. Leave plenty of room for your hollies to grow, or it will be a yearly chore to prune them. Because of the spines on the leaves, pruning holly is no small task. Full sun is best, but Chinese holly will tolerate slight shade.

HOW TO PLANT

Most Chinese hollies are purchased in containers, not balled and burlapped. If the plant has been in a pot for more than two years,

ZONE
6,7,8

the root ball will be severely "potbound" and the white roots will be densely packed inside. It is very important to loosen and untangle these roots before planting. The planting hole should be dug 3 times as wide as the root ball. Spread the roots in the hole before putting soil back in place. Make sure the main stem of the holly is not buried more deeply in the earth than it grew in the pot. Pack the soil around the roots by hand, then water well. Spread mulch under the new plant to conserve moisture.

CARE AND MAINTENANCE

Once a Chinese holly is established in the right spot, it will grow for years without problems. Apply 1 tablespoon of 10–10–10 fertilizer per foot of height in spring and again in midsummer. A holly hedge protected from natural rainfall beneath the overhang of your roof will need water during a drought. To keep a Chinese holly small, prune moderately in July. Water is rarely needed except once a week for a month after the shrub has been planted.

ADDITIONAL ADVICE FOR CARE

If shade causes lower limbs to die, a Chinese holly's bare trunk can be hidden with ferns or Japanese hollies. If the shrub needs to be drastically reduced in size, plan to cut off everything down to a height of 12" in late February. A naked stump will remain, but green branches will quickly sprout. When they are 12" long, cut off the tips to force new, smaller branches.

ADDITIONAL CULTIVARS AND SPECIES

Ilex cornuta 'Burfordii' was discovered in Westview cemetery in Atlanta. The original plant is parent to millions of Burford holly shrubs. *Ilex cornuta* 'Rotunda' is an excellent barrier shrub, as its spines make it impassable to children, pets, and adults. If you want a "friendlier" Chinese holly, try *Ilex cornuta* 'Carissa,' with its single spine per leaf.

Ilex crenata

Japanese Holly

Height: 2'–10' Width: 2'–8'
Evergreen shrub

In contrast to the Chinese hollies, whose leaves are large and have sharp-needled spines, Japanese hollies have small leaves, generally 1" long and 1/2" wide. If left to grow as large as possible, some Japanese hollies can reach 12' tall, but these hollies are usually pruned regularly to form a 3' to 5' foundation shrub or a massed hedge. Unlike the red berries of other hollies, the berries are black and inconspicuous. Because they are so common, Japanese hollies are the underappreciated green backbone of thousands of home and commercial landscapes. After it is pruned, a holly branch will sprout 3 or 4 smaller branches in short order. This makes the plant adaptable to any pruned shape. Japanese hollies have a very attractive natural shape, but they are often mistakenly pruned into "green meatballs" in a landscape. Several cultivars have red or gray twigs that contrast with the green leaves of the plant. The limb structure of Ilex crenata *'Convexa' and that of 'Buxifolia' makes these plants look like boxwoods. Both are called "Box Holly."*

WHEN TO PLANT

Hollies are very easy to transplant. Fall planting is better in theory, but spring planting from nursery pots seems to work well, too. If the shrub is watered regularly, even summertime planting can succeed.

WHERE TO PLANT

Japanese holly makes a fine foundation shrub, but will look better if it is not planted as a solid line of shrubs side-by-side in front of your house. Break up the monotony of green with a small camellia or an azalea in a similar size. Japanese hollies are often planted when a house is new and no shade is in sight. After a decade, shade from nearby trees will cause the hollies to become bare and "leggy" underneath.

ZONE
6,7,8

How to Plant

Most Japanese hollies are purchased in containers, not balled and burlapped. If the plant has been in a pot for more than two years, the root ball will be severely "potbound." When taken out of the pot, the white roots will seem to be circling around endlessly. It is very important to loosen and untangle the roots before planting. The planting hole should be dug 3 times as wide as the root ball. Spread the roots in the hole before putting soil back in place. Make sure the main stem of the holly is not buried more deeply in the earth than it grew in the pot. Pack the soil around the roots by hand, then water well. Spread mulch under the plant to conserve moisture.

Care and Maintenance

Once a Japanese holly is established in the right spot, it will grow for decades without problems. Apply 1 tablespoon of 10–10–10 fertilizer per foot of height in spring and again in midsummer. A holly hedge that is protected from natural rainfall beneath the overhang of your roof will need water during times of drought. Electric hedge trimmers are "Public Enemy Number One" of Japanese hollies. The trimmers do make pruning hollies easier, but just a few years of regular shearing will result in a dense outer shell of greenery growing around an interior of naked brown twigs.

Additional Advice for Care

If a constantly sheared Japanese holly shrub needs to be reduced in size, most of the foliage will have to be taken off, leaving nothing but "brownery" in view. A better way to prune is to use a hand pruner to remove long branches regularly each summer. If a hole is left in the exterior of the holly, it will quickly be filled by adventuresome branches on either side.

Additional Cultivars and Species

Ilex crenata 'Helleri' is an old-fashioned standard for low (1' to 3') growth. *Ilex crenata* 'Hetzii' is taller (3' to 5') and is adaptable to just about any site. *Ilex crenata* 'Green Luster' grows much wider than tall. *Ilex crenata* 'Beehive' was selected from thousands of seedlings at Rutgers University for its good-looking foliage and hardiness.

Ilex verticillata

Winterberry

Height: 6'–10' Width: 6'–8'
Evergreen berrying shrub

Until recently, winterberry has been rare in Georgia landscapes. It is not evergreen as are the Japanese and Chinese hollies, but its multitudes of intense red berries are eye-catching in early winter after the autumn tree leaves have fallen. The bark is a warm gray color; older stems, which zigzag a little, exhibit an interesting twisting appearance. Berries from all hollies supply the food needs of chickadees, blue jays, and other birds for several weeks in winter. A week of warm weather early in December may lead to mass intoxication among the birds. The berries can ferment and the birds are affected by the alcohol. It's not unusual to see a small flock fly up from a holly bush, then land quickly on the ground and sit dazed until the intoxicating effects have worn off. Like all hollies, winterberries are dioecious, which means the male and female flowers are on separate plants. Make sure you have both kinds if you want prodigious berry production.

WHEN TO PLANT

As is true of most hollies, a winterberry is supremely easy to plant or transplant. In theory, fall planting is better, but this holly seems to do well with spring planting, too.

WHERE TO PLANT

Winterberry is a remarkably adaptable shrub. It can tolerate wet, even swampy, spots without complaint. Low spots in the landscape, where rainwater accumulates frequently, are excellent for winterberry. Ferns and other moisture-loving but sun-averse plants will thrive in its shade.

HOW TO PLANT

Dig a hole 3 times as wide as the root ball. Spread the roots in the
hole before putting soil back in place. Make sure the main stem of
the holly is not buried more deeply in the earth than it grew in the
pot. Pack the soil around the roots by hand, then water well. Mulch
with pine straw or bark chips under the new plant to conserve moisture. If you can, plant a mass of shrubs behind the winterberry.
Good background companions are Prague viburnum (*Viburnum x
pragense*), osmanthus (*Osmanthus fragrans*), and Leyland cypress (x
Cupressocyparis leylandii)

CARE AND MAINTENANCE

Once a winterberry is established in the right spot, it will grow easily without problems. Apply 1 tablespoon of 10–10–10 fertilizer per
foot of height in spring and again in midsummer. Water is rarely
needed except for a few times after the shrub has been planted.
Pruning is almost never needed except when you wish to change a
mature shrub into a tree form.

ADDITIONAL ADVICE FOR CARE

The berries of *Ilex verticillata* are useful in Christmas decorations
because they cluster around bare stems. In the fall, cover the shrub
with bird netting to keep the birds away. Gather the branches as
needed, placing them in water immediately to keep the berries from
shriveling and falling off.

ADDITIONAL CULTIVARS AND SPECIES

Ilex verticillata 'Winter Red' is most common in the nursery trade.
The leaves are dark green and the berries are profuse. *Ilex verticillata
x Ilex serrata* 'Sparkleberry' is another outstanding red-berried deciduous holly. *Ilex verticillata x Ilex serrata* 'Apollo' is usually available
in nurseries as a male pollinator for female hollies.

Ilex vomitoria

Yaupon Holly

Height: 8'–15' Width: 6'–10'
Evergreen shrub with berries

It's a good thing that most purchasers don't know the Latin name for this excellent native shrub. If they did, they might overlook its hardy nature and beautiful red berries while wondering if it will make them sick. In fact, the epithet vomitoria *refers to a drink made by Native Americans to be used in celebrations. The roasted leaves of this plant were boiled and made into a body-cleansing tonic that only a committed anthropologist could enjoy. Japanese hollies (*Ilex crenata*) are commonly used as foundation plants, but yaupon holly can achieve the same look with half the attention to pruning and watering. Birds are not as attracted to yaupon's scarlet berries as they are to other holly berries. The berries glisten like jewels under the green leaves and remain until spring.*

WHEN TO PLANT

Yaupon is one of the most adaptable shrubs in a Georgia landscape. It can be planted in fall or in spring with equal success. Its native character means a yaupon holly will grow well in windy coastal sites, even next to the ocean. In sandy soils, fall planting will allow more time to grow an extensive root system.

WHERE TO PLANT

If your Japanese holly or Kurume azalea no longer prospers as a foundation plant, consider replacing it with yaupon holly. It grows densely in full sun but can survive, with slow growth, in shade. Since it can be pruned to any size, it can function as a tall screen plant, or it can form a short, rounded mass. A wet or dry problem site is a good place to try a yaupon holly.

ZONE
6,7,8

HOW TO PLANT

Dig a hole 3 times as wide as the root ball. Spread the roots in the
hole before putting the soil back in place. Make sure the main stem
of the holly is not buried more deeply in the earth than it grew in
the pot. Pack the soil around the roots by hand, then water well.
Mulch which has been spread under the new plant will conserve
moisture. Transplanted yaupon hollies seem to thrive immediately
in their new homes as long as they are cut back by half before digging. Because the roots are shallow, dig a wide, shallow root ball
instead of a deep, round one under the plant to be moved.

CARE AND MAINTENANCE

Little fertilizer is needed by a yaupon holly. Apply 1 tablespoon
of 10–10–10 per foot of height to a newly planted shrub in March,
June, and September. After the first year, using the same amount,
fertilize in April and June. Water is needed for only a few weeks
after planting. Light pruning can be done any time, but if you want
to make the plant more dense, prune in March. Drastic pruning
can be done in February, and regrowth will be rapid if the original
plant was healthy. Cut back new sprouts by half after they reach
12" in length.

ADDITIONAL ADVICE FOR CARE

No pests seem to bother yaupon holly. Occasionally black vine
weevils will chew round notches in leaf edges. If the damage is
objectionable, contact your local Extension office to learn about
control measures.

ADDITIONAL CULTIVARS AND SPECIES

Because of its distinctive shape, weeping yaupon holly (*Ilex
vomitoria* 'Pendula') is a mainstay of commercial landscapers. *Ilex
vomitoria* 'Shillings Dwarf' grows only 3' high and 3' wide, and is
an excellent choice for a foundation shrub.

Illicium spp.

Anise

Anise-tree

Height: 6'–10' Width: 5'–10'
Evergreen shrub

Anise is an attractive, easy-to-care-for evergreen plant that grows perfectly well in a landscape spot that is damp and shady. When crushed, its foliage smells of licorice. The shrub is multi-trunked and irregularly branched, but it forms an upright oval shape that is useful for screening. In light shade, it typically grows to a height of 8' tall and 6' wide. You can let it grow naturally or it can be sheared to a hedge. Two species of anise are commonly available: Florida anise, Illicium floridanum, *and small anise-tree,* Illicium parviflorum. *To tell the two apart, look at the stem at the base of a leaf. The leaf stem of a Florida anise is red, while the leaf stem of a small anise-tree is green. Another major difference between the two is in their flowers. Florida anise grows 1" star-shaped, maroon blossoms that emerge at the base of the leaves in late spring. The flowers resemble deep red asters and the blooms are followed by brown, waxy seed capsules. When they are dry, the seed pods open rapidly, throwing the seeds several feet from the mother plant. Small anise-tree has inconspicuous yellow flowers.*

WHEN TO PLANT

If possible, plant in fall while the soil is still warm. If this is impossible, plant in spring after the last frost.

WHERE TO PLANT

Anise does best in spots where it can get full morning sunshine and some shade during the afternoon. It can grow in full sun, but thick mulch and regular watering will be needed. The high shade of pine or poplar trees is a perfect setting, especially if the ground stays moist most of the time. Some gardeners with sensitive noses find the April blooms of Florida anise to be less pleasant-smelling than its foliage.

HOW TO PLANT

Moist, well-drained soil is essential for good growth. Dig a planting hole 5 times as wide as the root ball of your plant. Since an anise has shallow roots, the hole need not be more than 12" deep. If the area is completely boggy, add 2 to 3 bags of compost or soil conditioner to the soil. The resulting mound will keep the anise roots above standing water. If the anise is container-grown, try to untangle the circling roots and spread them in the hole before filling it with soil.

CARE AND MAINTENANCE

For the first two years after planting, fertilize 3 times a year with 1 tablespoon of 10–10–10 fertilizer per foot of plant height. After your anise is established, one application of fertilizer each spring will suffice. Although anise can be sheared with hedge trimmers, the damaged leaves are not attractive. A better technique is to prune out individual branches with hand pruners, cutting back to smaller branches or buds. Pests are rare. Black vine weevils will occasionally make 1/4" notches in the edges of leaves, but the damage is usually not serious.

ADDITIONAL ADVICE FOR CARE

Since anise likes shady locations, shade-loving companions should be selected. Nandina (*Nandina domestica*), deciduous holly (*Ilex verticillata*), and common azaleas are good choices. Perennial flowers such as astilbe, ferns, and hosta can be planted underneath. Anise seeds can be collected and planted in the fall.

ADDITIONAL CULTIVARS AND SPECIES

Illicium floridanum 'Hally's Comet' is reputed to have more abundant flowers than the species.

Juniperus spp.

Juniper

Height: 6'–12' Width: 3'–15'
Evergreen shrub

Junipers are shrubs that get no respect. They are common as dirt, tough as nails, and they are green year round. They are sheared into balls, tortured into pom-pons, and are given the toughest of steep slopes to beautify. If a broadleafed shrub were able to perform so well, it would be hailed throughout the country, yet junipers are not honored at all. We rarely appreciate the terrific durability and variability of this everyday shrub. Though some of the junipers make good solitary specimen shrubs, most junipers are planted as groundcover. Junipers are widely used on the sides of interstate highways and on the clay banks surrounding shopping malls in Georgia. Junipers are inexpensive and they may be common, but they get the landscape job done without complaint.

WHEN TO PLANT

A juniper can be planted at any time other than the heat of summer. But even if one is planted in summer, it's a good bet that it will survive with a bit of watering. For best results, plant in early spring in north Georgia and in spring or fall in south Georgia.

WHERE TO PLANT

Plant a juniper in full sunshine. Nothing looks more pitiful than a juniper trying to grow in the shade. Junipers are selected for their growth habit, either upright or creeping. Read the plant information tag to determine how large your plant will grow. The plant's ultimate width is the spacing you should use between plants when you plant a group.

HOW TO PLANT

It is a myth that a juniper can grow easily in hard clay soil. As is true of any other plant, a juniper grows much faster if given a good

ZONE
6,7,8

root environment. If you are planting juniper on a slope, first try to form 18"-wide terraces along its length. Dig a hole at least twice the size of the root ball and form a slight basin around the hole to catch water as it runs downhill. Before purchasing a juniper, examine its roots. If they are densely matted in the pot, look for another plant. A newly rooted, vigorously growing juniper will become established much faster than one that has been sitting in a nursery for two years.

CARE AND MAINTENANCE

In general, junipers do not require any more care than you choose to give them. For the first two years, fertilize 3 times a year with 1 tablespoon of 10–10–10 fertilizer per foot of plant height. After your juniper is established, 1/4 cup of 10–10–10 per foot of height each spring will be enough. Pruning is done in spring when new green shoots are growing, typically in early May. Remember the difference between "above ground" drainage and "root zone" drainage. You might think that a juniper is well-drained when growing on a clay bank while the plants at the bottom of the slope are drowning.

ADDITIONAL ADVICE FOR CARE

Spider mites can infest a weakened juniper. Clip a branch and slap it against a piece of white paper. If you see tiny pink creatures scurrying for cover, you know the juniper has spider mites. Call your local Extension office for control measures. Phomopsis disease reveals itself in spring when new shoots die back 6" to 10". Control this disease by removing the shoots.

ADDITIONAL CULTIVARS AND SPECIES

You may choose from dozens of junipers. Read the plant information tag to determine how large yours will grow. *Juniperus chinensis* 'Blue Point' is an easy-to-find upright variety. *Juniperus horizontalis* 'Blue Rug' and 'Bar Harbor' are two low-growing, spreading groundcover junipers.

Lagerstroemia indica

Crapemyrtle

Height: 3'–20' Width: 3'–15'
Deciduous flowering shrub or tree

When Atlanta won the rights to host the 1996 Olympics, the first thought of landscapers was: "I hope the crapemyrtles will still be in bloom that summer!" Fortunately, they were, and thousands of visitors to the South envied our ability to enjoy these graceful flowering plants in July and August. A crapemyrtle has three elements of beauty: its flowers, its bark, and its fall foliage color. Flower color ranges from pure white ('Natchez') to medium purple ('Powhatan'). Several crapemyrtles have bark which peels off to reveal a cinnamon or gray underbark in winter. Fall leaf color on these shrubs is outstanding all over Georgia, ranging from bright yellow to deep red. Crapemyrtles are as underappreciated in Georgia as tropical hibiscus is in Miami. Many tourists recognized the flowers of our crapemyrtles but did not realize that it can grow into a perennial shrub or small tree. In Northern states, crapemyrtle is frozen to the ground each winter.

WHEN TO PLANT

Plant a crapemyrtle in spring or fall. Pine straw or pine chip mulch is important during the first year to conserve moisture in summer. Thereafter, the mulch will help keep errant lawnmowers from bumping the thin bark of the shrub.

WHERE TO PLANT

Certainly full sun is the best environment for a crapemyrtle. The shrub makes a fine specimen plant, especially if a walkway is nearby so the bark can be seen up close. The smaller varieties can be planted in a mass. The Atlanta Botanical Garden has planted 'Natchez' crapemyrtles on either side of a sidewalk to make a wonderful shady 'allee' during the summer.

HOW TO PLANT

Container-grown crapemyrtles are easy to find, but they may not bloom for a couple of years. They may spend their first few years

ZONE
6,7,8

making vigorous growth rather than flower buds. Balled-and-burlapped specimens are also common, and they may bloom sooner. Dig a hole 3 times as wide as the root ball and to a depth equal to the height of the root ball. No organic matter needs to be added as long as the soil is thoroughly broken up. Remove any burlap and twine that shows after a balled-and-burlapped crapemyrtle is placed in its hole. Water the soil thoroughly to settle it around the roots, then spread pine straw or pine bark mulch over the whole area.

CARE AND MAINTENANCE

Too much fertilizer can hinder the growth of crapemyrtle blooms. Apply 1 tablespoon of 10–10–10 per foot of plant height in April each year. Although the plant is fairly drought-tolerant, water a new plant during the summer after it has been planted. It is a popular myth that a crapemyrtle requires pruning every January to produce blooms. In fact, pruning is only advised if the plant is too large for its growing site. Remove the small sprouts from the trunks of multi-trunked crapemyrtles each winter. If you must prune drastically, select an appropriate height and remove all branches above that point.

ADDITIONAL ADVICE FOR CARE

Powdery mildew is a disease that affects older varieties of crapemyrtle. During some summers, the foliage will be thickly covered with white powder. This does no lasting harm, but blooms will be greatly reduced. Aphids love to suck sap from crapemyrtle leaves. They secrete a sticky "honeydew" which covers lower leaves. Sooty mold may turn these leaves black. Check with the local Extension office for controls.

ADDITIONAL CULTIVARS AND SPECIES

The National Arboretum has released several outstanding selections of disease-resistant crapemyrtle. 'Natchez,' 'Muskogee,' 'Lipan,' 'Tonto,' 'Yuma,' and 'Sioux' are among the best. Avoid purchasing a plant simply labeled "White Crapemyrtle" or "Pink Crapemyrtle." These are most assuredly lower-quality plants.

Loropetalum chinense

Loropetalum

Chinese Fringeflower

Height: 2'–6' Width: 2'–8'
Evergreen flowering shrub

The common loropetalum has deep-green leaves that remain on the shrub all year long. The flowers are white or slightly cream-colored and they appear in mid-spring. The recently introduced purple-leaved varieties have bright (screamingly bright!) fuchsia blooms. A member of the witch-hazel family, the white flowers of common loropetalum are strap-like and approximately 1" long. The newer purple-foliaged, pink-flowered varieties will undoubtedly attract enough attention from the general public that loropetalum will be common in landscapes within a few years. As its scientific name indicates, loropetalum was brought over from China in the late nineteenth century. It has not been extensively planted, although it is an excellent shrub. It grows rapidly, has flowers, and is generally care-free and pest-free. It is usually hardy from Atlanta southward, but a severe winter in the northern third of Georgia will freeze many loropetalums to the ground. Fortunately, a loropetalum will make quick regrowth the following year.

WHEN TO PLANT

In south Georgia, loropetalum can be planted in fall or in spring. Since it is susceptible to cold injury when young, it is best to plant in mid-spring in the northern half of the state.

WHERE TO PLANT

Loropetalum can tolerate a very wide range of environmental conditions. It will grow faster in full sun, but it can grow very nicely in shade. Moist, well-drained soils are best, but loropetalum also grows well in clay or in sandy soil. It can be used as a solitary specimen or as part of a larger shrub grouping. In extreme south Georgia, it can be trimmed into a small tree.

ZONE
6,7,8

How to Plant

Dig a hole 3 times as wide as the root ball of the plant. There is no need to add soil amendments as long as the soil is thoroughly broken up. When the shrub is out of its pot, gently untangle some of the larger roots and spread them in the hole before filling it with earth. Water immediately after planting and spread mulch under the plant. Attempt to keep the soil evenly moist for at least 4 weeks. If planted in sandy soil or in full sun, drought stress may occur in summer. Pay attention to the leaf color during the summer. When leaves appear dull instead of glossy, it's time for a long soaking.

Care and Maintenance

Fertilize a loropetalum twice each year, in spring and in late summer. Use 1 tablespoon of 10–10–10 fertilizer for each foot of plant height. Mulch under the plant is important to avoid moisture stress, but do not pile the mulch high against the trunk. Pine straw in a layer 3" thick is an excellent mulch material. Pruning is usually not necessary unless a wayward shoot extends far out beyond the rest of the plant. In that case, simply prune it off just above a lower branch or bud.

Additional Advice for Care

Plan ahead when planting a loropetalum in the colder parts of the state. Shelter from cold winds can be provided by choosing a site in a protected corner on the east side of a house. In winter, if temperatures below 15 degrees are predicted, cover the shrub with an old bedsheet. Make sure the edges of the sheet touch the ground on all sides and are held down by rocks or limbs.

Additional Cultivars and Species

Several selections of purple-leafed loropetalum have recently been introduced and patented by large nurseries. 'Plum Delight,' 'Razzle Dazzle,' 'Hines Purpleleaf,' and others are common. The National Arboretum has released two selections: 'Burgundy' has bronze-purple leaves with dark-pink flowers, and 'Blush' has light-pink foliage and pink flowers.

Nandina domestica

Nandina

Heavenly Bamboo

Height: 18"–8' Width: 18"–5'
Evergreen shrub

What a difference a name makes! When a plant peddler rolled his wagon up to a rural farmhouse, he had to have a good pitch to persuade the woman of the house to part with her egg money. "What about this bridal wreath spirea? It's really pretty in the spring! If you buy it along with these zinnia seeds, I'll throw in a rooted cutting of heavenly bamboo!" Unless the farm wife knew that heavenly bamboo *was the same plant as the common nandina growing by the front steps, she might fall for the beautiful name. Nandina can offer wonderful textural relief to a group of other shrubs. In December it will produce an abundant and attractive crop of red berries. One of the most shade-tolerant shrubs, common nandina can be used as a foundation shrub or as a screen plant. The introduction of dwarf cultivars, particularly the red-foliaged ones, has made nandina a shrub sought after by many gardeners. Though it may not be as divine as the old plant peddler claimed, nandina possesses fine qualities.*

WHEN TO PLANT

Plant your nandina in fall or in spring. If you are transplanting an old nandina to a new spot, it will be hard to keep soil on its roots. The roots are not very fibrous, and soil falls off easily. The solution is to cut back the stems to 18" and plant it bare root. Given some shade and a few waterings, your nandina will take root, sprout, and do well.

WHERE TO PLANT

Though tolerant of shade, common nandina can grow easily in full sunshine. In sandy soils or on dry sites, this nandina appreciates irrigation during July and August. The dwarf forms that have red winter leaves do best in full sun so the leaf color is most pronounced.

How to Plant

Dig a hole 3 times as wide as the root ball. Spread the roots in the hole before putting the soil back in place. Be sure the main stem of the nandina is not planted more deeply in the earth than it grew in the pot. Pack the soil around the roots by hand, then water well. Spread mulch under the new plant to conserve moisture. Good companions for common nandina are the coarser-leaved shrubs that like shade. Leatherleaf mahonia (*Mahonia bealei*), aucuba (*Aucuba japonica*), and hydrangea (*Hydrangea macrophylla*) are fine choices. Red-leafed cultivars can be planted as border plants around an ever-green for a good color contrast.

Care and Maintenance

Nandina seems to do fine with no fertilizer, but the shrub will make bigger groups of berries if it is given added nutrients. Apply 1 table-spoon of 10–10–10 per foot of height to a newly planted shrub in March, May, and July. After the first year, fertilize in April and June with the same amount of fertilizer. Water is needed for only a few weeks after planting. Prune out the oldest stems in March when a bush has grown too tall. For the most attractive shape, cut one of the stems at 6", one at 12", one at 18", and so on in six-inch increments.

Additional Advice for Care

The plant peddler could not afford to sell plants that had to be pampered. Nandina is remarkably free of any reported insect or disease pests.

Additional Cultivars and Species

Nandina domestica 'Gulf Stream' is a common dwarf form that exhibits brilliant red leaves in winter. *Nandina domestica* 'San Gabriel' grows up to 24" high and has green leaves that look almost ferny.

Photinia x fraseri

Red Tip Photinia

Height: 8'–15' Width: 6'–10'
Evergreen shrub

Few plants in April can match the shimmering red foliage of the over-used but still attractive red tip photinia. The shrubs grace million-dollar mansions and dilapidated shacks, favoring all residents equally with their spring glory. If red tip photinias were not used so often, they would be regarded as wonderful specimen shrubs. Unfortunately, because they are so easy to propagate and sell by the thousands, red tips are as common as weeds in Georgia landscapes. Like Burford holly, the red tip photinia originated in the South. Fraser Nurseries in Birmingham, Alabama, discovered this attractive hybrid of Chinese photinia (Photinia serrulata) and began propagating it from cuttings. The red tip photinia leaf disease situation points to the dangers of overplanting a particular plant. Photinia leaf spot would be a minor problem if there were not so many susceptible shrubs nearby to infect. Rare is the gardener who has not seen the serious defoliation this fungus can cause on a large shrub.

WHEN TO PLANT

If you choose to gamble on this shrub, plant in mid-fall or early spring. Examine individual leaves on the plant you are considering from top to bottom for the tell-tale purple spots that indicate photinia leaf spot. Do not purchase a plant with any sign of disease.

WHERE TO PLANT

A red tip photinia can grow in almost any soil. Full sunshine will stimulate the most vibrant new growth, but a red tip can grow in dense shade, thought it will grow slowly. It makes no sense to plant a red tip within 100 yards of a diseased plant. Leaf spot is so virulent that your plant will be sure to get it. Isolated plants can grow for years without disease; the plants around Hartsfield International Airport in Atlanta are good examples.

HOW TO PLANT

Dig a hole 3 times as wide as the root ball. Spread the roots in the hole before putting the soil back in place. Make sure the main stem of the photinia is not buried more deeply in the earth than it grew in the pot. Pack the soil around the roots by hand, then water well. Pine straw or pine bark mulch under the new plant will help conserve moisture. When used for a screening hedge, plant red tip photinias 4′ apart.

CARE AND MAINTENANCE

Fertilize 3 times a year with 1 tablespoon of 10–10–10 fertilizer per foot of plant height. After the plant is established, 1/4 cup of 10–10–10 per foot of height each spring will suffice. Although a photinia can be sheared with hedge trimmers, the damaged leaves are not very attractive. A better technique is to prune out individual branches with hand pruners, cutting back to a smaller branch or bud. If you do this after the red leaves have begun to turn green, you'll get another flush of red foliage later. Insect pests are rare. Occasionally black vine weevils will make 1/4″ notches in the edges of leaves but damage is never serious.

ADDITIONAL ADVICE FOR CARE

If your red tip does get leaf spot, regular applications of fungicide in the spring can keep it at bay to some extent. Call your local Extension office to learn about effective controls. If you cannot accomplish the regular spraying that is required, replace the photinia with a holly or other evergreen. Some have achieved disease-control success by removing the lower limbs of a tall shrub to form a photinia tree.

ADDITIONAL CULTIVARS AND SPECIES

There are no commonly available improved selections of the original red tip photinia. Chinese photinia (*Photinia serrulata*) grows into a shrub that is much wider than red tip photinia. The spring foliage is not nearly as red as *Photinia x fraseri*. It is less susceptible to leaf spot and can be used more often as a screen hedge.

Rhododendron prunifolium

Plumleaf Azalea

Height: 7'–10' Width: 6'–8'
Deciduous flowering shrub

Japanese azaleas put on a stunning performance in spring, but what azaleas offer blossoms during the sweltering heat of summer? In July and August, when few blooms on any other shrubs are evident, a plumleaf azalea presents bright red flowers on glossy green foliage. Plumleaf azalea is native to west Georgia. It is found around Callaway Gardens, lining the streams that meander down the flanks of Pine Mountain. Even though it thrives in the South, it is hardy all the way up to Kentucky and Virginia. The best use of plumleaf azalea is beneath tall pines and hardwoods, where little but English ivy and scraggly underbrush grows. Scatter a few of these gems in an overgrown backyard area, clear a path nearby, and you will have an instant native plant trail. Add some Christmas fern (Polystichum acrostichoides), *some wild ginger* (Asarum shuttleworthii), *and a few summersweet* (Clethra alnifolia) *to make an enticing garden area.*

WHEN TO PLANT

Plant a plumleaf azalea in early fall before the soil has cooled. If a small specimen must be transplanted from another site, dig it in late November after the leaves have fallen. Instead of forming a root ball under the shrub to be moved, excavate a wide "root pancake" of roots and soil around the shrub.

WHERE TO PLANT

Since plumleaf azalea might need water during establishment, try to place it in a spot where where a hose will reach. Remember that the blooms appear during the hottest part of the year, so afternoon shade is essential. The eye-catching color of the azalea's blossoms will be enhanced if the plant can be placed in front of a dense green backdrop.

HOW TO PLANT

Azaleas need an enriched, moist soil that is well drained. The best
way to get such soil is to dig a hole 5' wide and mix 4 cubic feet of
soil conditioner with the soil removed from the hole. The resulting
mound could be a perfect planting spot for every member of the
rhododendron family. If the plant's roots are densely packed in the
pot, untangle and spread them in the hole before soil is packed
around them. Make sure your azalea is planted neither deeper nor
higher than it was grown in the pot. For a month after planting,
inspect it weekly to make sure the root ball has not become exposed
and dry. Mulch heavily with pine straw, but be sure to pull the
mulch back from the plant stem 3" on all sides.

CARE AND MAINTENANCE

Little fertilizer is needed except for a few light applications during
the first year of establishment. Spread 1 tablespoon of 10–10–10 per
foot of plant height in March, June, and August of the first year.
Thereafter, 2 tablespoons of 10–10–10 per foot of height applied in
April and June should suffice. Buds for next year's flowers form
during the summer, so pruning at any time during the year will
reduce blooms in the current year or the following summer.
Fortunately, plumleaf azalea forms an attractive shape naturally,
so little but the removal of dead wood is necessary.

ADDITIONAL ADVICE FOR CARE

The bright blooms of plumleaf azalea attract butterflies and hummingbirds. Try planting trumpetcreeper (*Campsis radicans*) and
cross vine (*Anisostichus cupreolata*) nearby to attract these and other
pollinators.

ADDITIONAL CULTIVARS AND SPECIES

Rhododendron prunifolium 'Cherry Bomb' and *Rhododendron prunifolium* 'Peach Glow' are occasionally found in nurseries.

Rhododendron spp.

Spring-flowering Azalea

Height: 2'–8' Width: 4'–10'
Flowering shrub

Who can forget the stunning shades of white, pink, red, and lavender that grace the cities and suburbs of Georgia in April? Combined with the clouds of pure white dogwood blooms that hang overhead, the beauty is enough to cause a Northern visitor to call home, sell the house, and become a Southerner. The masses of azaleas in the older suburbs of Atlanta and other Georgia cities are beloved parts of our landscapes. Hundreds of years of hybridization plus the springtime availability of azaleas mean that a distinctive azalea is within reach of everyone. There are both evergreen and deciduous azaleas as well as small-leafed and large-leafed types. In general, the large-leafed azaleas are more likely to be damaged from extreme cold than are the small-leafed ones. The deciduous azaleas tend to have a more open form than do most evergreen azaleas.

WHEN TO PLANT

Plant azaleas in fall so the roots can become established before the following summer. If you want a specific color, plant in April when the shrubs are blooming in garden centers. You will be able to select the exact pastel shade you want. Plan to water a spring-planted azalea weekly until June.

WHERE TO PLANT

Afternoon shade is a requirement for azaleas. Select a site with natural moisture or nearby irrigation. Evergreen azaleas are often used as shrubs along the foundation of a home. It is best to combine them with other evergreens in order to avoid the monotony of a single leaf texture. Consider the eventual size of your azalea when planting. If azaleas grow too large, some may have to be removed.

HOW TO PLANT

Azaleas need an enriched, moist soil that is well drained. The best way to get such soil is to dig a hole 5' wide and mix 4 cubic feet of

ZONE
6,7,8

soil conditioner with the soil removed from the hole. The resulting mound could be a perfect planting spot for every member of the rhododendron family. If the plant's roots are densely packed in the pot, untangle and spread them in the hole before soil is packed around them. Make sure your azalea is planted neither deeper nor higher than it was grown in the pot. For a month after planting, inspect it weekly to make sure the root ball has not become exposed and dry. Mulch heavily with pine straw, but be sure to pull the mulch back from the plant stem 3" on all sides.

CARE AND MAINTENANCE

After the light fertilizer applications needed during the first year of establishment, azaleas require only a moderate application of fertilizer each year. Spread 1 tablespoon of 10–10–10 per foot of plant height in March, June, and August in the first year. Thereafter, 2 tablespoons of 10–10–10 per foot of height applied in April and June should suffice. Buds for next year's flowers form during the summer; pruning after July will reduce blooms in the following spring. All azaleas form a dense, rounded shape naturally, but if pruning seems necessary, do it in May or June.

ADDITIONAL ADVICE FOR CARE

There are thousands of azalea cultivars. If the name is not noted when you plant a cultivar, it will be an impossible task to determine the variety later. Use wide plastic garbage bag ties to attach tags to lower branches. A tag should contain brief but vital information about the azalea to which it is attached.

ADDITIONAL CULTIVARS AND SPECIES

Entire groups of azalea hybrids are named for their original hybridizers. Glenn Dale, Robin Hill, and Girard hybrids are a few of the many you will find. Exbury azaleas are a common deciduous type. The Satsuki hybrids flower in May, weeks later than do most azaleas. In Japanese, "satsuke" means "fifth month."

Rhododendron

Height: 4'–15' Width: 4'–15'
Evergreen flowering shrub

The Latin name for rhododendron perfectly describes its form: Rhodo means "rose" and dendron means "tree." Rose-tree is the perfect name for this grand lady of the April landscape. The flower color of different varieties ranges from pure white through yellow, orange, pink, red, and lavender. Beware if you find yourself planting more than four. That might be a sign that you have become fascinated with the possibilities of this genus and want to plant nothing but rhododendrons in your yard! Only in the Pacific Northwest do rhododendrons prosper the way they do in Georgia. The massive spring displays at Callaway Gardens are famous around the world. With a bit of soil preparation, your landscape can have the same stunning effect. What's the difference between a rhododendron and an azalea? Gardeners know that both are members of the genus Rhododendron. Azalea flowers are funnel-shaped, rhododendron flowers are bell-shaped. Rhododendrons generally have larger and more leathery leaves than do azaleas.

WHEN TO PLANT

Early spring seems to be the best time to plant rhododendrons. Perhaps this is because the roots are fine and fast-growing. The warming soil stimulates the roots to explore their new surroundings at the same time the leaves are becoming accustomed to their new light level.

WHERE TO PLANT

Landscapes which have become more shady over the years offer an excellent spot for a rhododendron. Morning sunshine followed by afternoon shade is ideal. There are many shade-loving plants that make good rhododendron companions. Camellia (*Camellia japonica*), Solomon's-seal (*Polygonatum commutatum*), toad lily (*Tricyrtis hirta*), and ferns are top choices for partners in the shade.

How to Plant

Dig a hole 5 times as wide as the root ball, no less than 4' across. Remove 1/3 of the native soil and add to it 4 cubic feet of soil conditioner or compost. Mix everything together to make a raised mound in which to plant. All rhododendrons have very fine, fibrous roots. Although they will spread shallowly out from the stem when planted in the earth, in a container the roots make a dense web inside the pot walls. When you take a plant out of the pot, use a sharp knife inserted halfway down the side of the root ball to cut through the roots down to the bottom. The roots can then be flared out in all directions when planted. Pack soil on top of the roots, then water.

Care and Maintenance

Mulch must be used to keep moisture in the soil during the summer. Spread a 2" layer of shredded leaves on top of the soil underneath your rhododendron. Pull the mulch back from the stem 3" to avoid stem rot. Apply 1 tablespoon of 10–10–10 fertilizer per foot of height in spring and again in midsummer. Drip irrigation or soaker hoses are a good investment in the long-term health of your plant. Snake the soaker hose throughout the beds where you have planted rhododendrons and azaleas. They and their companions will enjoy a good soaking each week in July and August. If needed, prune a rhododendron in May after flowering.

Additional Advice for Care

Sometimes the shade over a rhododendron will become much too dense and the lower limbs of the shrub will die. If this happens, move the plant, or remove some lower limbs of nearby trees. When sunshine is restored, the rhododendron can be cut back by half in early March so it will resprout.

Additional Cultivars and Species

Rhododendron catawbiense 'Nova Zembla' grows 8' tall and has large red flowers. *Rhododendron* 'Scintillation' has light pink flowers and is tolerant of Georgia heat. *Rhododendron* 'Ramapo' grows only 2' tall and has violet-purple flowers.

Spiraea x bumalda

Bumald Spirea

Height: 18"–30" Width: 3'–5'
Deciduous flowering shrub

*There are several species of spirea that are common in Georgia landscapes. Bumald spirea and Vanhoutte spirea (*Spirea x vanhoutei*) are among the best. Bridal wreath spirea (*Spiraea prunifolia*) was introduced into Georgia just after the Civil War. Cuttings of this plant are so easy to root that the plant followed families as they moved all over the rural South during the rebuilding of farms and cities. Even the humblest sharecropper cabin had a tough-as-nails bridal wreath spirea growing beside the chimney. The problem with most spireas, including bridal wreath spirea, is that the foliage is not particularly attractive after the flowers fade. Bumald spirea is a hybrid that has the best foliage and flower features of both its parents. Like most spireas, the foliage of a bumald spirea is bluish-green at maturity. Flower color ranges from light pink to carmine. A great advantage is that the flowers will continue to appear from late May through early August if you give the plant a good shearing in June.*

WHEN TO PLANT

Plant bumald spirea in spring in north Georgia. In south Georgia, it can be planted in spring or fall.

WHERE TO PLANT

Give your spirea full sunshine and room to spread out. You can even consider it a groundcover plant and use it to cover a slope. Good companion shrubs in a mass grouping include summersweet (*Clethra alnifolia*) and fothergilla (*Fothergilla gardenii*).

HOW TO PLANT

Dig a hole 3 times as wide as the root ball of the plant. There is no need to add soil amendments as long as the soil is thoroughly broken up. When the shrub is out of its pot, gently untangle some of

the larger roots and spread them in the hole before filling it with earth. Water immediately after planting and spread mulch under the plant. Attempt to keep the soil evenly moist for at least 4 weeks. If the plant is in sandy soil and in full sun, water during the summer to avoid drought stress.

CARE AND MAINTENANCE

Apply 1 tablespoon of 10–10–10 per foot of height to a newly plant-ed spirea in March, June, and August. After the first year, using the same amount, fertilize in March and June. Once it is established, your spirea will be able to withstand considerable drought. You can water in summer if you want to promote the appearance of more flowers. After the first flowers have begun to fade, use hedge clip-pers to trim 6" of foliage off the entire plant. The new growth that appears will give you a second flush of flowers in July.

ADDITIONAL ADVICE FOR CARE

It is easy to propagate a spirea. Take a look underneath a mature plant, and you'll probably find several sprouts ready to transplant. To make a spirea spread quickly over a large area, bury the tips of the longest branches in the earth. They will root and grow vigorous-ly within a year.

ADDITIONAL CULTIVARS AND SPECIES

Spiraea x bumalda 'Anthony Waterer' is by far the most common cultivar. You might also find *Spiraea x bumalda* 'Goldflame.' It has brilliant orange-red leaves in spring and light pink flowers during the summer.

Lilac

Height: 6'–10' Width: 5'–8'
Deciduous flowering shrub

One of the first plants a transplanted Northerner misses in the South is the lilac. Northerners remember the armloads of blooms and the scent at their childhood homes. They react with concern when they see no lilacs appear in spring in Georgia. They wonder why such a glorious plant is neglected here! The answer is simple: the same cold weather that drives some folks to move and make residence in Georgia is essential to make most lilacs bloom. The buds need hundreds of "chill hours" in order to make flowers. Lilacs occasionally do well in the Georgia mountains, but further south these plants produce nothing but leaves. If the summer is dry, not only will there be no blooms, but powdery mildew disease will cover the leaves and disfigure the plants. Fortunately, there are a few varieties which can bloom with little cold (see below for details). Several have done well at Barnsley Gardens in Adairsville, and they have a chance of flourishing in middle Georgia. If you want to see what all the fuss is about, take on the challenge of growing lilacs.

WHEN TO PLANT

Lilacs are certainly cold-hardy—they thrive in Chicago and northward— but they suffer when temperatures fluctuate in February from 60 degrees in the daytime to 20 degrees at night. For this reason it is best to plant in spring after the coldest weather has passed.

WHERE TO PLANT

Even when planted at the edge of your landscape, the scent of a lilac will fill your yard and home. You can adjust the intensity of the smell indoors by placing the shrub fairly close to the most-used outside door. A full-sun site on the north or northeast side of the house is best for chilling the flower buds in winter.

SHRUBS

HOW TO PLANT

Dig a hole 3 times as large as the root ball of your lilac. Add one bag of soil conditioner to form a low mound in which to plant. Untangle the roots if necessary and spread them in the hole before filling it with soil. Pack the soil in place and water thoroughly. Add more soil if the earth settles around the roots. Mulch with pine straw.

CARE AND MAINTENANCE

Conditions in Georgia result in such rampant lilac growth that it is almost shameful to stimulate the plants with fertilizer. Try 1 tablespoon of 10–10–10 fertilizer per foot of plant height in April and June. When your plant has reached its desired size, cut back to a single fertilization in April. Drier summers result in fewer flowers, so plan to water regularly during June, July, and August. If blooms appear, remove them as soon as they begin to fade. After flowering, prune back to the first two side branches below the spot where the flowers grew. Once the shrub is large, completely remove a couple of older stems each year.

ADDITIONAL ADVICE FOR CARE

After a lilac has been in one spot for a few years, sprouts will appear near the base. These may be left alone if you want a bigger plant, or they may be dug up and transplanted in spring.

ADDITIONAL CULTIVARS AND SPECIES

Syringa vulgaris 'President Lincoln' and *S. meyeri* 'Miss Kim' have done well at Barnsley Gardens. *S. vulgaris* 'Blue Boy' and 'Lavender Lady' were developed in California for mild winter environments. Another lilac to try is cut-leaf lilac, *Syringa laciniata*. Its blooms are not as large as those of Northern lilacs, but it blooms reliably each year.

Viburnum plicatum var. *tomentosum*

Doublefile Viburnum

Height: 8'–10' Width: 8'–10'
Deciduous flowering shrub

The flowers on a doublefile viburnum are unlike those on any other shrub. The limbs on this viburnum grow in horizontal layers up the trunk, each tier higher and smaller than the last, resulting in an effect like a tall, layered green cake. When the flowers come in April, they emerge on top of each branch, covering it all the way to the tip. Then it appears the green cake has white icing—a spectacular sight! Doublefile viburnum is a "dogwood season extender." Its blooms arrive after most dogwoods blossoms have fallen. A large specimen can be mistaken for a beautiful dogwood that has arrived late at the spring blossom party. A doublefile viburnum is elegant. The horizontal lines of its branches offer good contrast to the more upright shrubs along your property line.

WHEN TO PLANT

In north Georgia, plant your doublefile viburnum in spring. In south Georgia, fall planting allows the roots to grow before summer arrives.

WHERE TO PLANT

An excellent place for doublefile viburnum is the high corner of a house whose lot slopes from one side to the other. The viburnum will do best on a site that has moist, well-drained soil. Do not put it too far from a water hose. A prolonged summer drought can cause stem dieback.

HOW TO PLANT

Dig a hole 5 times as wide as the root ball. Spread the roots in the hole before putting the soil back in place. Make sure the main stem of the viburnum is not planted more deeply in the earth than it grew in the pot. Pack the soil around the roots by hand, then water well.

ZONE
6,7,8

Pine straw or pine bark mulch under the new plant will help conserve moisture.

CARE AND MAINTENANCE

Little fertilizer is needed by a doublefile viburnum after it has
become established. Apply 1 tablespoon of 10–10–10 per foot of
height to a newly planted shrub in March, June, and August. After
the first year, using the same amount, fertilize in April and June.
Water once a week for 3 weeks after planting, then watch the plant
for signs of water stress. The leaves hang almost vertically from the
branches, but they will look markedly more droopy when the shrub
is dry. Pruning is rarely needed. The viburnum will usually make a
wonderful shape without assistance.

ADDITIONAL ADVICE FOR CARE

Watch your viburnum in late July for red berries. You'll have to keep
an eye out for them because birds find them delicious.

ADDITIONAL CULTIVARS AND SPECIES

Viburnum plicatum var. *tomentosum* 'Shasta' is by far the best doublefile viburnum. It has large flowers and very graceful, layered,
declining branches. The variety 'Mariesii' is also outstanding. Its
limbs grow so strongly horizontal that in bloom it looks like a table
covered with a white tablecloth.

Viburnum x pragense

Prague Viburnum

Height: 8'–12' Width: 8'–10'
Evergreen shrub

Prague viburnum is almost as hardy as Burford holly, but it is not used often enough in Georgia landscapes. Both plants are large and evergreen and both have attractive berries. Either can be used as a foundation shrub at the high corner of a house whose lot slopes from one side of the yard to the other. Perhaps the infrequency of use is due to the fact that there are so many other good viburnums from which to select. But Prague viburnum is considered the "best of the best" in the South. Prague viburnum lacks the fabulous scent of Koreanspice viburnum (Viburnum carlseii), but its flowers and berries are outstanding. The flower buds, borne in flat clusters, are pink when they appear in April and quickly turn white after opening. The berries are red, but change gradually to black by late October. You have to be quick to enjoy the berries—birds sometimes enjoy their taste faster than humans can enjoy their sight. If you are looking for an indestructible evergreen shrub, Prague viburnum should be high on your list.

WHEN TO PLANT

Plant your Prague viburnum in late fall or in early spring. The leaves may be a little discolored when you visit a nursery in fall, but this will not be apparent once the plant has become established in your landscape.

WHERE TO PLANT

Prague viburnum can grow well in a wide variety of conditions and types of soil. Berries will be more numerous in full sun, but the shrub can tolerate a surprising amount of shade. It is an "edge-of-the woods" shrub, so place it there if you have that choice. The deep-green, leathery foliage provides a good background for all blooming perennials. Good companions are Japanese anemone (*Anemone hupehensis*) and lantana (*Lantana camara*).

ZONE
6,7,8

How to Plant

If you want years of little care, take the time to dig a planting hole 5 times as large as the root ball of your new plant. If the soil you remove from the hole is all clay, mix in 2 cubic feet of soil conditioner or compost. Pack the earth back around the roots. Water occasionally for the first month. Spread a layer of pine straw mulch or wood chips under your viburnum to conserve moisture.

Care and Maintenance

The shrub will have better-looking leaves and more berries with regular fertilization. Apply 1 tablespoon of 10–10–10 fertilizer per foot of height in March, June, and August. Plan on watering during the heat of summer for the first two years. Unless your viburnum is in a hot, dry site, it may not require watering after that. Prague viburnum grows to a nice rounded form without major pruning. In very rich soil, however, the vigorous sprouts may be removed as they occur to give a more manicured look.

Additional Advice for Care

Prague viburnum is remarkably free of insect or disease problems. On a windy site in winter, leaf scorch can sometimes occur. The damaged leaves will be quickly hidden in spring.

Additional Cultivars and Species

Koreanspice viburnum (*Viburnum carlseii*) is nondescript most of the year, but a single shrub can spice up a neighborhood with its sweet scent in March. Snowball viburnum (*Viburnum macrocephalum*) has large, round, white flower heads in early May that are remarkably similar to those found on a common hydrangea.

Vitex agnus-castus

Chastetree

Height: 7'–10' Width: 8'–10'
Deciduous flowering shrub

Visitors to the Georgia Agricultural Pavilion at Centennial Olympic Park always stopped in surprise before the chastetree on display. It looked so much like a butterfly bush, but it obviously was not. Its light green leaves were topped by 6"-long, light blue flower spikes. It looked like a very fine shrub . . . but why had the visitors never seen one before? Georgia homeowners are rapidly discovering the chastetree. Its blue flowers in mid-summer are very attractive, and its lacy, open growth make it an excellent centerpiece for a raised landscape island. As the years go by, nurseries will sell more of this plant, and gardeners will find it easy to distingish a chastetree from a butterfly bush.

WHEN TO PLANT

As is true of the butterfly bush, chastetree cán be damaged by a severe winter. Plant in spring in north Georgia, and in fall in south Georgia.

WHERE TO PLANT

Plant your chastetree in full sunshine, making sure there is enough room for it to grow to its full size. Chastetree flowers are good forage for bumblebees, so plant your shrub away from your patio if you don't care for bees. At the Agriculture Pavilion, chastetree was planted with 'Zuni' crapemyrtles on each side and 'New Gold' lantana covering the ground in front.

HOW TO PLANT

Dig a hole 3 times as wide as the root ball of the plant. There is no need to add soil amendments as long as the soil is thoroughly broken up. When the shrub is out of its pot, gently untangle some of the larger roots and spread them in the hole before filling it with

earth. Water immediately after planting and spread mulch under the plant. Attempt to keep the soil evenly moist for at least four weeks. If planted in sandy soil and full sun, drought stress may occur in the first summer. Be sure to water regularly under these conditions.

CARE AND MAINTENANCE

For the first two years after planting, fertilize with 1 tablespoon of 10–10–10 fertilizer per foot of plant height in March, May, and July. After your chastetree is established, apply the same amount of fertilizer once in April and once in June. In the extreme north part of Georgia, winter cold may freeze most of the limbs off a chastetree. It may be necessary to cut it back to 12" tall each spring. Since blooms emerge on new branches, cold damage does not affect the flowering. In south Georgia, you may select one or two upright stems and form your shrub into a small tree.

ADDITIONAL ADVICE FOR CARE

Few insects or diseases attack a healthy chastetree. If a nearby tree grows larger and begins to give it deep shade, it may develop leaf spot.

ADDITIONAL CULTIVARS AND SPECIES

Vitex agnus-castus 'Latifolia' has larger leaves and longer flowers than others of the species. *Vitex agnus-castus* 'Alba' produces white flowers.

x *Cupressocyparis leylandii*

Leyland Cypress

Height: 8'–40' Width: 4'–8'
Fast-growing needled evergreen

Leyland cypress is one of the most attractive fast-growing screen plants in Georgia. Its bluish-green foliage grows densely from near ground level up to the tip. The plant itself is strongly columnar: even at a height of 40' it will be only 8' wide at the base. Although common in Georgia, Leyland cypress is a hybrid which originated in Wales. Its parents are members of the cypress and the falsecypress families. Around 1890, an amateur botanist recognized that six seedlings found near a cypress tree did not exactly resemble their parent. His brother-in-law, a Mr. Leyland, took the seedlings to his property nearby, where their growth and appearance greatly excited the horticultural community. The rooted cuttings have been sold throughout the world. Leyland cypress has been widely used as a replacement for red tip photinia shrubs. Growing conditions in Georgia promote large Leyland cypress trees. These same growing conditions and the popularity of this plant contain the potential to be its downfall (see below).

WHEN TO PLANT

Plant in fall or spring. If the chosen site is windy, spring planting is better: the foliage is apt to become dried out during the winter when roots are not able to supply moisture to the green foliage.

WHERE TO PLANT

As a screen or hedge, Leyland cypress has few equals. In full sun it will grow densely, but in shade the foliage tends to be more loose and open. If you need a screen plant in shade, either plant large (6' to 8') plants or use a hemlock instead. Plant container-grown plants 4' apart. It is a good idea to have a nearby source of water for summer irrigation.

HOW TO PLANT

For a chance at long life, it is imperative that Leyland cypress be planted in excellent soil conditions. For even a one-gallon plant, dig a hole 5′ wide and 12″ deep. If you are planting a hedge, simply dig a 5′-wide planting bed the length you intend the hedge to be. There is no need to add soil conditioner if the earth is thoroughly broken up. Place the root ball in the proper spot and fill around it with soil. Pack the ground around the roots and water very well.

CARE AND MAINTENANCE

Without fertilizer, Leyland cypress grows fast. With fertilizer, it grows even faster. It is probably better for the shrub to receive minimal fertilizer as it grows. Apply 1 tablespoon of 10–10–10 per foot of plant height in March, June, and August until it reaches the height you prefer. Leyland cypress can be pruned to any height that you can maintain with yearly trimming. It is difficult, but possible, to shorten a 10′ shrub to a 6′ hedge. The top will recover its oval shape in just a few years. Watering is of key importance for Leyland cypress in the summer. The roots must not be allowed to dry out in the summer heat.

ADDITIONAL ADVICE FOR CARE

Leyland cypress is susceptible to a disease called bot canker against which there is little defense. This disease infects individual branches and moves in the sap to the trunk. Death is inevitable if the trunk is infected. If you see brownish-red, dying branches, prune them out immediately, going back 6″ into the green part of the branch.

ADDITIONAL CULTIVARS AND SPECIES

x *Cupressocyparis leylandii* 'Haggerston Gray' has green foliage with a slightly gray cast. x *Cupressocyparis leylandii* 'Castlewellan' has golden-yellow foliage.

CHAPTER EIGHT

Trees

*He that planteth a tree is a servant of God. He provideth a
kindness for many generations, and faces that he hath not
seen shall bless him.*

—Henry van Dyke

*T*HE HOMES THAT BABY BOOMERS BOUGHT several years
ago have been decorated more than once inside. Curtains have
been hung and rehung. Rooms have been painted and repainted.
Furniture has been bought, used, and given to charity. All this may
have gone on inside a home while the outside landscape looks the
same as it did a decade ago.

Many have realized that it is just as creative and enjoyable to
decorate the outdoors as it is indoors. It is trendy these days to talk
about garden *rooms*. Instead of opening the front door and walking
onto a one-color, two-dimensional lawn, homeowners have discovered the excitement of walking into an outdoor room with colors
and textures that change every day and every season. With good
planning, a landscape's yearly change in appearance can happen
without discarding the old decorations. It's as if your furniture and
curtains never need replacing!

Step back from your landscape and think of it as an outdoor
room. The trunks of tall trees form the contours of the walls, and
their limbs and leaves contribute a light-filled green ceiling. The
smaller, flowering trees supply the paintings that hang on the walls.

A healthy tree enhances your outdoor room, while an unhealthy
one degrades it. Here are some guidelines for growing healthy trees.

PLANTING
*"Planting a tree is simple. Just dig a hole and stuff the roots in it the way
our parents did . . . right?"*

Wrong! Some of the most significant research on tree planting has been done in just the last twenty years. Scientists have tested whether organic matter added to the planting hole makes any difference in the health of the tree. They have determined if pruning the branches off a small tree will help bring it in balance with the balled and burlapped roots. Researchers have determined the seasons a tree really needs nutrients and the times when fertilizing is just a waste of time. Here are some of their conclusions:

Adding organic matter to the planting hole makes no difference. In fact, if amendments are added, the tree roots may decide to remain within the planting hole (where they are vulnerable to drought) and never explore the surrounding soil. Roots *will* move into soil that contains lots of oxygen, so the best recommendation is to dig a hole *wide* rather than deep, pulverizing the soil thoroughly.

The branch tips on a small tree produce plant hormones that direct the growth of roots. If you prune a tree to compensate for lost roots, the tree cannot tell the roots to begin growing. Don't prune a new tree for a year after planting except to remove damaged limbs or to correct its shape.

Roots need lots of calcium and phosphorus to grow well. But spreading lime and fertilizer on top of the soil after a tree is planted is futile, because the nutrients dissolve into the root zone very slowly. Add lime and phosphorus to the earth as you shovel it back into the hole. The roots will be able to use the nutrients immediately.

PRUNING

We have a natural instinct to avoid pruning a plant. *"If I cut off that limb, the tree will bleed to death and die, just as I would if I lost an arm!"*

This thought is understandable, but it is mistaken. Very rarely does pruning do any permanent damage. Even trees that are pruned at the "wrong" time will take little notice of this mistake. The following rules can guide you through almost every pruning situation.

WHAT:	WHEN:
Removing major limbs	Any time from December through February
Light pruning, flowering trees	During the two months after the flowers have disappeared
Light pruning, other trees	Any time, but don't remove more than 1/4 of the total foliage

WHAT:	HOW:
Large limbs	Look for the collar of bark that surrounds the base of the limb. Make your first cut underneath the limb and 12" from the trunk. Make the second cut on the top of the limb, above the first cut. The limb will fall, leaving a 12" stub. Make final cut 1/8" outside the bark collar, leaving a large "bump" on the trunk.
Small limbs	Make cut 1/8" beyond a limb you intend to leave on the tree.

Wound dressings?

Unlike animals, plants don't heal, they seal. Once you make a cut, the tree will seal off the damaged area internally. Tar smeared over a cut will dry out and crack eventually, making a fabulous home for boring insects and diseases. Use your tar to repair your roof!

Watering

It is a myth that trees have long tap roots that can reach underground water sources. In fact, most of a tree's roots are within twelve inches of the soil surface. Two weeks of drought and high temperatures in the summer will dry the soil and kill small roots. A tree may take years to recover from a prolonged period without water. The best way to insure the health of your trees is to water them deeply in the summer. Buy a soaker hose and an inexpensive water timer. When daytime temperatures rise above 90 degrees and no rainfall is expected, water according to these calculations:

DISTANCE FROM TRUNK TO BRANCH TIPS	GALLONS PER WEEK
1' to 5'	8
5' to 10'	60
10' to 20'	200
20' to 35'	750
35' to 50'	1000

Acer barbatum

Florida Maple

Height: 20'–25' Width: 20'–25'
Deciduous shade tree

Many gardeners are not familiar with Florida maple, but it is a good tree to know. It is similar to Acer saccharum, *the sugar maple, but it is smaller and grows much better in the sweltering Georgia heat. While sugar maples grown south of Macon down to the Florida state line will suffer during the summer, a Florida maple thrives on mountainsides and in swamps from Virginia to north Florida. The fall color of a Florida maple is not quite as brilliant as that of a sugar maple, but it is a bright yellow that most people find pleasing. When grown in the open, a Florida maple's trunk will be short and its limbs will naturally form a graceful oval above it. Maples belong to the genus* Acer, *which means "hard" or "sharp." The Romans used maple wood for their pikes and lances because of its strength and light weight.*

WHEN TO PLANT

Florida maple can be purchased in a container or with roots balled and burlapped. Try to plant in mid-autumn, while the earth is still warm, or in early spring, just before the earth becomes warm. Midsummer is a terrible time to plant, as the leaves require more moisture than the roots can possibly supply when the weather is hot, and leaf scorch will result.

WHERE TO PLANT

Plant in full sun or in light shade. Do not plant a maple where the roots cannot spread out in all directions. Florida maple is sometimes affected by air pollution, so do not plant it near a busy street.

HOW TO PLANT

The planting hole for a Florida maple should be at least 3 times and preferably 5 times as large as the tree root ball, though it need be no deeper than the depth of the root ball. Research has shown no benefit from adding soil conditioner to the earth you'll shovel back into the hole unless your tree will be part of a larger bed. It is smart, however, to add 1 cup of lime per foot of hole diameter and 1 table-spoon of 0–46–0 fertilizer per foot of hole diameter. Once the root ball is in place, cut away all of the visible burlap, twine, or wire. Fill the hole with soil and water thoroughly. Spread a 2"-thick layer of pine straw or wood chips over the entire planting area.

CARE AND MAINTENANCE

While your maple tree is young, small amounts of fertilizer applied regularly will help it grow. Measure the thickness of the trunk 4' from the ground. Apply 1 cup of 10–10–10 fertilizer per inch of thickness in March, May, and September. Sprinkle the fertilizer all the way out under the branches. Once the tree is mature, little fertil-izer is needed. If summer temperatures rise above 95 degrees, give the tree a heavy watering each week. Light pruning can be done at any time, while major limb pruning should be done in January. If the tree needs support, a stake 18" on either side of the trunk will keep it upright for a year.

ADDITIONAL ADVICE FOR CARE

Japanese beetles sometimes chew on Florida maple leaves. Their damage is not noticeable except on young trees. Call your local Extension office to find out about appropriate controls. Leaf scorch or sun scald may affect young trees if they are not regularly watered for the first year.

ADDITIONAL CULTIVARS AND SPECIES

In an argument that may be of interest only to scientists, some main-tain the Florida maple is just a smaller variety of sugar maple. Whether this is true or not, Florida maple is a fine tree for most parts of Georgia.

Acer griseum

Paperbark Maple

Height: 15'–30' Width: 10'–20'
Deciduous shade tree

Two Georgia trees are commonly appreciated for their peeling bark: Betula
nigra *'Heritage' river birch and* Lagerstroemia indica *'Natchez' crapemyrtle. A third should be added to this group: the paperbark maple. Its bark
may be the most attractive of them all. The young trunk and stems of a
paperbark maple are a rich reddish-brown color. As the trunk and the major
limbs age, the bark becomes lighter in color, and it begins to peel back from
the stem. The gray-red color of the thin sheets of peeling bark contrasts
wonderfully with the polished cinnamon-red stem underneath. The rounded
and open appearance of a paperbark maple makes it noticeable at a distance.
After a snowfall, be sure to take photographs of the tree against the snow. If
you want to try planting other trees with interesting bark, look for Korean
Stewartia* (Stewartia koreana*), Tall Stewartia* (Stewartia monadelpha*),
and Lacebark Pine* (Pinus bungeana*). They may be difficult to find, but
they are worth the search.*

WHEN TO PLANT

Though you will not find this tree in every retail nursery, it can
be found in Georgia. Plant balled and burlapped trees in the fall.
Container-grown trees may be planted any time. Paperbark maple
grows slowly, so purchase the largest specimen you can afford.

WHERE TO PLANT

Paperbark maple is not a large tree, so it can be planted near
sidewalks and driveways where the bark can be appreciated by
passersby. Try to plant it in front of a solid, light color such as a
blank wall or a rolling lawn of Bermuda grass. In winter, the light
brown dormant Bermuda grass will contrast with the bark. To
achieve a similar effect in a small sunny space, plant maiden grass
(*Miscanthus sinensis*) nearby.

How to Plant

The tree planting hole should be at least 3 times and preferably 5 times as large as the tree root ball, though it need be no deeper than the depth of the root ball. Research has shown there is no benefit from adding soil conditioner to the earth you'll shovel back into the hole unless your tree will be part of a larger bed. It is smart, however, to add 1 cup of lime per foot of hole diameter and 1 tablespoon of 0–46–0 fertilizer per foot of hole diameter. Once the root ball is in place, cut away all of the visible burlap, twine, or wire. Fill the hole with soil and water thoroughly. Spread a 2" layer of pine straw or wood chips over the entire planting area.

Care and Maintenance

Small amounts of fertilizer applied regularly will help a young elm grow throughout the summer. Measure the thickness of the trunk 4' from the ground. Apply 1 cup of 10–10–10 per inch of thickness in March, May, and September. Once the tree becomes mature, little fertilizer is needed. If summer temperatures rise above 95 degrees, water the tree heavily each week. Light pruning may be done at any time. If you need to remove a major limb, do it in January. If the tree needs support, a stake 18" from either side of the trunk will keep it upright.

Additional Advice for Care

Paperback maple attracts no serious pests. An occasional caterpillar may chew on the leaves, but caterpillars are easy to control. Call your local Extension office for information on controlling these pests.

Additional Cultivars and Species

There are no known superior selections of paperbark maple. This plant will hybridize with other maples that have three leaflets, and the seedlings will exhibit characteristics of both parents. Breeding an improved paperbark maple could be a fine challenge for gardeners who enjoy exploring unusual plants.

Japanese Maple

Height: 2'–20' Width: 4'–20'
Deciduous tree

Thousands of years of cultivation and selection have resulted in the existence of literally hundreds of attractive Japanese maple cultivars. Leaf color ranges from bright red-purple to deep green. Some consider the leaf shape to be the most interesting part of the tree. Leaves can have broad, rounded lobes or finely divided, almost "ferny," foliage. Japanese maples can produce wonderful fall leaf color, but colors may not be as bright in the warmer parts of Georgia as in colder climates. There is a Japanese maple for almost any landscape. Smaller varieties such as 'Crimson Queen' and 'Beni Hime' can be used near a home's foundation. The taller ones are excellent specimen trees that draw a visitor's eye to their presence in a landscape. Foliage shape can be chosen to blend or to contrast with surrounding shrubbery. This maple is attractive when grown in a container. Its overall size will be smaller than when it is planted outdoors, but small size is desirable for a tree that will occupy a patio corner or grace an entranceway.

WHEN TO PLANT

Plant in fall just after the weather has begun to turn cool. The still-warm soil will encourage root growth before winter. If the roots are balled and burlapped, remove all string and wire around the trunk. After the tree is placed in its hole, use a sharp knife to cut away the burlap as far down as possible. Remove tree stakes after one year.

WHERE TO PLANT

Find a spot that receives direct morning sun but is shady in the afternoon. The intermittent shade of nearby large trees is desirable on hot afternoons. Do not plant in the middle of a lawn with no shelter from the wind. The east or north side of a home is usually ideal.

HOW TO PLANT

Japanese maple roots are shallow, but they quickly explore surrounding soil. For this reason, a planting hole should be at least 3

ZONE
6,7,8

times as large as the root ball: it is more important that the hole be wide than it be deep. If the planting spot is lower than the surrounding landscape, mix 4 cubic feet of topsoil with the soil you remove from the hole. Then shovel the soil back around the root ball, forming a mound in which to plant the tree. Spread mulch 1" to 2" deep around the tree, at least as far out as the branches will spread. If the tree is planted in spring, plan to provide it with plenty of water in the summer. A drought in July will almost certainly result in scorched leaves.

CARE AND MAINTENANCE

Japanese maples usually grow gracefully without much pruning. Long, vigorous sprouts should be removed or shortened back to side branches in January. Minor pruning can be done at any time. Japanese maples are not heavy feeders. Fertilize once in April with $1/16$ cup of 10–10–10 for every foot of height. Regular watering in summer is a must. Mulching with wood chips or pine straw is the easiest way to conserve moisture and to keep the roots cool.

ADDITIONAL ADVICE FOR CARE

The most common problem with Japanese maples is the appearance of scorched leaves in midsummer. The edges of the leaves first turn yellow, then brown and dry. This is a sign that not enough water is getting to the leaves. Determine whether the problem is lack of water in the ground or compaction around the plant, and correct the condition.

ADDITIONAL CULTIVARS AND SPECIES

Acer palmatum 'Atropurpureum' has wonderfully red leaves in the spring, but the color usually fades to a dark green in summer. *Acer p.* 'Bloodgood' has a crimson spring color which darkens to a deep red in summer. *Acer p.* 'Beni Hime' has miniature leaves and a twiggy branch structure. Any of the smaller 'Dissectum' varieties makes a nice texture variation in the landscape.

Acer rubrum

Red Maple

Height: 40′–60′ Width: 30′–50′
Deciduous tree

Red maples mark the beginning of spring. Their red flowers emerge in clusters along the branches in mid-February before their leaves appear. Red maples also mark the end of the growing season with fiery red leaves that stand out brilliantly against the yellow leaves of tulip poplars and the green needles of pine trees. A red maple is an excellent choice for a shade tree. It grows fast and does not have the brittle wood or weak limb structure of a silver maple. It can tolerate spots both wet and dry. The winged seeds are fascinating to children as they "helicopter" down from the branches in October, and they provide an important part of the fall diet of forest birds and small mammals.

WHEN TO PLANT

Red maple trees are easy to plant, whether balled and burlapped or grown in containers. Fall planting allows plenty of time for the roots to establish themselves, but an early spring planting may be just as successful as a fall one. From late fall to early spring, trees less than 6′ tall can be dug from the woods and transplanted into your yard.

WHERE TO PLANT

Since they do not grow as tall as pines, oaks, or poplars, red maples are excellent specimen and shade trees. The roots will adapt to wet conditions by running along the surface of the ground, so avoid planting one near a sidewalk or drive. A red maple provides excellent shade for the south or west side of a house. Windows will be protected from the glare of summer, but warm sunshine can enter during the winter.

HOW TO PLANT

It is important to allow plenty of room for the red maple's roots to grow. Dig a hole 6′ wide and 12″ deep, and thoroughly break up the soil. Set the root ball in the center of the hole. The top of the ball should be level with, or a little higher than, the undisturbed soil around the edges of the hole. If planting in spring, form a raised "doughnut" of soil around the outer edge of the root ball. This will ensure a concentration of water in the root ball for the first few months. After a year, the "doughnut" can be raked flat. Spread a 2" layer of wood chip mulch over the entire planting hole to keep the soil cool in summer and to protect the tree from drought.

CARE AND MAINTENANCE

Do not fertilize until the tree has been in the ground for three months. $1/8$ cup of 10–10–10 fertilizer applied in spring, summer, and fall should be sufficient for a young tree. A mature tree will probably not require fertilizer. Examine the form of the tree at planting time and perform some corrective pruning if necessary. Remove or head back limbs that try to "head for the sky." A desirable form offers 3 or 4 main limbs evenly spaced around the trunk, each 3' to 5' from the ground. Do not cut the growing tip of the main trunk, as weak limbs may sprout and crash to the ground during a wind storm decades in the future.

ADDITIONAL ADVICE FOR CARE

Red maples attract few serious pests, but two pests must be noted. Purple eye leaf spot disease will result in the appearance of groups of purple "eyes" on leaves. Leaf galls caused by insects may cause thousands of warty bumps on leaf surfaces. Neither can be prevented, but neither causes a decline in tree health.

ADDITIONAL CULTIVARS AND SPECIES

The common red maple does not always have a pretty red fall color. For beautiful color in fall, *Acer rubrum* 'Red Sunset' is a good selection. *Acer r.* 'October Glory' is well formed and has excellent fall color as well. *Acer r.* 'Columnare' grows much narrower than other red maples, almost like a Bradford pear.

Betula nigra

River Birch

Height: 20'–50' Spread: 20'–30'
Deciduous shade tree

A river birch is an excellent specimen tree when planted in the center of a landscape. It is small in comparison to oak and pine trees. Three single-trunked birches planted in a group make a better statement than one birch planted by itself. On the other hand, for a small lot you may prefer a multi-stemmed single plant. A river birch tolerates areas that do not drain well, but after a few years of growth it can also stand considerable dryness. The grayish-white bark peels away from the trunk in paper-thin layers. The brown bark revealed underneath adds to the tree's attractiveness in the winter. A river birch is much more "informal" than a dogwood or white pine. The branches are vigorous but do not arise symmetrically from the trunk. River birch is the only member of the **Betula** *family which can stand the heat of Georgia summers. This species is found in swamps and along streams throughout much of the Southeast. The branches bear small, brown, cone-shaped "catkins," the reproductive parts of the tree, in early spring.*

WHEN TO PLANT

Plant in fall after the weather has begun to turn cool. The still-warm soil will encourage root growth before winter. If the roots are balled and burlapped, remove all string and wire around the trunk. Use a sharp knife to cut away the burlap as far down as possible after the tree has been initially placed in its hole.

WHERE TO PLANT

Because it grows so upright, river birch is often seen planted near the corner of an expensive, newly constructed home. This will be recognized as a big mistake after several years when the limbs begin to batter the wall and nearby windows! A river birch tolerates wet spots and is the perfect choice for shading a gazebo that overlooks a backyard koi pond.

How to Plant

The most important predictor of success in growing a river birch is the width of the planting hole. It should be at least 3 times and preferably 5 times as big as the tree root ball. It need be no deeper than the depth of the root ball. Unless your tree will be part of a larger bed, research has shown no benefit from adding soil conditioner to the earth you'll shovel back into the hole. It is smart, however, to add 1 cup of lime per foot of hole diameter and 1 tablespoon of 0–46–0 fertilizer per foot of hole diameter. Fill the hole with soil and water thoroughly. Spread a 2" thick layer of pine straw or wood chips over the entire planting area.

Care and Maintenance

If planted correctly, a river birch will not suffer in full sun. But if the roots do not have room to expand, a dry summer month will cause substantial leaf drop. This is not a major problem, even if half the leaves fall. If you are unable to irrigate, a wide layer of mulch around the tree will help conserve moisture. Fertilize in March and in midsummer with 10–10–10. Apply 1/8 cup for every foot of height each time you fertilize until the tree reaches full height. Pruning is usually not needed after the first few years. To expose its peeling white bark, remove the tree's lower limbs when it grows tall.

Additional Advice for Care

If your birch's leaves are yellow rather than green during the summer, the pH of the soil may be too low. Have the soil tested by your local Extension office and add lime to bring the pH above 6.0. Leaf spot may cause the leaves on common river birches to drop in hot, wet weather, but 'Heritage' river birch is resistant to this problem.

Additional Cultivars and Species

Betula nigra 'Heritage' is an excellent river birch selection. The bark is whiter than regular river birches, and the leaves are dark green. It was discovered on a residential lawn in St. Louis in 1968 by Earl Culley, a local nurseryman there. He received permission to propagate, name, and distribute this selection throughout the country.

Cercis canadensis

Eastern Redbud

Height: 20'–30' Width: 25'–35'
Deciduous tree

The redbud with its heart-shaped leaves stands out beautifully in a land-scape. The bright pink-purple blooms that emerge on bare twigs before almost any other flowering tree are an early herald of spring. As the sum-mer progresses, the tree develops another interesting feature, its seed pods. Redbud is a member of the legume family, the same family that contains soybeans, peanuts, and kudzu. Like these plants, a redbud can collect nitro-gen from the atmosphere and turn it into useful fertilizer around its roots. The appearance of its seed pods is proof of its bean family membership. The seeds are eaten by birds and forest animals. Adventurous gardeners report that the flowers are quite tasty when added to salads, and that the seed pods can be made into fritters.

WHEN TO PLANT

Redbud can be purchased in a container or with its roots balled and burlapped. Try to plant in mid-autumn, while the earth is still warm, or in early spring, just before the earth becomes warm. Midsummer is a terrible time to plant, as redbud leaves need more moisture than the roots can possibly supply at this time of year.

WHERE TO PLANT

Redbuds will grow in full sun as well as in light shade. In full sun, the limbs will grow together densely; when grown in shade, the tree's form is loose and open. The trees seem to do best when plant-ed near the eastern sides of taller trees. The resulting afternoon shade protects a redbud's leaves from the mid-August "droops."

HOW TO PLANT

A redbud will not do well in poorly drained soil. Dig a hole 3 times as large as the root ball of the tree. Do not mix anything with the

ZONE
6,7,8

TREES

soil; simply pulverize the clods of earth in the hole with a spade. If the planting spot is lower than the surrounding landscape, add 4 cubic feet of topsoil to the planting hole to make a mound that will keep the roots above standing water. Place the top of the root ball level with or a little below the earth surrounding it. Water heavily to settle the soil. A month later, inspect the tree to see if the soil has settled around the root ball, exposing the top surface of the ball. If this has happened, add more soil.

CARE AND MAINTENANCE

Fertilize twice each year with 10–10–10 fertilizer, in spring after the leaves have fully opened, and again in late June. Use 1/8 cup of fertilizer for every foot of plant height. After the tree has reached its desired height, fertilize it only in the spring. A redbud will usually grow into a well-shaped tree with little pruning. It does not grow to a great height, so it is desirable when multiple trunks appear. Two or three strong, upright limbs growing out in different directions from the main trunk will branch and rebranch as directed by nature.

ADDITIONAL ADVICE FOR CARE

The redbud's pods provide food for wildlife, but they are messy when they fall. Do not plant a redbud close to a driveway, sidewalk, or patio unless you enjoy slipping and sliding!

ADDITIONAL CULTIVARS AND SPECIES

Cercis canadensis 'Alba' displays blooms that are white instead of the intense pink-purple of most redbuds. *Cercis canadensis* 'Forest Pansy' has intensely purple leaves in spring that fade to a dark green in summer. *Cercis canadensis* 'Silver Cloud' displays irregular variegations on its leaves. It grows much better in shade than in full sun.

Chionanthus virginicus

Fringe Tree

Grancy Gray-beard

Height: 10'–15' Width: 8'–10'
Deciduous flowering tree

Do you have a memory of an older friend or relative with a grizzled gray beard? If you can imagine this beard made of dark green leaves flecked with pure white flowers instead of dark hair flecked with lots of gray, you will have a vision of the fringe tree—also known as the Grancy gray-beard. This tree's white flowers are held in masses just beyond its leaves; its thin, elongated flower petals hang from tiny, threadlike stems. The contrast of the white flowers against the new, vibrant green leaves is striking. Because they bloom in May, fringe tree flowers are a good followup to the dogwood blooms of early spring. When a slight breeze appears, the whole tree will start shaking, looking almost like a disco mirror ball in your spring landscape. The flowers are slightly fragrant, and some plants seem to give off more perfume than others. Fringe tree grows in the wild from New Jersey to Florida. It was found in the catalog of America's earliest nurseryman, John Bartram, and was cultivated at Thomas Jefferson's Monticello.

WHEN TO PLANT

Fringe tree is usually purchased with the roots balled and burlapped. Try to plant in mid-autumn, while the earth is still warm, or in early spring, just before the earth becomes warm.

WHERE TO PLANT

Fringe tree is found in the wild along stream banks or near swamps, but it can be planted in full sunshine without problems. It seems to be comfortable growing in relatively dry places as long as water is supplied a few times during the summer.

How to Plant

The most important predictor of planting success is the width
of the planting hole. It should be at least 3 times and preferably 5
five times as large as the root ball, though it need be no deeper than
the depth of the root ball. Research has shown there is no benefit
from adding soil conditioner to the earth unless your tree will be
part of a larger bed. It is smart, however, to add 1 cup of lime per
foot of hole diameter and 1 tablespoon of 0–46–0 fertilizer per foot
of hole diameter. Once the root ball is in place, cut away all of the
visible burlap, twine, or wire. Fill the hole with soil, then water
thoroughly. Spread a 2" layer of pine straw or wood chips over the
entire planting area.

Care and Maintenance

While a fringe tree is still young, small amounts of fertilizer applied
regularly will help it grow throughout the summer. Measure the
thickness of the trunk 2' from the ground. Apply 1 cup of 10–10–10
fertilizer per inch of thickness in March, May, and September. Once
the tree is mature, little fertilizer is needed. If summer temperatures
rise above 95 degrees, give the tree a heavy watering each week.
Light pruning may be done at any time. Fringe tree is variable in its
form. Some plants tend to be large bushes and some grow immediately into small trees. Decide early which form you want and prune
accordingly.

Additional Advice for Care

One reason that fringe tree is not grown more often is that cuttings
are sometimes difficult to root and seeds are almost impossible to
germinate. As propagation scientists develop more propagation
tricks, you will see this attractive tree become more popular.

Additional Cultivars and Species

No cultivars are generally available. It is interesting to know that the
scientific name for fringe tree, *Chionanthus*, comes from the Greek
words *chion* (snow) and *anthos* (flower). Watch your tree in May to
see if *snowflower* could be another common name for this tree.

Cornus florida

Flowering Dogwood

Height: 10'–20' Width: 10'–25'
Deciduous flowering tree

Is there any tree more strongly associated with spring in Georgia than the flowering dogwood? In mid-April when azaleas and dogwoods are at their peak, out-of-state visitors have been known to call their families and announce that they'd better start packing for a move to Georgia! Dogwoods grow wild in every part of Georgia, usually as understory trees beneath towering pines and hardwoods. Their white flower bracts glow in the April gloom along highways and roads from the mountains to the coast. The bright red berries that follow the flowers are quite attractive in September while the leaves are still on the tree. They are attractive to squirrels as well, who drop them, half-eaten, onto patios and sidewalks. Seeds that survive the squirrels are widely scattered by birds and will grow wherever conditions are favorable. Although a small dogwood can be transplanted out of the woods, it may never equal the beauty of a superior selection. Nursery trees labeled "White Dogwood" are usually inferior.

WHEN TO PLANT

A dogwood is usually purchased with the roots balled and burlapped. Try to plant in mid-autumn, while the earth is still warm, or in early spring, when the earth will soon become warm. Midsummer is a terrible time to plant, even from a container. The leaves require more moisture than the roots can possibly supply at this time of year.

WHERE TO PLANT

It is true that a dogwood may find a way to prosper in full sunshine, but placing one in the heat is asking for trouble. The best site is on the eastern or northern side of larger trees or a house so there will be shelter from the hot sun. It is common to plant azaleas near dogwoods, but also try fothergilla (*Fothergilla gardenii*) or witchhazel (*Hamamelis x intermedia*) as dogwood companions.

ZONE
6,7,8

HOW TO PLANT

The tree planting hole should be at least 3 times and preferably 5 times as large as the tree root ball, though it need be no deeper than the depth of the root ball. Research has shown there is no benefit from adding soil conditioner to the earth you'll shovel back into the hole unless your tree will be part of a larger bed. It is smart, however, to add 1 cup of lime per foot of hole diameter and 1 tablespoon of 0–46–0 fertilizer per foot of hole diameter. Once the root ball is in place, cut away all of the visible burlap, twine, or wire. Fill the hole with soil and water thoroughly. Spread a 2″ layer of pine straw or wood chips over the entire planting area.

CARE AND MAINTENANCE

Small amounts of fertilizer applied regularly will help a young dogwood grow throughout the summer. Measure the thickness of the trunk 3' from the ground. Apply 1 cup of 10–10–10 per inch of thickness in March, May, and September. Once the tree becomes mature, little fertilizer will be needed. If summer temperatures rise above 95 degrees, water the tree heavily each week. Light pruning may be done at any time. If you need to remove a major limb, do it in January. If the tree needs support, a stake 18″ from either side of the trunk will keep it upright. Stake the trunk in a way that will permit it to slightly sway.

ADDITIONAL ADVICE FOR CARE

Spot anthracnose is a leaf disease that causes small purple spots on the leaves and flowers in April. Dogwood discula is a serious disease that has killed many dogwoods along the Eastern coast. Both diseases can be controlled with fungicide, but the best way to prevent disease is to keep the tree well-watered in summer.

ADDITIONAL CULTIVARS AND SPECIES

Cornus florida 'Cloud 9' flowers profusely when young. *Cornus florida* 'Green Glow' has green leaves splotched with lighter green. *Cornus florida* 'Cherokee Chief' has deep red flower bracts.

Cornus kousa

Korean Dogwood

Height: 10′–20′ Width: 10′–20′
Deciduous flowering tree

Gardeners do a double-take when they see a dogwood still in bloom in May. At second glance they may recognize it as a Korean dogwood, a tree that blooms weeks later than the common dogwood. Unlike the common dogwood, the Korean dogwood comes into its glory after its leaves have emerged. The leaves of a Korean dogwood are more slender than those on a common dogwood, and they appear to be a deeper green. The leaf tips are more pointed than the tips of a Florida dogwood. While the seeds of a common dogwood are individuals borne in a loose cluster, those of a Korean dogwood are smaller and grow tightly together. In fall, the seed may look like a red raspberry rising above the branch tip. You might be tempted to taste the fruit, but Dr. Michael Dirr, Professor of Horticulture at the University of Georgia, reports that he honestly prefers the taste of a chocolate bar to that of a Korean dogwood seed!

WHEN TO PLANT

A dogwood is usually purchased with the roots balled and burlapped. Try to plant in mid-autumn, while the earth is still warm, or in early spring, when the earth will soon become warm. Midsummer is a terrible time to plant, even from a container. Dogwood leaves require more moisture than its roots can possibly supply in midsummer.

WHERE TO PLANT

Korean dogwood can tolerate more sunshine than can a common dogwood. Avoid the temptation, however, to place it in full sunshine. With some afternoon shade, the tree's form will grow open and upright. As the tree ages and becomes more rounded, you'll appreciate its contribution to a mixed shrub border.

HOW TO PLANT

The tree planting hole should be at least 3 times and preferably 5 times as large as the tree root ball, though it need be no deeper than the depth of the root ball. Research has shown there is no benefit from adding soil conditioner to the earth you'll shovel back into the hole unless your tree will be part of a larger bed. It is smart, however, to add 1 cup of lime per foot of hole diameter and 1 tablespoon of 0–46–0 fertilizer per foot of hole diameter. Once the root ball is in place, cut away all of the visible burlap, twine, or wire. Fill the hole with soil and water thoroughly. Spread a 2" layer of pine straw or wood chips over the entire planting area.

CARE AND MAINTENANCE

Small amounts of fertilizer applied regularly will help a young tree grow throughout the summer. Measure the thickness of the trunk 4' from the ground. Apply 1 cup of 10–10–10 per inch of thickness in March, May, and September. Once the tree becomes mature, little fertilizer will be needed. If summer temperatures rise above 95 degrees, water the tree heavily each week. Light pruning may be done at any time. If you need to remove a major limb, do it in January. If the tree needs support, a stake 18" from either side of the trunk will keep it upright. Stake the trunk in a way that will allow it to slightly sway.

ADDITIONAL ADVICE FOR CARE

Korean dogwood is resistant to the dogwood disease *Discula* that has killed so many flowering dogwoods along the east coast, and it seems to resist dogwood borer as well. But it is no match for "lawn-mower disease"! Keep a wide band of mulch around the trunk so mowers and string trimmers will not come too close.

ADDITIONAL CULTIVARS AND SPECIES

Cornus kousa var. *chinensis* 'Milky Way' has numerous flowers and a bushy form that is nice for smaller landscapes. *Cornus kousa* 'Moonbeam' has flower bracts that can spread up to 8" wide!

Cryptomeria japonica 'Yoshino'

Japanese Cryptomeria

Height: 30'–60' Width: 10'–25'
Evergreen needled tree

It is surprising that Japanese cryptomeria is not more widely planted in Georgia. It is evergreen and thus makes a fine screen. It is tall and symmetrical, making it an impressive specimen tree. It is more narrow than wide, so it can be placed near homes and buildings without fear of eventual encroachment. When the lower limbs are removed, the reddish brown bark on the trunk is very attractive. But even with all of these good traits, cryptomeria is rarely part of a landscape. Many landscapers suspect that the reason is just its name: cryptomeria sounds like a code-breaking tree. More gardeners should break the code and plant this very adaptable tree! One good use for cryptomeria is in the island that divides two lanes of a roadway. Though it would not have the clouds of white flowers that accompany a planting of Bradford pears, it would also not be affected by the limb breakage that is usually a Bradford's destiny.

WHEN TO PLANT
Japanese cryptomeria is usually purchased with the roots balled and burlapped. Try to plant in mid-autumn, while the earth is still warm, or in early spring, when the earth will soon be warm. If planted in the spring, do not put your cryptomeria in a windy spot. In such a site the foliage will scorch and become unattractive.

WHERE TO PLANT
Plant a cryptomeria in full sunshine. In shade it becomes thin and ragged. Cryptomeria could also be used in spots where a Leyland cypress would be too large. When used as a screen, plant two staggered rows with the trees 10' apart.

HOW TO PLANT
The most important predictor of tree planting success is the width of the planting hole. It should be at least 3 times and preferably 5 times

as big as the tree root ball. It need be no deeper than the depth of the root ball. Unless your tree will be part of a larger bed, research has shown no benefit from adding soil conditioner to the earth you'll shovel back into the hole. It is smart, however, to add 1 cup of lime per foot of hole diameter and 1 tablespoon of 0−46−0 fertilizer per foot of hole diameter. Once the root ball is in place, cut away all of the visible burlap, twine, or wire. Fill the hole with soil and water thoroughly. Spread a 2" layer of pine straw or wood chips over the entire planting area.

CARE AND MAINTENANCE

While a tree is still young, small amounts of fertilizer applied regularly will help it grow. Measure the thickness of the trunk 4' from the ground. Apply 1 cup of 10−10−10 fertilizer per inch of thickness in March, May, and September. Sprinkle the fertilizer all the way out under the branches. Once the tree is mature, little fertilizer is needed. If summer temperatures rise above 95 degrees, give the tree a heavy watering each week. Light pruning can be done at any time. To make the foliage more dense, shear off half the length of the new green branch tips in May. If you need to remove lower limbs, do it in January.

ADDITIONAL ADVICE FOR CARE

Bagworms can affect all of the needled evergreens, and Japanese cryptomeria is no exception. These wingless moths devour needles, gluing some to their webbed home for camouflage. Look for 3" long bags of needles hanging from branch tips in August. If you find them on a cryptomeria or any other tree, pick them off and destroy them.

ADDITIONAL CULTIVARS AND SPECIES

One of the best cultivars for Georgia is *Cryptomeria japonica* 'Yoshino.' It is fast growing, has blue-green summer foliage, and will grow strongly in a wide variety of situations.

Ginkgo biloba

Ginkgo

Maidenhair Tree

Height: 40′–70′ Width: 30′–50′
Deciduous shade tree

A view of the bright yellow carpet of fall leaves under a ginkgo tree is a memory that can last a lifetime. Several huge ginkgo trees grow on the University of Georgia campus. They have impressed visitors at autumn football games for decades. A ginkgo tree has an attractive form. The central trunk grows vigorously for 20 years, usually producing small branches that emerge on all sides. This produces a nice conical shape while avoiding the widely spread limbs of oaks or maples. The ginkgo tree is one of our oldest trees. We know from fossil records that it was native to North America and grew here 150 million years ago. But climate changes caused it to die out here in favor of Asian climates. It was reintroduced back here from China in 1784. The malodorous fruit produced by female trees can be cleaned of its flesh, producing a white nut which is eaten in the Orient: 'Ginkgo' means 'silver fruit' in Chinese.

When to Plant

A ginkgo can be purchased as a bare root whip, but is more often found with roots balled and burlapped. Try to plant in mid-autumn, while the earth is still warm, or in early spring just before the earth becomes warm. Always buy from a nursery; if you transplant a seedling sprout from under a tree, you won't know if it is a male or female for many years.

Where to Plant

Plant in full sun for best growth and appearance. The shade cast by a ginkgo is not very dense, so groundcovers and bulbs grow very well beneath the ginkgo. It you plant any upright shrubs or perennials under the branches, these plants will ruin the carpet of gold that comes each autumn.

How to Plant

The tree planting hole should be at least 3 times and preferably 5 times as large as the tree root ball, though it need be no deeper than the depth of the root ball. Research has shown there is no benefit from adding soil conditioner to the earth you'll shovel back into the hole unless your tree will be part of a larger bed. It is smart, however, to add 1 cup of lime per foot of hole diameter and 1 tablespoon of 0–46–0 fertilizer per foot of hole diameter. Once the root ball is in place, cut away all of the visible burlap, twine, or wire. Fill the hole with soil and water thoroughly. Spread a 2″ layer of pine straw or wood chips over the entire planting area.

Care and Maintenance

Small amounts of fertilizer applied regularly will help a young tree grow throughout the summer. Measure the thickness of the trunk 4′ from the ground. Apply 1 cup of 10–10–10 per inch of thickness in March, May, and September. Once the tree becomes mature, little fertilizer is needed. If summer temperatures rise above 95 degrees, water the tree heavily each week. Light pruning may be done at any time. If you need to remove a major limb, do it in January. If the tree needs support, a stake 18″ from either side of the trunk will keep it upright. Stake the trunk in a way that allows it to slightly sway.

Additional Advice for Care

Ginkgo trees can be either male or female. The ripe fruit borne by a female tree has a nauseating smell. Avoid the female tree, buying only from a reputable nursery. If a young tree is damaged, it may send up two competing trunks. If you see this begin to happen, choose the straightest trunk and prune the other one out in January.

Additional Cultivars and Species

Ginkgo biloba 'Autumn Gold' is a symmetrical tree with excellent clear yellow fall color. *Ginkgo biloba* 'Fastigiata' is more columnar than other ginkgos. It is a good tree with which to line a winding parkway.

Koelreuteria spp.

Goldenraintree

Height: 20'–40' Width: 20'–30'
Deciduous flowering tree

Goldenraintree was introduced to the Americas from China before the Revolutionary War, but it is a late arrival in Georgia landscapes. Now that it has been used frequently by the state highway department along Georgia interstates, it will become more common in other places as well. The yellow flowers that cover goldenraintree in June are quite unusual, as are the clusters of papery, lantern-like seed pods that follow the flowers. Goldenraintree is the perfect size for a suburban landscape: it grows relatively fast, but does not grow so large that it will overpower a house. Because it is very attractive, it is desirable to place it in a spot near a flow of pedestrian or automobile traffic. The rosy pink seed capsules of bouganvilla goldenraintree retain enough color to form a wash of color on the sidewalks and pavement when they fall in September. It is said that the ancient Chinese planted a goldenraintree beside a gravesite they wished to reserve for an important statesman.

WHEN TO PLANT

Goldenraintree is usually purchased with its roots balled and burlapped. Try to plant in mid-autumn, while the earth is still warm, or in early spring, when the earth will soon become warm. Midsummer is a terrible time to plant, as the tree's leaves require more moisture than its roots can possibly supply at this time of year.

WHERE TO PLANT

Goldenraintree grows best in full sunshine, but it can tolerate a wide variety of soils and temperatures. Good planting companions include ornamental grasses such as maiden grass (*Miscanthus sinensis* 'Gracillimus') or fountain grass (*Pennisetum alopecuroides*). Loose soil underneath your tree will allow a few tree seedlings to sprout. These seedlings can be dug up in December to share with friends.

How to Plant

The tree planting hole should be at least 3 times and preferably 5 times as large as the tree root ball, though it need be no deeper than the depth of the root ball. Research has shown there is no benefit from adding soil conditioner to the earth you'll shovel back into the hole unless your tree will be part of a larger bed. It is smart, however, to add 1 cup of lime per foot of hole diameter and 1 tablespoon of 0–46–0 fertilizer per foot of hole diameter. Once the root ball is in place, cut away all of the visible burlap, twine, or wire. Fill the hole with soil and water thoroughly. Spread a 2" layer of pine straw or wood chips over the entire planting area.

Care and Maintenance

While a goldenraintree is still young, small amounts of fertilizer applied regularly will help it grow throughout the summer. Measure the thickness of the trunk 4' from the ground. Apply 1 cup of 10–10–10 per inch of thickness in March, May, and September. Once the tree becomes mature, little fertilizer will be needed. If summer temperatures rise above 95 degrees, water the tree heavily each week. This tree has a fairly open form. If you would like to make the leaves and limbs more dense, remove the branch tips each March to force more limbs to sprout. You can stop this kind of pruning after the third year.

Additional Advice for Care

Goldenraintree is attacked by no known pests. For attractive dried arrangements, harvest the pink seed capsules of bouganvilla goldenraintree when they are at their peak. Pour one pound of silica gel into a large plastic bag and hang a large spray of goldenraintree pods in the bag. This quick drying action will keep the color fresh.

Additional Cultivars and Species

The common goldenraintree, *Koelreuteria paniculata*, has brown seed pods. The bouganvilla goldenraintree, *Koelreuteria bipinnata*, displays pink seed pods which persist on the tree for several weeks. Each of these species displays yellow flowers for a few weeks in mid- to late summer.

Liquidambar styraciflua 'Rotundiloba'

Sweetgum

Height: 50'–80' Width: 30'–50'
Deciduous shade tree

Even children recognize the common sweetgum tree. They know from firsthand experience that prickly balls cover the ground beneath: "That's a gumball tree! Don't go barefoot over there!" The five-pointed, star-shaped leaves are another way to quickly identify this fast-growing tree. Sweetgums are not usually planned as part of a formal landscape. Often they are included in a landscape plan simply because they are already in place. They can provide needed shade. Though some do not think of the common sweetgum as a great tree, it should not be considered a weed. A small sweetgum growing in light shade will eventually become larger than most surrounding trees. Liquidambar styraciflua 'Rotundiloba' was discovered in North Carolina in 1930—it is notable because it has no gumballs! As its Latin name indicates, the five lobes on each leaf are round rather than pointed. This shade tree is an excellent candidate for a medium- to large-sized landscape.

WHEN TO PLANT

Common sweetgum is occasionally transplanted from the woods by gardeners looking for instant shade. 'Rotundiloba' can be purchased with the roots balled and burlapped. Try to plant in mid-autumn, while the earth is still warm, or in early spring just before the earth becomes warm.

WHERE TO PLANT

Plant in any sunny spot where you need a medium to large shade tree. If planted near a lawn, show mercy to barefoot children by keeping the turf grass well back from the branch ends. Sweetgum limbs are rather brittle, so the tree should not be planted near your house or deck.

☀	ZONE 6,7,8

HOW TO PLANT

The tree planting hole should be at least 3 times and preferably 5 times as large as the tree root ball, though it need be no deeper than the depth of the root ball. Research has shown there is no benefit from adding soil conditioner to the earth you'll shovel back into the hole unless your tree will be part of a larger bed. It is smart, however, to add 1 cup of lime per foot of hole diameter and 1 tablespoon of 0–46–0 fertilizer per foot of hole diameter. Once the root ball is in place, cut away all of the visible burlap, twine, or wire. Fill the hole with soil and water thoroughly. Spread a 2" layer of pine straw or wood chips over the entire planting area.

CARE AND MAINTENANCE

While the tree is still young, small amounts of fertilizer applied regularly will help it grow throughout the summer. Measure the thickness of the trunk 4' from the ground. Apply 1 cup of 10–10–10 per inch of thickness in March, May, and September. Once the tree becomes mature, little fertilizer will be needed. If summer temperatures rise above 95 degrees, water the tree heavily each week. Light pruning can be done at any time. If you need to remove a major limb, do it in January. If a young tree needs support, a stake 18" from either side of the trunk will keep it upright.

ADDITIONAL ADVICE FOR CARE

A young sweetgum will occasionally send up sprouts from its base. Remove these sprouts as they appear. To help a major limb attach strongly to the trunk, wedge a 1' forked branch between the trunk and a rapidly growing vertical branch. Try to make all branches grow at an angle that is 45 degrees to the main trunk.

ADDITIONAL CULTIVARS AND SPECIES

Liquidambar styraciflua 'Gumball' is a bush form of the common sweetgum tree. It has a rounded top and straight sides and grows to 8' in height.

Magnolia grandiflora

Southern Magnolia

Height: 40'–70' Width: 20'–40'
Evergreen flowering tree

*Only the flowering dogwood may be more strongly associated with the
South than is the magnolia. The magnolia's huge, fragrant white flowers
appear in June. From the 1930s to the 1960s, no high school prom in
Georgia was complete without magnolia flower centerpieces on the tables.
Children appreciate some of the less celebrated properties of a magnolia.
The drooping branches make wonderful secret rooms for sharing secrets and
the branches are spaced perfectly for climbing. The red seeds from the big
seedpods can be strung with needle and thread to make necklaces. For a
creative holiday decoration, mount a large electric star on the end of a 10'
length of rigid electrical conduit. Extend the conduit up through the center
of the magnolia until the star is above the treetop. Tie the conduit to the
trunk and wrap the tree with bright lights. You'll have a huge Christmas
tree that can be seen throughout the neighborhood!*

WHEN TO PLANT

A southern magnolia is usually purchased with the roots balled
and burlapped. Try to plant in mid-autumn, while the earth is still
warm, or in early spring, when the earth will soon become warm.
Midsummer is a terrible time to plant, as the tree's leaves require
more moisture than its roots can possibly supply at this time of year.

WHERE TO PLANT

This tree's glossy green leaves can be a good backdrop for summer-
flowering shrubs like chaste tree (*Vitex agnus-castus*) or smokebush
(*Cotinus coggygria*). But don't expect a common southern magnolia
to stay small. It should be planted well away from your house, as a
nice 15' specimen may eventually become an overpowering monster
that is 50' tall.

How to Plant

The tree planting hole should be at least 3 times and preferably 5 times as large as the tree root ball, though it need be no deeper than the depth of the root ball. Research has shown there is no benefit from adding soil conditioner to the earth you'll shovel back into the hole unless your tree will be part of a larger bed. It is smart, however, to add 1 cup of lime per foot of hole diameter and 1 tablespoon of 0–46–0 fertilizer per foot of hole diameter. Once the root ball is in place, cut away all of the visible burlap, twine, or wire. Fill the hole with soil and water thoroughly. Spread a 2" layer of pine straw or wood chips over the entire planting area.

Care and Maintenance

Small amounts of fertilizer applied regularly will help a young tree grow throughout the summer. Measure the thickness of the trunk 4' from the ground. Apply 1 cup of 10–10–10 per inch of thickness in March, May, and September. Once the tree becomes mature, little fertilizer will be needed. Some people like to remove lower limbs, but leaving these limbs on the tree serves the purpose of hiding the mess of each year's fallen leaves.

Additional Advice for Care

A huge magnolia may occasionally frustrate a homeowner when it fails to produce many flowers. This magnolia is almost always a tree that has been transplanted from the woods; it is much better to purchase an excellent nursery specimen. The magnolia's leathery leaves and tough seed cones are difficult for a lawnmower to shred, and they decompose so slowly that they should not be added to a compost pile.

Additional Cultivars and Species

There are several excellent cultivars of magnolia. *Magnolia g.* 'Claudia Wannamaker' is commonly available. *Magnolia g.* 'Bracken's Brown Beauty' displays rather small leaves that grow densely on the tree. The best compact tree is *Magnolia g.* 'Little Gem.' It begins to flower the first year, and it only grows 10' to 20' tall.

Saucer Magnolia and Star Magnolia

Saucer magnolia: Height: 20'–30' Width: 15'–25'
Star magnolia: Height: 10'–20' Width: 10'–15'

The saucer magnolia and star magnolia are plants loved by Georgia garden gamblers. Their blooms appear very early in the spring, and if gardeners are lucky, the blooms can be enjoyed for several days. But if the gardeners do not rub their lucky shovels, unexpected temperatures below 32 degrees will turn the flowers to gelatinous brown mush overnight. Saucer magnolia (Magnolia x soulangiana) has large 3" to 4" flowers that are usually a light pinkish white inside and a darker pink or purple color on the outside. Star magnolia (Magnolia stellata) is a large shrub, but it can be pruned into a small tree shape. The 3" blooms are pure white and slightly fragrant. Either plant can be quite a conversation piece in February, when no other large plant is in bloom. In years when Mother Nature is cold and cruel, gardeners lament the magnolia's untimely passing.

WHEN TO PLANT

Both magnolias will bloom when they are still young. You may succumb to the beauty of a magnolia flowering in the nursery and find yourself tempted to plant it immediately after you have purchased it. Instead of tempting fate, keep your tree in its pot for a few weeks until its blooms are gone and freezing is not a danger, and then plant it.

WHERE TO PLANT

Plant your magnolias in full sunshine. To avoid damage when temperatures are just above freezing on a windy February night, find a spot that is sheltered from early spring gusts. Either plant can be used as a solitary specimen tree or planted with others in a row to line a street.

How to Plant

The tree planting hole should be at least 3 times and preferably 5 times as large as the tree root ball, though it need be no deeper than the depth of the root ball. Research has shown there is no benefit from adding soil conditioner to the earth you'll shovel back into the hole unless your tree will be part of a larger bed. It is smart, however, to add 1 cup of lime per foot of hole diameter and 1 tablespoon of 0–46–0 fertilizer per foot of hole diameter. Magnolia roots are thick and tough. Try to unwind them a little before placing them in the planting hole. Fill the hole with soil and then water thoroughly.

Care and Maintenance

While the tree is still young, small amounts of fertilizer applied regularly will help it grow throughout the summer. Measure the thickness of the trunk 4' from the ground. Apply 1 cup of 10–10–10 per inch of thickness in March, May, and September. Once the tree becomes mature, little fertilizer will be needed. If summer temperatures rise above 95 degrees, water the tree heavily each week. Light pruning can be done at any time after a magnolia flowers. If you need to remove a major limb, do it in January.

Additional Advice for Care

The limbs and flowers of a magnolia on an exposed site may be damaged by cold weather. In June, prune out the limbs that were killed during the previous cold season, leaving the living branches. In July, remove any small, spindly branches along the trunk. Leave only the most vigorous and well-placed new branches.

Additional Cultivars and Species

Magnolia x soulangiana 'Brozzonii' has huge (10") mostly white flowers. The flowers appear later than the flowers of the species, so frost damage is avoided. *Magnolia x soulangiana* 'Lennei' has blooms that are white inside and dark purple outside. *Magnolia stellata* 'Royal Star' has pure white flowers which emerge later than those of the other star magnolias.

Malus spp.

Flowering Crabapple

Height: 10'–20' Width: 15'–25'
Deciduous flowering tree

Flowering crabapple is attractive during at least three seasons of the year. There are dozens of different types of 'named' crabapple. On some types, the flowers begin appearing in mid-April, while other types reserve their blooms until early June. The foliage of various crabapples can range from light to dark green. In fall, masses of red fruit remind us that the crabapple's blossoms are only one colorful reason to plant this tree. A weeping crabapple's bare limbs will ornament the fourth season. The different species of crabapple freely pollinate each other. 'Named' plants are selections which have shown notable advances in beauty or resistance to disease. Leaf diseases are the most common assaults on a crabapple's health. Fortunately, there are several crabapples commonly available that are tremendously resistant to disease. Crabapple scab disease can completely defoliate a tree by July; never purchase an 'unnamed' tree. Plants that are simply labeled "White Crabapple" or "Pink Crabapple" are almost certain to be a disappointment in years to come.

When to Plant

Crabapples are usually purchased with the roots balled and burlapped. Try to plant in mid-autumn, while the earth is still warm, or in early spring, just before the earth warms up. Mid-summer is a terrible time to plant, as the leaves require more moisture than the roots can possibly supply at this time of year.

Where to Plant

Full sun will produce the fastest growth and most profuse flowering. Select a spot that will remain sunny for several years. Look for neighboring trees that might overshade your crabapple after time, and plant the crabapple far enough from them so that shade and root competition won't become a problem.

ZONE
6,7,8

How to Plant

Dig a hole three times as large as the root ball of the tree. There is no
need to mix anything with the soil; simply pulverize the clods of
earth in the hole with a spade. Place the top of the root ball level
with or a little below the soil surrounding the hole. Remove any
wire or twine that was used to secure the burlap wrapping. Once
the tree is in the hole, try to cut away all of the burlap you can see.
Water heavily in order to settle the soil. A month later, inspect the
tree to see if the soil has settled around the root ball, exposing the
top surface of the ball. If this has occurred, add more soil around the
root ball.

Care and Maintenance

Once a crabapple is established, it will grow with little care. For the
first few years, fertilize twice each season with 10–10–10 fertilizer,
applying 1/8 cup of fertilizer for every foot of tree height. The first
fertilization should be in April, after the leaves have fully opened;
wait until late June for the next application. Prune a crabapple tree
to maintain a spreading, rounded form. Pencil-sized 'water sprouts'
can be pruned out every spring. Do not prune heavily after early
June, or you'll find you have removed next year's flowers!

Additional Advice for Care

After your tree has been in the ground for at least a year, examine its
form in January. Look for sprouts that seem to be trying to grow
parallel to the central trunk. These potential "co-dominant trunks"
should be removed without delay. When the tree gets older, a co-
dominant trunk is only weakly attached to the tree, and it might
split away in a storm.

Additional Cultivars and Species

Malus 'Callaway' crabapple was selected as a markedly superior tree
at Callaway Gardens by Mr. Fred Galle, the azalea expert. *Malus*
'Donald Wyman' and *Malus* 'Dolgo' are almost as disease-resistant
as 'Callaway.' Avoid *Malus* 'Hopa,' as it has remarkably little resistance to crabapple scab.

Metasequoia glyptostroboides

Dawn Redwood

Height: 70'–100' Width: 15'–25'
Deciduous shade tree

The dawn redwood was found growing wild in China in 1941, but the fossil record shows that this tree is millions of years old. When you look at a dawn redwood, imagine pterodactyls flying above and a brontosaurus munching on nearby giant ferns. The scene you are imagining is straight out of the Pliocene era. A dawn redwood is an excellent fast-growing shade tree for a larger landscape. It can grow 4' per year under good conditions. This symmetrical tree tapers rapidly from top to bottom, presenting a cone-shaped form. It's hard to believe it can attain this graceful shape without any pruning. The leaves of a dawn redwood are soft needles 1/2" long arranged on 6" branchlets. The leaves fall from the tree each year, but the foliage seems to drop straight down to the ground, making autumn raking a breeze.

WHEN TO PLANT

A dawn redwood is usually purchased with the roots balled and burlapped. Try to plant in mid-autumn, while the earth is still warm, or in early spring, when the earth will soon become warm. Midsummer is a terrible time to plant, as the tree's leaves require more moisture than its roots can possibly supply at this time of year.

WHERE TO PLANT

Dawn redwood grows too large for most residential landscapes, but it is a fine addition to a golf course or office park where plenty of room is available. Several of these trees were planted near a tall office building in Decatur. Here they do a fine job of integrating the building with the smaller structures around it.

HOW TO PLANT

The tree planting hole should be at least three times and preferably five times as large as the tree root ball, though it need be no deeper than the depth of the root ball. Research has shown there is no benefit from adding soil conditioner to the earth you'll shovel back into the hole unless your tree will be part of a larger bed. It is smart, however, to add 1 cup of lime per foot of hole diameter and 1 tablespoon of 0–46–0 fertilizer per foot of hole diameter. Once the root ball is in place, cut away all of the visible burlap, twine, or wire. Fill the hole with soil and water thoroughly. Spread a 2" layer of pine straw or wood chips over the entire planting area.

CARE AND MAINTENANCE

Small amounts of fertilizer applied regularly will help a young tree grow throughout the summer. Measure the thickness of the trunk 4' from the ground. Apply 1 cup of 10–10–10 per inch of thickness in March, May, and September. Once the tree becomes mature, little fertilizer will be needed. If summer temperatures rise above 95 degrees, water the tree heavily each week. Light pruning may be done at any time. If you need to remove a major limb, do it in January. If the tree needs support, a stake 18" from either side of the trunk will keep it upright. Stake the trunk in a way that allows it to slightly sway.

ADDITIONAL ADVICE FOR CARE

Dawn redwood is sometimes confused with the bald cypress tree. A way to tell them apart is to look at the branchlets and think "A-B-C: Alternating = Bald Cypress." Bald cypress branchlets are arranged alternately on either side of a branch. The dawn redwood branchlets are opposite each other. "O-D-R: Opposite = Dawn Redwood."

ADDITIONAL CULTIVARS AND SPECIES

There are no cultivars. The dawn redwood has survived for many years. Perhaps it is the best selection Mother Nature herself could make from an entire species!

Pine

Height: 15'–90' Width: 10'–25'
Evergreen needled tree

Pine trees grow in all parts of Georgia. Tall loblolly pines grow by the millions on pulpwood plantations in the south. Gnarled Virginia pines battle the elements in the north. On farms throughout Georgia where cattle once grazed, thousands of identical white pines grow to be harvested for Christmas trees. Because they are evergreen, pines are valuable as tall screen plants. Their characteristics vary, but the following three are most often used. Loblolly pine (Pinus taeda) is often called Georgia pine because it is so common across the state. It grows tall rapidly. After a few years, the foliage will be too far above the ground to provide much screening. The shade under a loblolly pine is excellent for plants that need partial shade. White pine (Pinus strobus) has soft, green-gray needles. It grows to 60', and its branches are symmetrically whorled around its trunk. Virginia pine (Pinus virginiana) makes a dense, dark-green screen only 20' tall. Its lower limbs will remain on the tree if it is grown in full sunshine.

WHEN TO PLANT

All pines are easy to plant in fall or in early spring. Whether you plant a container-grown tree or one that has been balled and burlapped, it seems to establish itself quickly and begin growth immediately.

WHERE TO PLANT

Pine trees grow best in full sunshine. The narrow needles are not as adept at capturing sunshine as are the leaves of the broadleafed trees. Hardwoods planted near pines will eventually catch up with the pines and kill them with their shade. White pine and Virginia pine form the best screens. If you have room, the trees should be planted in two staggered rows with 10' between plants. Some can be removed later when they become crowded.

How to Plant

On a pulpwood plantation, a seedling pine is planted by simply making a slit in the ground with an ax and stuffing its roots in the cut. When you're planting thousands of treees, you don't worry if a few do not survive the planting process! You should dig a hole 3 times as wide as the root ball to a depth the same as the ball. Add 1 cup lime plus 1 tablespoon 0–46–0 per foot of hole diameter to the soil before you shovel it back around the roots. Once a balled and burlapped root ball is in place, cut away all visible burlap, twine, or wire. Fill the hole with soil, then water thoroughly. Spread pine straw or wood chips over the planting area.

Care and Maintenance

Pine trees will grow rapidly if they are fertilized lightly and regularly. Measure the thickness of the trunk 4' from the ground. Apply 1 cup of 10–10–10 fertilizer per inch of thickness in March, May, and September. Once the tree is mature, little fertilizer is needed. If summer temperatures rise above 95 degrees, water your tree heavily each week. Pines can be sheared for better shape in May when new growth at the ends of the branches is 3" long. Try to cut all of these "candles" in half, forcing them to resprout and make dense foliage.

Additional Advice for Care

Loblolly pine trees grow well everywhere. White pines and Virginia pines are best grown in the northern half of the state. White pines will often flourish for twenty years and then rapidly turn brown. Heat and drought seem to play significant parts in "white pine decline."

Additional Cultivars and Species

It is easy to tell which kinds of pines you have in your landscape. Notice that the needles grow on the branch tips in bundles of 2, 3, or 5 individual needles. Virginia pine has 2 needles per bundle, loblolly pine has 3 needles, and white pine has 5 needles.

Prunus caroliniana

Cherrylaurel

Height: 20'–30' Width: 15'–20'
Evergreen shade tree

*Occasionally a cherrylaurel will offer just what is needed in a landscape;
at other times, it is considered a weed tree. Cherrylaurel is more tolerant
of shade that any other broadleafed tree. It even grows relatively fast in
the shade. For this reason alone, it deserves consideration for a shaded site
where no other tree will work. Some hesitate to use cherrylaurel because
of its seeds. Its fruit is a small purple berry which appears in copious quan-
tities in October, much to the delight of the native bird population. Birds
cannot digest the hard seeds inside the fruit and cherrylaurel seedlings
appear wherever birds alight. Fortunately, these sprouts are easy to identify
and, unlike oak seedlings, they are a snap to pull and remove in the spring.
Cherrylaurel flowers are vaguely attractive in early April but their fragrance may be perceived as "sickeningly sweet." Though it has some
problems, cherrylaurel can be counted on for deep green foliage and years
of life with little care.*

WHEN TO PLANT

Cherrylaurel is usually purchased with the roots balled and
burlapped. Try to plant in mid-autumn, while the earth is still
warm, or in early spring, just before the earth becomes warm.

WHERE TO PLANT

Cherrylaurel can form a thick screen, hedge, or windbreak for your
landscape. Trees should be planted 6' to 10' apart. Be sure you leave
some room to maneuver underneath the trees so that seedlings can
be pulled each year. In the coldest part of Georgia, cherrylaurel may
lose its leaves in winter, or it may even be frozen to the ground. It is
a good idea to protect the tree from strong winds in the extreme
north part of the state.

ZONE
6,7,8

HOW TO PLANT

The tree planting hole should be at least 3 times and preferably 5 times as large as the tree root ball, though it need be no deeper than the depth of the root ball. Research has shown there is no benefit from adding soil conditioner to the earth you'll shovel back into the hole unless your tree will be part of a larger bed. It is smart, however, to add 1 cup of lime per foot of hole diameter and 1 tablespoon of 0–46–0 fertilizer per foot of hole diameter. Once the root ball is in place, cut away all of the visible burlap, twine, or wire. Fill the hole with soil and water thoroughly. Spread a 2" layer of pine straw or wood chips over the entire planting area.

CARE AND MAINTENANCE

Small amounts of fertilizer applied regularly will help a young cherrylaurel grow throughout the summer. Measure the thickness of the trunk 4' from the ground. Apply 1 cup of 10–10–10 per inch of thickness in March, May, and September. Once the tree becomes mature, little fertilizer is needed. If summer temperatures rise above 95 degrees, water the tree heavily every week. Cherrylaurel can be pruned to a tree shape or to a thick rounded hedge. To keep the foliage densely growing in a shady spot, prune off branch tips every March.

ADDITIONAL ADVICE FOR CARE

Cherrylaurel attracts few insect or disease pests. You may sometimes see hundreds of tiny holes in the leaves, as if someone aimed a shotgun at your plant. This bacterial disease is called "shothole," and it is best prevented by keeping the foliage dry. Fungicides offer little help in controlling this problem.

ADDITIONAL CULTIVARS AND SPECIES

Prunus caroliniana 'Bright 'n' Tight' has leaves that are smaller than those of the species, and the foliage is dense. *Prunus caroliniana* 'Cherry Ruffles' grows to 15' and has deep-green, ruffled leaves.

Kwanzan Cherry

Height: 15′–20′ Width: 15′–25′
Deciduous flowering tree

The flowering cherry is regarded with reverence in its native Japan. This tree has been important in Japanese landscapes for centuries, and it has become a symbol of friendship between the Japanese and other cultures. In 1909, Japan made a gift of 2000 cherry trees to the city of Washington, D.C. Since that time, cherries have spread throughout the United States. The Cherry Blossom Festival in Macon was started after a cherry tree burst into bloom on the property of civic leader Mr. Bill Fickling, Sr. Today, flowering cherries offer one of the most spectacular blooming displays in spring. The Kwanzan cherry is known for its masses of double ruffled pink flowers which appear in April. Though it seems ignoble to bring this up, it must be mentioned that the slippery fallen blooms should be cleaned immediately from a deck or patio.

WHEN TO PLANT

A Kwanzan cherry may be purchased in a large container or with the roots balled and burlapped. A balled and burlapped tree should be planted in mid-autumn, while the earth is still warm. A container-grown tree may also be planted in mid-autumn, or it may be planted in early spring just before the earth becomes warm.

WHERE TO PLANT

Kwanzan cherry does best in full sun or very light shade. It is most important to avoid siting it in low spots that might flood in the spring, as a flood just a few days long in April can cause severe damage. The tree's rapidly growing roots will accumulate poisonous compounds if growing in saturated soil that cannot breathe.

HOW TO PLANT

It is important to select a site with good drainage. The planting hole should be at least 3 times and preferably 5 times as large as the root

ball, though it need be no deeper than the depth of the root ball. Research has shown there is no benefit derived from adding soil conditioner to the earth you'll shovel back into the hole unless your tree will be part of a larger bed. But do add 1 cup of lime per foot of hole diameter and 1 tablespoon of 0–46–0 fertilizer per foot of hole diameter. If you must plant in a low spot, first add 6 cubic feet of topsoil to the planting area to keep the roots out of standing water. A thin layer of mulch over the roots will help conserve moisture.

CARE AND MAINTENANCE

While the tree is still young, small amounts of fertilizer applied regularly will help it grow throughout the summer. Measure the thickness of the trunk 4' from the ground. Apply 1 cup of 10–10–10 per inch of thickness in March, May, and September. Once the tree becomes mature, little fertilizer will be needed. If summer temperatures rise above 95 degrees, water the tree heavily each week. Light pruning can be done at any time. If you need to remove a major limb, do it in January. If a young tree needs support, a stake 18" from either side of the trunk will keep it upright.

ADDITIONAL ADVICE FOR CARE

Bacterial canker and bot canker are common cherry diseases that appear as oozing areas on the trunk. Increasing the soil pH can help fight these diseases if they occur. To treat a large tree, mix 5 lb. of pickling lime in 5 gallons of water and sprinkle the mixture under the branches. Then apply 50 gallons of water to wash the mixture down to the roots. Repeat this procedure 5 months later.

ADDITIONAL CULTIVARS AND SPECIES

Kwanzan cherry (*Prunus* 'Sekiyama') is certainly the best-known of this family of flowering cherries, but there are others to be discovered. *Prunus* 'Amanogowa' is quite columnar, perhaps 20' high and only 5' wide. *Prunus* 'Royal Burgundy' has deep pink flowers and an attractive mahogany red trunk.

Prunus x yedoensis

Yoshino Cherry

Height: 20′–30′ Width: 25′–40′
Deciduous flowering tree

Yoshino cherry is another of the spectacular flowering cherries brought over from Japan in the early 1900s. In April, abundant white flowers cover the ends of the branches. The flowers appear before the leaves, and some have described the effect as a luminous white cloud floating in the landscape beneath taller trees. Unlike those of the Kwanzan cherry, Yoshino cherry flowers are fragrant, exuding a slight almond smell. In Japan, where cherry trees are so much a part of daily life, flowering cherries are referred to as "Sato-Zakura," or village cherries. A Yoshino cherry is propagated by grafting a cutting onto another cherry trunk or by rooting small cuttings. If you find a Yoshino cherry with a swollen "knot" approximately 4′ from ground level, it is likely a grafted tree. Because the lower cherry rootstock can send up sprouts that do not resemble the Yoshino, it is best to buy trees that have been produced by rooted cuttings.

WHEN TO PLANT

A Yoshino cherry may be purchased growing in a large container or with the roots balled and burlapped. Try to plant balled and burlapped trees in mid-autumn, while the earth is still warm. Container-grown trees may be planted in fall or in early spring just before the earth becomes warm.

WHERE TO PLANT

Preferred conditions for the Yoshino cherry range from full sunshine to light shade. Shrubs that bloom at the same time as the cherry are good companions. The flowers of azaleas, rhododendrons, and nearby dogwood trees make a wonderful color combination.

HOW TO PLANT

It is important to select a site with good drainage. The planting hole should be at least 3 times and preferably 5 times as large as the root ball, though it need be no deeper than the depth of the root ball. Research has shown there is no benefit derived from adding soil conditioner to the earth you'll shovel back into the hole unless your tree will be part of a larger bed. It is smart, however, to add 1 cup of lime per foot of hole diameter and 1 tablespoon of 0−46−0 fertilizer per foot of hole diameter. If you must plant in a low spot, first add 6 cubic feet of topsoil to the planting area to keep the roots out of wet soil. A thin layer of mulch over the roots will help conserve moisture in summer.

CARE AND MAINTENANCE

While the tree is still young, small amounts of fertilizer applied regularly will help it grow throughout the summer. Measure the thickness of the trunk 4' from the ground. Apply 1 cup of 10−10−10 per inch of thickness in March, May, and September. Once the tree becomes mature, little fertilizer will be needed. If summer temperatures rise above 95 degrees, water the tree heavily each week. Light pruning can be done at any time. If you need to remove a major limb, do it in January. If a young tree needs support, a stake 18" from either side of the trunk will keep it upright.

ADDITIONAL ADVICE FOR CARE

In April, tent caterpillars sometimes make their webs at the end of cherry branches. To combat these pests, use a forked branch to wind up the webs and expose the caterpillars to predators. Even if the tent caterpillars consume lots of foliage, there will not be permanent damage. New leaves will appear after the pests disappear in May.

ADDITIONAL CULTIVARS AND SPECIES

Prunus x yedoensis 'Akebono' is smaller than 'Yoshino' and its flowers are a soft pink rather than white. *Prunus x yedoensis* 'Shidare Yoshino' has gracefully arching branches that "weep" to the ground.

Pyrus calleryana 'Bradford'

Bradford Pear

Height: 20′–30′ Width: 15′–25′
Deciduous flowering tree

The glossy green leaves and clouds of springtime blooms of a Bradford pear make the tree wonderfully attractive. This tree is so beautiful that there is hardly a subdivision in Georgia that does not sport a dozen Bradford pears. But as is true of Leyland cypress and red tip photinia, it is a tree that is used so often it may actually make a landscape appear less interesting. The rapid growth of this tree can lead to devastating limb breakage in ice and wind storms. It is not uncommon to see a tree split in half by the weight of a limb that was weakly attached to the main trunk. Its rapid growth also makes it susceptible to a major disease: fire blight. Many people can overlook the shortcomings of this plant when they see a street lined on both sides with Bradford pear trees in full flower. The sight of billowing white clouds of flowers close to the earth on a warm April day can take your breath away.

WHEN TO PLANT

Bradford pear trees are usually sold with the roots balled and burlapped. The larger sizes are best planted in fall so the roots can grow in warm soil before winter. Smaller trees less than 10′ tall can be planted in spring if water can be provided during the summer.

WHERE TO PLANT

This is unmistakably a "full sun" tree. When grown in shade, the tree will lose its shape and become spindly. Never plant it where it will grow too tall for the surroundings. Pruning it shorter (*topping*) can lead to vigorously growing but weakly attached upper limbs which can fall out of the tree during a thunderstorm.

HOW TO PLANT

Establishment and growth will be much quicker if the tree is planted in a hole that is three times as large as the root ball. The top of the root ball should be level with the soil on either side of the hole.

Remove any wire or twine that was used to secure the burlap wrapping. Once the tree is in its hole, try to cut away all of the burlap you can still see. A tree planted in the spring may need to be staked for its first year. Two stakes driven on opposite sides of the trunk and 2' away from it provide ample support. The trunk should be able to move freely. It should not be lashed so rigidly that it can't sway in the wind.

CARE AND MAINTENANCE

To avoid the disaster of major limb breakage, pruning and training should begin as soon as the tree is planted. Though the lower limbs are small at first, in ten years they will grow to be 10" in diameter. Note the three or four best limbs of all those growing approximately 4' from the ground. Remove all smaller limbs that are growing within 16" of these best limbs. Insert wooden "spacers" between the main trunk and the limbs that are left so they will spread outwards at a 45-degree angle. A Bradford pear does not need much fertilizer. Faster growth would lead to weak limb structure and increased problems with disease.

ADDITIONAL ADVICE FOR CARE

Bradford pear plantings occasionally become roosts for migrating birds in the fall. The noise each evening and the resulting mess are often unbearable. If birds invade your trees, scare them away immediately with noisemakers and horns. If you can keep them from becoming accustomed to this roost, they'll find trees somewhere else.

ADDITIONAL CULTIVARS AND SPECIES

Pyrus calleryana 'Bradford' is only one of several named selections of callery pear. *Pyrus calleryana* 'Autumn Blaze' has good color in fall, while *Pyrus calleryana* 'Aristocrat' has stronger limbs. *Pyrus calleryana* 'Whitehouse' is much more columnar than 'Bradford.' Its limbs grow close to the main trunk

Oak

Height: 40'–80' Width: 50'–90'
Deciduous shade tree

*Dozens of oaks grow well in Georgia. Instead of selecting just one for description, we will take a look at several that will grow well in most landscapes. Sawtooth oak (*Quercus acutissima*), about 40' tall, is one of the smaller oaks. It is a good choice for a street tree or a fast-growing shade tree. The acorn cap is distinctive, resembling a woven straw hat. Shumard oak (*Quercus shumardii*) and scarlet oak (*Quercus coccinea*) are two of the best oaks for red fall leaf color. The brown leaves may hold onto the tree until spring forces them off. Red oak (*Quercus rubra*) is easy to transplant and grows rapidly into a large tree. Squirrels love multitudes of acorns. Live oak (*Quercus virginiana*) is the state tree. Its limbs spread out horizontally from the trunk. A mature tree, often seen in Savannah, can appear to cover acres and is the perfect tree for children to climb and play under on a hot summer day. Live oak grows with difficulty in the northern half of Georgia.*

WHEN TO PLANT

Oaks are usually sold with the roots balled and burlapped. Try to plant in mid-autumn, while the earth is still warm, or in early spring, when just before the earth becomes warm. A landscape company might plant an oak at any time. Be sure to water a young oak regularly during the summer.

WHERE TO PLANT

Plant your oak in full sunshine. Before you plant, think about the space needs of your tree. Check on all sides for sun-loving plants which might become shaded by the oak, and look overhead for telephone and electrical lines. Don't forget that it is difficult to grow grass in the shade of a mature oak.

ZONE
6,7,8

How to Plant

The tree planting hole should be at least 3 times and preferably 5 times as large as the tree root ball, though it need be no deeper than the depth of the root ball. Research has shown there is no benefit from adding soil conditioner to the earth you'll shovel back into the hole unless your tree will be part of a larger bed. It is smart, however, to add 1 cup of lime per foot of hole diameter and 1 tablespoon of 0–46–0 fertilizer per foot of hole diameter. Once the root ball is in place, cut away all of the visible burlap, twine, or wire. Fill the hole with soil and water thoroughly. Spread a 2" layer of pine straw or wood chips over the entire planting area.

Care and Maintenance

While the tree is still young, small amounts of fertilizer applied regularly will help it grow throughout the summer. Measure the thickness of the trunk 4' from the ground. Apply 1 cup of 10–10–10 per inch of thickness in March, May, and September. Once the tree becomes mature, little fertilizer will be needed. If summer temperatures rise above 95 degrees, water the tree heavily each week. Light pruning can be done at any time. If you need to remove a major limb, do it in January. If a young tree needs support, a stake 18" from either side of the trunk will keep it upright.

Additional Advice for Care

The major cause of death for mature oak trees is damage by construction crews. If you plan to build on a wooded lot, tell your builder which trees must be protected. Direct your builder to build a wire fence under the branch ends of a designated tree and to prohibit machinery in the area bounded by the wire. If only 12" of soil is removed from around a tree, its essential feeder roots will be eliminated.

Additional Cultivars and Species

Water oak (*Quercus nigra*) may grow in a wide variety of soil types and will tolerate wet or dry sites. Though it has little fall color, it grows very fast and is a fine shade tree.

351

Canadian Hemlock

Height: 40'–70' Width: 25'–40'
Evergreen tree

Gardeners from Western states marvel at the diversity of broadleafed trees in our state. Maple, flowering cherry, poplar, crabapple, and dogwood trees are just a few of our trees that present a remarkably diverse landscape selection. On the other hand, a Westerner may criticize the narrow range of needled trees that grow in Georgia. The spruce, fir, and larch trees in the Western states provide a good contrast in form and color to broadleafed trees. Here, after our pines, there isn't much else! Except in the mountains, it is difficult to keep spruce and fir alive in Georgia. Larch is almost unknown here. We do find Canadian hemlock, however, in the northern third of the state. This excellent evergreen is an exceptionally graceful tree that has several uses in the landscape. Hemlock may be pruned to a hedge or allowed to grow into a tall, green pyramid. Though it grows in full sunshine in its native habitat, it only tolerates filtered shade in Georgia. It is a fine choice to grow in the shade of mature broadleafed trees whose trunks don't completely hide the disarray in your neighbor's backyard.

WHEN TO PLANT

Canadian hemlock is usually purchased with its roots balled and burlapped. Try to plant in mid-autumn, while the earth is still warm, or in early spring, when the earth will soon become warm. Midsummer is a terrible time to plant, as the tree's leaves require more moisture than its roots can possibly supply at this time of year.

WHERE TO PLANT

Plant in the shade of hardwoods or tall pines. Morning sunshine is fine, but avoid summer's baking glare after mid-afternoon. The growth of a hemlock will be slow in dense shade, so purchase the largest tree you can afford. If using hemlock as a screen, stagger the trees and plant them 10' apart. As they grow larger, a few may be removed as needed.

How to Plant

Hemlocks require good drainage around their roots. You can achieve good drainage in clay soil by first digging a planting hole 5 times as big as the tree root ball; it need be no deeper than the depth of the root ball. Add 10 lb. of pea gravel and 1 cubic foot of soil conditioner for every foot of hole diameter. Add 1 cup of lime per foot of hole diameter and 1 tablespoon of 0–46–0 per foot of hole diameter as well. Once the root ball is in place, cut away all visible burlap, twine, or wire. Fill the hole with the improved soil and water thoroughly. Spread a 2" layer of pine straw or wood chips over the entire planting area.

Care and Maintenance

Small amounts of fertilizer applied regularly will help a young tree grow throughout the summer. Measure the thickness of the trunk 4' from the ground. Apply 1 cup of 10–10–10 per inch of thickness in March, May, and September. Once the tree becomes mature, little fertilizer is needed. If summer temperatures rise above 95 degrees, water the tree heavily each week. Light pruning may be done at any time, but will not be necessary unless you are forming a hemlock hedge. If you need to remove a major limb, do it in January.

Additional Advice for Care

We cannot overemphasize the need for excellent drainage as well as watering during the summer. During the first year, check your hemlock weekly for signs of stress. Hemlock pests are few in Georgia— its only enemy here is the environment. Woolly adelgid insects are devastating to hemlocks in the North, but they haven't reached Georgia yet!

Additional Cultivars and Species

Tsuga canadensis 'Sargentii' is a smaller, weeping form of hemlock, 10' high and 15' wide. It has been described as "a ghost sweeping across the landscape." Carolina hemlock (*Tsuga caroliniana*) may be hardier in Georgia landscapes than Canadian hemlock, and it is reputed to be even more tolerant of shade, but finding it at a nursery may be a challenge.

Ulmus parvifolia

Chinese Elm

Lacebark Elm

Height: 40'–50' Width: 40'–50'
Deciduous shade tree

Elms were once the predominant street tree in cities throughout the American Northeast and Midwest. American elms were tough and durable. Their limbs ascended upward from a sturdy trunk, then arched gently at the tips. Sometimes rows of elms lined both sides of a street and their branches intertwined over the street's center. When the European bark beetle arrived on this continent and began to spread Dutch elm disease, millions of elms began to die. The search began for a substitute tree and for disease-resistant selections of American elm. One of the best substitutes is the Chinese elm (which should not be confused with the inferior Siberian elm). Though smaller than the American elm, Chinese elm has similar ascending branches and it is resistant to pests. Its bark is noticeably different. Small patches of bark drop off to reveal a beautiful, mottled combination of gray, green, and brown. The pattern is like a jigsaw puzzle with a random but always pleasing combination of colors.

WHEN TO PLANT

Chinese elm is usually purchased with the roots balled and burlapped. Try to plant in mid-autumn, while the earth is still warm, or in early spring, just before the earth becomes warm. Even trees planted at the "wrong" time in midsummer may withstand the stress and establish themselves if they are watered occasionally.

WHERE TO PLANT

Plant your Chinese elm in full sunshine in any spot that needs shade. The leaves are a deep green and make a nice contrast to the bricks when the tree is planted in front of a large brick home. When deciding how far away it should be placed from other plants or structures, remember that the tree grows rapidly.

TREES

How to Plant

The tree planting hole should be at least 3 times and preferably 5 times as large as the tree root ball, though it need be no deeper than the depth of the root ball. Research has shown there is no benefit from adding soil conditioner to the earth you'll shovel back into the hole unless your tree will be part of a larger bed. It is smart, however, to add 1 cup of lime per foot of hole diameter and 1 tablespoon of 0–46–0 fertilizer per foot of hole diameter. Once the root ball is in place, cut away all of the visible burlap, twine, or wire. Fill the hole with soil and water thoroughly. Spread a 2" layer of pine straw or wood chips over the entire planting area.

Care and Maintenance

Small amounts of fertilizer applied regularly will help a young elm tree grow throughout the summer. Measure the thickness of the trunk 4' from the ground. Apply 1 cup of 10–10–10 per inch of thickness in March, May, and September. Once the tree becomes mature, little fertilizer is needed. If summer temperatures rise above 95 degrees, water the tree heavily each week. Light pruning may be done at any time. If you need to remove a major limb, do it in January. If the tree needs support, a stake 18" from either side of the trunk will keep it upright. Stake the trunk in a way that allows it to slightly sway.

Additional Advice for Care

Chinese elm is resistant to Dutch elm disease and other pests. Make sure the tree you have decided to buy is a true Chinese elm. The inferior Siberian elm is occasionally called Chinese elm. Some horticulturists prefer to refer to Chinese elm as Lacebark elm.

Additional Cultivars and Species

Ulmus parvifolia 'Athena' was selected by the Georgia Gold Medal Plant committee as a superior tree that deserves to be used more often. It has a broad and rounded crown. *Ulmus parvifolia* 'Alee' has an upright, arching crown similar to that of the American elm. *Ulmus parvifolia* 'Burgundy' displays good purple fall foliage.

CHAPTER NINE

Vines

I REMEMBER MY INTRODUCTION TO GARDENING *with vines. Right after college, when a friend and I had a landscaping business in Maryland, we spent hours battling wisteria that had taken over a client's garden. We hacked, sawed, and dug for hours, barely beginning to eradicate this tenacious pest. It was this experience that led us to dub wisteria "hysteria." Then when I moved to Georgia, I encountered kudzu. Introduced from Asia as a groundcover to help control erosion, kudzu is now the ubiquitous weed of the South. Since these early encounters I have discovered that there is a wide selection of ornamental vines, not on the noxious weed list, that will thrive in Georgia gardens. While the list that follows is not exhaustive, it includes some of the tried-and-true. Once you get started with vines, you'll find out just how rewarding they can be.—E.L.G.*

Versatile vines. Evergreen, deciduous, flowering, clinging, twining, scrambling, and rambling, they offer us opportunities to take maximum advantage of our vertical gardening space. Whether clematis draped over a fence or trumpetcreeper climbing a tree, vines add another dimension to the garden. Some need supports like arbors, pergolas, fences, walls, or trees, while others will grow happily among shrubs or other climbing plants, creating interesting combinations of foliage and flowers. Vines provide screening, act as living fences, mask mistakes, and cover unsightly rockpiles or tree stumps. Some make effective groundcovers, too.

CHOOSING THE RIGHT VINE FOR THE RIGHT SPOT

Annual vines are a good way to experiment with adding certain colors and textures to the garden without making a long-term commitment. Many are easy to grow from seed. Impatient gardeners may want to start with young plants. All recommended here thrive in our hot summers and fill the garden with color.

At the end of the season, many set seed which can be stored and planted the following spring. Remember—annual vines will produce the largest leaves and flowers when they are planted in full sun.

Perennial vines reward us with flowers, foliage, and sometimes ornamental bark in the winter. Take care when selecting a spot for them to grow and flower, as many of them do not like to be disturbed.

Twining Versus Climbing

Vines like clematis have petioles which act like tendrils, leaf-like appendages that reach out and grab onto strings or other supports. Vines like wisteria and bittersweet climb by twining themselves around a structure. Then there is a group of vines that produce root-like holdfasts that attach to surfaces like stone, brick, or wood. Included in this category are trumpetcreeper and the climbing hydrangea.

Training and Pruning

Most vines need a support to climb or twine on. This can be as simple as a chain-link fence or as elaborate as a hand-sculpted metal arbor. For woody vines like five-leaf akebia or Carolina jessamine, copper wire is a strong, flexible material to use in the beginning. Copper, as it weathers, soon turns a color that disappears. The wire should not girdle plants. For clematis and many annual vines, twine or string should be adequate.

When it comes to pruning, there are a few general rules. If the vine flowers on two-year-old wood (as does *Clematis armandii*) prune it back as soon as it finishes flowering. If it blooms on the current season's growth, prune it in early spring before new growth begins. In some cases you will need to prune during the growing season to remove wild shoots that go off in all directions or to keep a particular vine in bounds.

Akebia quinata

Fiveleaf Akebia

Height: 20'–40'
Flowers: chocolate-purple Blooms: March–April
Fruit: purple sausaged-shaped pods Yields: September–October

This little-known vine gets its common name, fiveleaf akebia, from the five rounded leaflets that make up its compound leaf. It has a fine texture during the growing season and a coarser texture in winter. It is a deciduous climber whose new leaves emerge with purple tinges and turn blue-green as they mature. In early spring, the three-sectioned chocolate-purple flowers appear just as the vine is leafing out. Their spicy vanilla scent is released on warm days. More ornamental than the flowers are the curious 2 1/4" to 4" sausage-shaped fruits that appear, if you are lucky, at the end of the summer and then ripen September to October. There is disagreement about what determines whether akebia will set fruit or not, but chances are better when there are two individual plants so that cross-pollination can occur. Although akebia is tough and adaptable and grows in dry or moist soils in sun or shade, it seems to resent being disturbed once it is planted. A fast cover, it is suited for arbors, fences, walls, or other structures.

WHEN TO PLANT

Plant akebia in the spring or fall. If you want to propagate akebia, softwood cuttings taken in early summer will root easily.

WHERE TO PLANT

Plant akebia where you want a vine to provide quick cover or add an interesting texture. Pergolas, arbors, or fences are all good structures to use for training this vine. Akebia will thrive in sun or shade.

HOW TO PLANT

Don't amend the soil. Akebia is happy in a wide range of soil types. Dig a hole the depth of the container. Water after planting and stand back to watch it grow.

CARE AND MAINTENANCE

Prune akebia to keep it in bounds. Early spring before it leafs out is a good time to prune.

ADDITIONAL ADVICE FOR CARE

In the warmer parts of Georgia, akebia will probably be semi-evergreen.

ADDITIONAL CULTIVARS AND SPECIES

Akebia quinata 'Alba' has white flowers and white fruits. *A. quinata* 'Rosea' has much lighter flowers than other akebia.

Bignonia capreolata (Anisostichus capreolata)
'Tangerine Beauty'

Cross Vine

Height: 30'–50'
Flowers: peachy-orange Blooms: March through April

*'Tangerine Beauty' is a selection of the native cross vine that is seen cling-
ing to the trunks of trees in the woods throughout Georgia. A handsome
addition to the garden, this vine gets its common name from the cross-
shaped mark that is visible when you cut the woody stem in half. In bud,
the 2"–3" long flowers resemble long, narrow balloons. Once they begin to
open in early spring, they look more like funnels with yellow throats.
Mostly evergreen, the foliage starts out a bright, light green, and becomes
dark and leathery as it matures. In the winter, it turns shades of red and
purple. Even the tendrils and rootlets—the parts of the vine that grab onto
structures or other plants—are showy, twisting and curling in all directions. Little disks at the ends of the tendrils act like suction cups, easily
clinging to surfaces such as wood and cement. A tough vine, 'Tangerine
Beauty' grows in sun or shade and will tolerate wet soils. To get the best
flower production, plant it where it will get full sun. Although fast growing, cross vine is much easier to keep in bounds than its aggressive relative
Campsis radicans.*

WHEN TO PLANT
Plant 'Tangerine Beauty' in the spring or fall.

WHERE TO PLANT
This adaptable vine will grow in heavy shade, but for best flowering, give it plenty of sun. It will also tolerate less-than-ideal soil
conditions, growing in wet or dry soils. For best results, plant it in a
well-drained, moderately fertile soil.

HOW TO PLANT

Dig a hole equal to the size of the container. This self-clinging vine will use its tendrils to attach to wood, stone, or any other porous surface. Plant it against a fence or wall, or let it sprawl over a stump. Tying it up against a structure when it is still a young plant will prevent it from growing along the ground. When growing up a tree, cross vine grows flat, forming a beautiful pattern with its leaves.

CARE AND MAINTENANCE

Prune this vigorous native after it flowers to shape and train it. *B.* 'Tangerine Beauty' does not suffer from any serious pest or disease problems and requires no special care. Applying a general fertilizer like 10–10–10 in early spring the first year it is planted will help give it a boost. Water once a week during periods without any rain.

ADDITIONAL ADVICE FOR CARE

This vine is easy to root from cuttings taken in June and July. The more sun cross vine gets, the better cover it will provide.

ADDITIONAL CULTIVARS AND SPECIES

Another vine that is also native is *Decumaria barbara*, the hydrangea vine. It has glossy, green foliage and small, white, fragrant flowers that appear in spring.

Campsis x tagliabuana 'Madame Galen'

Trumpetcreeper

Height: 20'–30'
Flowers: large orange trumpets Blooms: June–September

'Madame Galen,' a hybrid cross between the American native C. radicans *and its Japanese counterpart* C. grandiflora, *is a hardy selection with larger flowers. As is true of many plants, it was only after 'Madame Galen' received a European education that American gardeners began to appreciate it. First distributed by a nursery in France in 1898, 'Madame Galen' thrives in the hot, humid summers that we regularly experience in Georgia. When driving along a Georgia highway, you have probably seen the common native trumpetcreeper,* C. radicans, *growing up telephone poles, and you may have wondered what that bright orange flower was. With 'Madame Galen,' clusters of large orange 2" by 2" trumpets first appear in June and continue intermittently until September. A magnet for hummingbirds, this trouble-free vine is not for the gardener who is shy about pruning. Its compound leaves are divided, with 7 to 9 to 11 leaflets. Virtually free of disease and pests, 'Madame Galen' is excellent for screening, training over structures, and covering stumps and rockpiles.*

WHEN TO PLANT
Plant trumpetcreeper in the spring or fall.

WHERE TO PLANT
This is a plant that will grow almost anywhere that it touches the soil. A lot of sun will make it flower best. Give it a structure to grow up or something to grow over like a rock wall or a pile of rocks.

HOW TO PLANT
There is no need to amend the soil. If the soil is too rich, trumpetcreeper may threaten to cover everything in sight, including all your other plants. Dig a hole equal to the size of the container.

ZONE
6,7,8

CARE AND MAINTENANCE
Don't be afraid to prune this vine. In fact, you will have to prune it to keep it in bounds. The flowers appear on new growth each year, so prune it back hard to the height of a few buds in early spring. Don't fertilize this plant unless you want to make more work for yourself.

ADDITIONAL ADVICE FOR CARE
Trumpetcreeper is the perfect vine to cover a dead tree stump or a telephone pole. Make sure you plant it where you will be able to appreciate the blooms. Sometimes they occur high up on the vine.

ADDITIONAL CULTIVARS AND SPECIES
Campsis 'Crimson Trumpet' has clusters that are a pure, glowing red color. *Campsis radicans* 'Flava' produces yellow flowers throughout the summer.

Clematis armandii

Armand Clematis

Height: an evergreen climber, 20′ or more
Flowers: creamy white Blooms: March–April

In Georgia, particularly in Zone 7 and south, this evergreen clematis is a choice vine that perfumes the air with its sweetly scented flowers in early spring. Each flower is 2" to 2½" wide and has 4 to 7 sepals that look like petals. The scent of the flowers has been compared to that of almonds. The dramatic foliage of armand clematis looks good almost year round, except during the coldest winter months. The compound leaves with their 3 leaflets are dark, shiny, and leathery. Individual leaflets vary in size from 3" to 6" long and grow up to 2" wide. This clematis makes a perfect living trellis on which to train another summer-blooming clematis. We can thank the great plant explorer E.H. Wilson for many wonderful plants like Clematis armandii. *Named after the missionary Armand David of China, this elegant vine was introduced by Wilson in 1900. Many of the vines, trees, and shrubs he collected for the Arnold Arboretum at Harvard University can be found in our gardens today.*

WHEN TO PLANT

Plant *Clematis armandii* in late spring when the soil temperatures begin to get warm.

WHERE TO PLANT

This evergreen climber needs a support like an arbor, fence, or wall to grow on. Clear fishing line attached to a wall with masonry nails will give it something to hold to. Unlike many clematis that are very particular about soil, the armand clematis will grow in a moderately fertile soil that is moist but well-drained. Plant this vine in full sun. In the coldest parts of Georgia, protect it from winter winds.

ZONE
7,8

VINES

HOW TO PLANT

Dig a hole equal to or larger than the size of the container. To ensure good drainage, add some broken clay pots or gravel to a depth of about 2" to 4" in the bottom of the hole. Make sure you water regularly, especially during dry periods. A light covering of mulch will help keep the roots cool. As this clematis matures, it tends to lose its leaves at the base. Planting it behind an evergreen shrub will help mask the vine's unsightly "bare ankles."

CARE AND MAINTENANCE

Because this clematis flowers on two-year-old wood, prune lightly after it flowers. Fertilize with a general 10–10–10 in the spring and lightly in the fall. This vigorous clematis sends tendrils in all directions, looking for a support. Check it often so you can prevent it from taking over your garden.

ADDITIONAL ADVICE FOR CARE

There are many wonderful clematis worth including in your garden. One is the fast-growing *Clematis montana*, called the mountain clematis. This vigorous clematis grows to 30' and produces a profusion of white flowers, 2" in diameter, in spring. Another is *C. montana* var. *rubens*. It has pale pink flowers.

ADDITIONAL CULTIVARS AND SPECIES

Two selections of *Clematis armandii* that are worth trying if you can find them are 'Appleblossom,' with its bronze young foliage and pink flowers, and 'Snowdrift,' with its pure-white flowers.

365

Clematis maximowicziana

Sweetautumn Clematis

Height: 30′
Flowers: fragrant, white Blooms: late summer–fall

It is a challenge to keep up with the name changes this carefree vine has gone through. Whatever its scientific name is at the moment, sweetautumn clematis is worth seeking out for its perfume, a scent that fills the air and reminds us that fall is just around the corner. Beginning in late August, clouds of 1″ white flowers cover this active climber that scrambles up trees or over other plants. The silver seedheads can be used for flower arrangements or left on the vine for winter interest. If you want to train this clematis to grow up a wall or other structure, remember to start early in the season before the vines become a tangled mess. Use twine that will decompose or plastic-covered ties. Prune this clematis in early spring to tidy it and encourage healthy new growth and flowers. You can also prune it as soon as it finishes flowering, but if you do that, you will sacrifice the showy seedheads. Unlike other types of clematis that are finicky about their location, sweetautumn thrives with little or no care.

WHEN TO PLANT

Plant sweetautumn clematis in the spring when the soil begins to warm.

WHERE TO PLANT

Plant sweetautumn clematis where you can get the most enjoyment from its fragrant flowers. Because this plant is almost weed-like in its growth, there is no need to improve the soil before you plant. Full sun or partial shade are best for maximum flowering in moderately fertile soil.

How to Plant

Dig a hole to the depth of the container. Please note that, unlike most types of clematis that prefer cool roots and hot tops, sweet-autumn clematis requires no special care when planting. Water it well after planting, and prune out any dead or broken stems. If you want it to grow up a structure, use ties to train it when the plant is still young.

Care and Maintenance

Prune back to a desired size in early spring before the vine begins to grow. This will encourage healthy, strong growth and good blooms. If you forget to prune, there is no need to worry: it will still bloom and grow like crazy.

Additional Advice for Care

Large, sturdy shrubs like wiegela or climbing roses provide a living support for the sweetautumn clematis.

Additional Cultivars and Species

A number of small-flowering species of climbing clematis offer scented flowers, including the lesser-known *C. flammula* and *C. rehderiana*.

Dolichos lablab (Dipogon lablab)

Hyacinth Bean Vine

Height: grows to 20′–30′
Flowers: lavender Blooms: in summer
Seed pods: purple to magenta Yields: in fall

A favorite of Thomas Jefferson, the eye-catching hyacinth bean vine is a star in the summer garden when it becomes covered with spikes of purple pea-like flowers. With autumn comes the grand finale, the arrival of the show-stopping 4″ seed pods in brilliant magenta. This heat-lover is perfect for Georgia gardens where summers are long and hot. Fast-growing hyacinth bean will cover an arbor or trellis, or twine itself around other plants almost overnight. Adding to its ornamental appeal are its purple stems and nearly heart-shaped, dark-green leaves with purple veins. Although gardeners today grow hyacinth bean as an ornamental, this Egyptian native was used in the ancient world as fodder for cattle. The genus name Dolichos *is ancient Greek for a form of pea;* lablab *is the common name of the plant throughout much of Africa. If it is happy where it grows, this member of the legume family will probably reward you with new seedlings every year. Once the pods have ripened and matured, you can collect seed to sow for next year.*

WHEN TO PLANT

Plant seeds in the spring after the last frost. Collect seeds from the previous year's plant if there are any left clinging to the dead vine.

WHERE TO PLANT

Plant the hyacinth bean where it can twine around a post or up a structure. A moderately fertile soil in a location with plenty of sun is fine.

ZONE
6,7,8

How to Plant

No special soil preparation is needed. Plant the seeds, with the "eye" (the lighter part of the seed) facing downward, about 3" to 4" apart. After the seedlings sprout, usually in 1 to 2 weeks, thin them out to a distance of just a few inches apart. Select those that exhibit the most color and discard the rest. Make sure that each plant has a structure to cling to, or the hyacinth bean will grab onto plants for support.

Care and Maintenance

The main requirements for growing hyacinth bean are heat and sun, both of which are easy to come by in Georgia. If you start seedlings indoors, give them a light watering with a liquid fertilizer such as 20–20–20 when you transplant them. If the soil is moderately fertile, more fertilizer should not be required, although mulch will help keep plants from drying out.

Additional Advice for Care

Sowing seeds directly where you want the vines to grow is best and avoids the step of having to transplant seedlings. If you start seedlings indoors to get a head start, use peat pots. Place the pots directly into the ground so you will not have to disturb individual plants. The seeds make great presents for gardening friends.

Additional Cultivars and Species

There is a selection that has white flowers, but it is not nearly as spectacular as the species.

Gelsemium sempervirens

Carolina Jessamine

Height: a hardy vine 10′–20′
Flowers: yellow, fragrant Blooms: February-April

Carolina jessamine has been grown for years, and there are good reasons for the popularity of this adaptable native. It offers shiny evergreen foliage and fragrant yellow flowers, and it grows in sun or shade. It is popular not only in Georgia gardens, but throughout the South. The most common use for this plant is as a twining vine. It has consumed many a mailbox, but it also graces arbors and fences. You may use it as a groundcover in an area where you can let it run wild. For example, it is a good groundcover in which to plant daffodil bulbs, as it masks their foliage when they're not in bloom, and works as well in areas where fall-blooming bulbs like orange-red suprise lilies await their cues. While this plant is a serviceable performer for many gardens, it should not be confused with Confederate jasmine, Trachelospermum jasminoides, an evergreen vine with powerfully fragrant flowers that is a treasure in the most southern parts of Georgia.

WHEN TO PLANT

Plant this vine in the early spring or fall.

WHERE TO PLANT

Plant it as a groundcover, or train it as a vine on an arbor or fence. Remember: the better the soil, the healthier the plant will be. This native will grow in full sun or shade, but will make a thicker cover when grown in the sun.

HOW TO PLANT

Carolina jessamine prefers a moist, well-drained soil that is moderately fertile, but it will also tolerate conditions that are less ideal. Dig a hole the size of the container in which the vine came. Give it plenty of room to spread out if you plant it as a groundcover.

CARE AND MAINTENANCE

Prune this vine after it flowers. Sometimes a hard pruning will help rejuvenate an older plant that has become a tangled mess. Water during periods of drought.

ADDITIONAL ADVICE FOR CARE

The American wisteria, *Wisteria frutescens*, is not as well-known as the Carolina jessamine, but it is perhaps more elegant. Because it is not as vigorous as its Asian counterparts, it may be a better choice for the garden. The 4"–6" blooms are fragrant. As is true of other wisteria, flower colors range from white to reddish-violet to deep purple.

ADDITIONAL CULTIVARS AND SPECIES

G. sempervirens 'Pride of Augusta,' a double-flowering form, and *G. rankinii*, a J.C. Raulston introduction, are not fragrant, but they flower in the spring and then again in the fall. They are not as hardy as the Carolina jessamine.

Hydrangea anomala subsp. *petiolaris*

Climbing Hydrangea

Height: a woody vine, 60'
Flowers: white Blooms: June-July

Although it may take a few years to establish itself in a garden, climbing hydrangea is worth the wait. It offers lustrous green foliage and white, sweetly scented flowers that are borne in flat clusters that are 6" to 10" in diameter. The handsome cinnamon-brown bark creates beautiful patterns in the winter landscape. This show-stopper can light up a woodland garden when its white flowers clothe a dark tree trunk reaching for the sky. It is equally impressive when planted against a brick wall in the sun. The dark green leaves, 2" to 4" long and nearly as wide, persist late into the season. Once the leaves drop, the peeling bark takes center stage. Although climbing hydrangea clings to surfaces with rootlike holdfasts, the plants may require extra support such as stakes and ties. This stately vine can transform the ordinary into a piece of art when trained to cover a wooden shed or garage. A word of caution: make sure that the structure on which you grow this vine is strong enough to support it, as it gets very woody when it matures. This is not a vine to plant for quick cover, but for the future!

WHEN TO PLANT

Plant container-grown plants in early spring or fall. This will allow the root system adequate time to become established before it becomes stressed by hot or cold weather.

WHERE TO PLANT

Plant climbing hydrangea in full sun or partial shade. For best results, plant it in a soil that is rich in organic matter, evenly moist, and well-drained. Although this vine will grow in shade, it may not produce as many flowers as when grown in sun.

ZONE 6,7

How to Plant

Unless you are blessed with a rich, well-drained soil, amend the area where you will plant this vine with organic matter and coarse sand. Till the ground, working the area to at least the size of the vine's container (even better is a hole 3 times the container's depth and width). Water well after planting. Use twine, jute, or copper wire, making sure the stakes and wires will not girdle the vine. Grow this vine next to a structure or wall.

Care and Maintenance

If you have amended the soil, the plant has probably gotten off to a good start. Climbing hydrangea should not require any pruning, as it is slow to become established. Once it is growing well, prune it after it flowers to a desired height or spread. Fertilize in early spring during the first couple of growing seasons with a 10–10–10.

Additional Advice for Care

Climbing hyrdrangea *sometimes* exhibits outstanding fall color with leaves that turn a rich yellow.

Additional Cultivars and Species

Schizophragma hydrangeoides 'Moonlight,' a cultivar with outstanding variegated foliage, has silver markings. It is different from *Hydrangea anomala* in that it does not send out protruding branches but remains flat.

Ipomoea alba

Moonflower

Height: an annual vine that grows 20′ or more
Flowers: white Blooms: open late afternoon–evening, close the
next morning

*The moonflower lights up the night garden and sweetens the air. Its spec-
tacular flowers start out as long tubes and open to flat, white trumpets that
are 6″ across. Each flower is divided into the five points of a star, reminiscent of the shape of a giant starfish. One of the most interesting features of
moonflower is the way it seems to open while you watch it. The flowers
seem to move before your very eyes. The only time the flowers lose their
elegance is after they have closed up the next day; then they look like wet
tissue paper. This fast-growing climber will twine itself around most types
of structures. Its heart-shaped foliage provides a lush background for its
dramatic flowers. No one knows why this morning glory relative enchants
us with its flowers only at night. Perhaps it needs a special moth for pollination, or perhaps it is because it originated in the tropics. Whatever the
reason, this delightful treat will reward you with fragrance and flowers
from summer into the fall with little care.*

WHEN TO PLANT

After the last frost date, sow seeds directly into the ground where
they will grow. Plant in groups of 2 or 3 about 1″ deep and 12″
apart. After germination, thin out the seedlings, keeping only the
strongest ones. Use peat pots so that when you transplant them to
the garden you will not disturb the seedlings.

WHERE TO PLANT

Plant the moonflower near windows and doors where you can
appreciate the perfume in the evening. A bright sunny location
is best. Moonflower will grow in a container or in the ground.
Combine it with other evergreen vines or roses for a dramatic effect.

HOW TO PLANT

A moderately fertile soil plus lots of sunshine are all this vine requires. If you are planting a moonflower that has been grown in a container, dig a hole equal to the size of the container. Like other tropical plants, moonflower grows best when the soil and air temperatures are warm, at least 55 degrees F. Too much fertilizer results in lots of foliage and fewer flowers. Unlike other annuals, once moonflower is planted, it can be forgotten, except for watering during dry spells.

CARE AND MAINTENANCE

Moonflower requires no special care, but it does need a structure to grow up or onto so that the flower display can be appreciated. Wait until after a hard frost before you harvest any seeds. Store them indoors in a cool, dry spot and sow them next spring. The seeds are tiny and plentiful. Begin with just one vine and you will find you have plenty to share with other gardeners.

ADDITIONAL ADVICE FOR CARE

Moonflower belongs to the morning glory family. While many morning glories quickly become invasive weeds, an equal number are showy, easy-to-grow annuals that bloom from early summer to frost.

ADDITIONAL CULTIVARS AND SPECIES

Other easy-to-grow relatives of the moonflower are *Ipomoea tricolor* 'Heavenly Blue,' a morning glory with sky-blue flowers, and *Mina lobata*, which has dark red flowers that fade to yellow. These annuals bloom in late summer into fall.

Ipomoea quamoclit

Cypress Vine

Height: an annual to 12' or more
Flowers: scarlet red Blooms: autumn to summer

This old-fashioned favorite is often offered for sale in the Georgia
Farmer's and Consumer's Market Bulletin, *a good source for many
heirloom plants. One envelope of seeds will produce more than you will
ever want or need. Fast growing, it has fine, feathery, cypress-like foliage.
Each 1½" scarlet-red flower looks like a little trumpet that ends in a star,
and seems designed especially for the hummingbirds that are drawn to it
throughout the summer. Because of its fine texture and bright summer
flowers, cypress vine is a good companion for spring-blooming vines like
wisteria and Carolina jessamine. Even without a structure to grow up,
cypress vine acts like a delicate veil that creeps along the lawn or climbs
over shrubs. While the cypress vine will quickly spread up or over an area,
it is also easy to control. Just selectively pull out individual plants if they
migrate to unwelcome spots. If you want to have cypress vine next year, let
seeds ripen on the plants. With any luck, you'll get seedlings in the spring.*

WHEN TO PLANT

After the last frost, sow seeds directly into the ground. Plant them
in groups of 2 or 3, about 1" deep and 12" apart. After germination,
thin out the seedlings, keeping only the strongest ones. If you start
them indoors, use peat pots and later plant the pots directly into
the ground.

WHERE TO PLANT

Plant cypress vine anywhere that you want a spot of bright color
in your summer or fall garden. Although it will grow in shade,
you will get better flower production if you plant it in full sun. You
can train it up a structure or use a spring-blooming shrub or tree as
a support. If you do this, you will get two seasons of bloom in a
small space.

How to Plant

Cypress vine will grow in almost any type of soil that is not constantly wet. Often it reseeds in a spot that is different from the one in which it was grown the previous year. Like its other morning glory relatives, this tropical can become a weed—but it is a welcome weed.

Care and Maintenance

Other than requiring water during periods of drought, this vine needs no special care. Let seeds ripen on the plant before you collect them. Usually seeds ripen after we have had at least one frost. Pull up the dead vines in late fall or early spring.

Additional Advice for Care

The cypress vine and the passionflower are two of the old-fashioned vines that are easy to grow and that survive with a minimum amount of care. The latter, also known as maypop, is the official wildflower of Tennessee and grows well in Georgia, too.

Additional Cultivars and Species

Closely related to the cypress vine is the cardinal flower (*Ipomoea quamoclit* x *multifida*), but its leaves are not as deeply divided as those of the cypress vine.

CHAPTER TEN

Water and Bog Plants

I REMEMBER HOW EXCITED I WAS *the first time I saw the cardinal flower blooming in the wild along the edge of a pond in a bald cypress swamp. It was late summer, and the brilliant red flowers stood out in the green-and-brown landscape. I still get a thrill when I see plants growing in their native habitats. Over the years I have incorporated into my own garden many of these plants, both perennials and shrubs, including the cardinal flower, turtlehead, Virginia sweetspire, and native azaleas. Not only are they ornamental, but many will grow in soils that are constantly moist. This makes them ideal for use in swampy areas, in bogs, along the edges of ponds, near streams, or in areas where drainage is a problem.*—E.L.G.

When you hear the term "water gardening," you may have visions of elaborate fountains and pools filled with exotic tropical water lilies and giant lotus. But aquatic plants such as these must be grown in enough water so that their crowns are submerged, and often they require special care. There is not enough space here to adequately address the subject of aquatic plants, so the plants recommended in this book are limited to marginal plants. Marginal plants are perennials that will grow in soils that are constantly moist during the growing season but do not have to grow in standing water.

Whether they occur naturally along streams or ponds, or are the result of drainage problems, damp soils present gardeners with a challenge. In this section we recommend plants that are easy to grow and offer ornamental flowers or foliage. Some, such as many of the water-loving iris, have ornamental flowers and ornamental foliage. Many of these marginal plants will also grow happily in the perennial border. Plants like *Iris pseudacorous*, with its vigorous habit and bold architectural foliage, provide a solution for areas that have poorly drained soils. These plants thrive for years with little or no care. They are happy when they grow in water along the edge of a pond where they provide a strong, vertical accent and help relate the pond to the rest of the garden. Some moisture-loving plants need full sun while some others grow happily in partial shade. Plants that thrive in partial shade are the royal fern, Japanese sweet flag, and the cardinal flower.

Other plants to consider for growing in moist soils along steams or ponds include the quick-spreading low groundcover *Mazus reptans* with its lavender flowers, and *Myosotis scoripoides*: when planted along the edge of a pond, in spring this creeper lights up the woodland with its tiny, bright-blue flowers marked with yellow eyes.

I have omitted certain plants such as horsetail, *Equisetum hyemale*. This is a striking plant with its green hollow stems, but with its stoloniferous habit, it can quickly take over an area. Use caution when growing this plant, or restrict it to a pot where it will be easier to contain.

The subject of water gardening is a vast one. Fortunately for Georgia gardeners, there are many hardy native and exotic plants that will thrive in moist soils with a minimum amount of care. Some of these moisture-loving plants will also grow in drier soils.

Acorus calamus 'Variegatus'

Striped Sweet Flag

Height: 2′–3′
Flowers: green, not showy

Striped sweet flag is an ideal choice for a bog garden, along the edge of a pond, or for a problem spot that won't dry out in your garden. The striking iris-like foliage provides a strong vertical accent. The leaves are broadly striped with creamy white, and often in spring they are flushed pink. Arranged in a fan-like fashion, the foliage provides a contrast for other larger-leaved moisture-loving plants like ligularia. Striped sweet flag also makes a good companion for perennials like yellow flag iris and the native cardinal flower. The rhizomes (underground stems) and leaves give off a cinnamon scent when they are crushed. Before the days of air freshener, the leaves of sweet flag were strewn on floors and walkways for their sweet smell. The rhizomes were also used for medicine. This easy-to-grow perennial is a must for the water garden, where it thrives in full sun or light shade. For a similar effect, the smaller (12″) golden Japanese sweet flag, A. gramineus 'Ogon,' has dark-green, grass-like foliage striped with gold.

WHEN TO PLANT

Plant sweet flag in the spring. It is easy to propagate from divisions.

WHERE TO PLANT

Plant sweet flag along the edge of a pond, in a swampy area of your garden, or anywhere that the soil is constantly moist. Some of the smaller varieties can be grown in pots and used as accents in the garden. Sweet flag is a good companion for the autumn fern, cardinal flower, iris, and shrubs like Virginia sweetspire.

HOW TO PLANT

Plant sweet flag in full sun or partial shade. The underground roots, called rhizomes, need soil to grow in but will tolerate being submerged in water. A soil that has lots of organic matter is best, but sweet flag is fairly adaptable.

CARE AND MAINTENANCE

Sweet flag requires no special care, just a moist soil and a moderate amount of light. It is easy to propagate by divisions in early spring. Make sure you get a piece of the rhizome and some roots with each division. If the tips get brown, cutting back the foliage early in the summer will encourage a new flush of growth.

ADDITIONAL ADVICE FOR CARE

They are not particularly showy, but the greenish flowers that appear in summer are reminiscent of small cattails. For a bold accent, the larger striped sweet flag, *A. calamus* 'Variegatus,' is best. *A. gramineus* 'Ogon' makes a good edging plant or can be used in combination with other perennials in a container.

ADDITIONAL CULTIVARS AND SPECIES

A. gramineus 'Variegatus' has green foliage with creamy white stripes and grows to 12". *Carex morrowii* 'Aurea Variegata,' the variegated Japanese sedge, is similar to sweet flag in the effect it creates, but it does well in a moist, well-drained soil and tolerates shade.

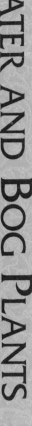

Chelone lyonii

Pink Turtlehead

Height: 3′
Flowers: pink Blooms: late summer to early fall

When you see this perennial in flower, it's easy to understand how it got its common name: turtlehead. Arranged in clusters at the tips of the stems, the individual rose-pink hooded flowers look like turtles with their mouths open. Although this native perennial is a good candidate for the flower border, it does best when it is planted in a soil that is rich in organic matter and constantly moist. Plant it along a stream or pond, at the edge of a woodland garden, or in the wild garden. The late-season flowers provide welcome color when few other perennials are blooming, and the 3"–7" long leaves make a handsome mass of green. Turtlehead also makes a good companion for other natives like cardinal flower, blue lobelia, ferns, and exotic iris like the Japanese and yellow flag. Growing up to 3' tall, turtlehead should not need staking unless it is planted in too much shade, causing plants to stretch and develop weak stems. Turtlehead is easy to propagate by division or tip cuttings and pinching back the plant in spring will help make a bushier plant.

WHEN TO PLANT

Divisions can be taken in the spring or fall. Tip cuttings, about 4"–6" long, should be taken in the spring or summer. For best germination, seeds require a 6-week cold treatment, with a temperature of 40 degrees F.

WHERE TO PLANT

Plant turtlehead in the flower border, along the sunny edge of a woodland garden, along a stream or pond, or in a naturalized garden. Turtlehead likes full sun or partial shade.

ZONE
6,7,8

How to Plant

For the best growth, plant turtlehead in a soil that is rich in organic matter and constantly moist. Give it plenty of room to grow as it forms a clump 2′ wide and 3′ high. Because it blooms late in the season, combine it with earlier-blooming perennials like *Myosotis scorpioides*, a perennial forget-me-not that grows naturally in water and in spring forms a carpet of bright-blue flowers, each with a yellow eye.

Care and Maintenance

Cutting back plants in spring will encourage bushy growth. For best growth, amend the soil with lots of organic matter. Planted in full sun, it is best to use a soil that is constantly moist.

Additional Advice for Care

Turtlehead blooms late in the season and should be planted in combination with spring-blooming perennials like marsh marigold and iris. It would also make a nice contrast for astilbes planted in the same area (but in a well-drained soil). Astilbes will bloom in spring before the turtlehead has put on a lot of growth.

Additional Cultivars and Species

Chelone glabra, called the swamp turtlehead, has pale, pinkish flowers and blooms on 4′ stems in August to September. *C. obliqua* is similar to *C. lyonii*.

WATER AND BOG PLANTS

Scarlet Rose Mallow and Marsh Mallow

Height: 3'–6'
Flowers: deep red, purple-red, pink and white Blooms: mid- to late summer

For a touch of drama in the summer garden, the scarlet rose mallow and the marsh mallow, some with blooms up to 10" across on 4'-tall plants, are among the largest flowers available. Native to swamps and marshes, both of these hibiscus will tolerate wet soils or average garden soil once they are established. Whether you plant them at the back of the flower border or along the edge of a pond, they are sure to attract attention with their huge saucer-like blooms in shades of pink, red, scarlet, and white. Mostly hardy, these relatives of the tropical hibiscus thrive in full sun or light shade. Planted individually or in groups, they provide a spectacular display. Both species will spread rapidly by seed in the garden. Despite the size of the plant, growing up to 6' or more, the scarlet rose mallow's lacy foliage is graceful in its effect. The 5"–6"-wide leaves are deeply divided into 3, 5, or 7 lobes, and the funnel-shaped flowers are borne on long stalks from the leaf axils.

WHEN TO PLANT

Plant the scarlet rose mallow and the marsh mallow in spring.
The species can be propagated by seed and the hybrids by divisions.
Collect seeds in the fall and store them in a cool, dry place until spring.

WHERE TO PLANT

Plant the scarlet rose mallow and the marsh mallow in a damp meadow, at the back of a large flower border, at the edge of a pond, or in naturalized areas. Although they will tolerate light shade, for best blooming plant both types in full sun. If space is limited, grow them in large pots, being sure to keep them well watered during the growing season.

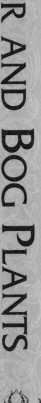

How to Plant

An average garden soil is adequate as long as it holds moisture. Soils that have some organic matter are best, but these hardy hibiscus are not too particular. During the summer, you may notice them blooming in the marshes. Once they are established, they can tolerate soils that are drier. Depending on the hybrid and how large it gets, space plants 18"–36" apart.

Care and Maintenance

If you plant these mallows in the flower garden, be sure to keep them well watered and apply a good layer of mulch in the winter, about 2"–4". In the coldest parts of Georgia, wait until spring to prune them back to the ground.

Additional Advice for Care

Hibiscus make up a large genus of plants ranging from woody types like the old-fashioned rose-of-sharon to the tropical types. Many of the large flowered hybrids available to gardeners are the result of crossing a number of the different native species. The result is larger flowers, longer blooming times, and heat resistance. Because many of the hybrids are sterile, they will be not spread by seed.

Additional Cultivars and Species

H. 'Southern Belle Mix' grows 5' tall with 10"-wide blooms in pink, white, and red. H. 'Dixie Bell Mix' offers dwarf plants to 3' with huge blooms. Other popular selections are H. 'Lord Baltimore' with 10" flowers, red with overlapping petals and deeply cut foliage. H. 'Lady Baltimore' has pink flowers with contrasting red centers.

Iris ensata and *Iris pseudacorus*

Japanese Iris and Yellow Flag

Height: 2′–5′
Flowers: white, blue, purple, lavender-pink, and yellow

Japanese iris blooms early to midsummer and yellow flag blooms in late spring to early summer. For bold architectural foliage and beautiful flowers, both the Japanese and yellow flag iris are outstanding choices. Planted as specimens or in a mass, their rich colors and graceful flowers add elegance to the garden. Both types will grow in a soil that is constantly moist, but the Japanese iris is more exacting in its requirements, preferring an acid soil that is rich in organic matter. Japanese iris are also heavy feeders, and because they require abundant moisture during the growing season, they thrive along streams, around ponds, near fountains, or in bogs. I know of one gardener who grows his in pots in children's swimming pools. This way they get plenty of moisture, and he can bring them into the garden when they bloom. The orchid-like flowers are magnificent from the moment the buds begin to swell until they open to flat-topped wide blooms, sometimes 6" across or more. The plants grow 18"–24" tall and thrive in full sun or partial shade.

WHEN TO PLANT
Plant divisions of yellow flag and Japanese iris in the spring or the fall. To germinate seeds of yellow flag, they need to be covered, and temperatures should be 72 degrees F. with high humidity. Yellow flag iris grown from seed take two years to flower. Cultivars of Japanese iris will not come true from seed.

WHERE TO PLANT
Both Japanese iris and yellow flag iris will grow in soils that are constantly wet, making them well suited for growing around streams, ponds, or fountains. They will also grow in more formal situations

like the flower border or in containers. Combine them with other moisture-loving perennials in a naturalistic planting.

HOW TO PLANT

Plant Japanese iris and yellow flag iris in full sun or partial shade. While both types of iris like constant moisture during the growing season, Japanese iris likes a well-drained soil during the winter. If you plant yellow flag iris in a dry soil, it is best to give it partial shade. Japanese iris require a soil that is rich in organic matter, but yellow flag iris will grow in an average garden soil and will also tolerate dry soils.

CARE AND MAINTENANCE

Both of these versatile iris require little in the way of pruning except to remove the spent flowers before they set seed. If yellow flag iris is planted in water, it can quickly spread to form a colony. To control its spreading, plant it in drier soils . . . and don't let it set any seed! Yellow flag iris forms vigorous clumps that seldom need dividing. Japanese iris benefits from regular fertilizing with a 10–10–10, and clumps should be divided every 3 to 4 years.

ADDITIONAL ADVICE FOR CARE

Yellow flag iris looks good in combination with the sky-blue flowers of the hardy bog salvia, *Salvia uliginosa*. By growing Japanese iris, yellow flag iris, and Siberian iris, you can extend the season of iris bloom in your garden from late spring into July. Other water-loving iris include *Iris virginica* and *Iris veriscolor*.

ADDITIONAL CULTIVARS AND SPECIES

There are numerous cultivars of Japanese iris available. Some have flowers as large across as small dinner plates. *I. ensata* 'Queen of the Blues,' 'Wine Ruffles,' and 'Gold Bound' are a few noteworthy selections. In the spring, the new foliage of *I. pseudacorus* 'Variegata' starts out striped with pale yellow markings. As it matures, the foliage turns green.

Lobelia cardinalis

Cardinal Flower

Height: 3'–4'
Flowers: scarlet red Blooms: late summer

Some of the best perennials for our Georgia gardens are also standouts in the wild. I still get excited when I see plants flowering in their native habitats, like the native cardinal flower which occurs throughout North America. Whether it's blooming along the edge of a lazy river or lighting up the banks of a bald cypress swamp with its scarlet red flowers, cardinal flower is a standout in the summer landscape. Partial shade, or at least shade from the late afternoon sun, and a moist soil that has been amended with lots of organic matter create the best environment for this beauty. Planted along a stream or in the flower border, it becomes a magnet for hummingbirds and bees. Easy to grow from seed or divisions, the cardinal flower forms large rosettes of foliage. The blooms occur on 2'-long stems, opening from the bottom over a period of about three weeks. Requiring the same conditions but blooming later than the cardinal flower is the big blue lobelia, L. syphilitica. *Thought to have medicinal properties at one time, this hardy perennial is now grown for its ornamental appeal.*

WHEN TO PLANT

Sow seeds in the spring when soil temperatures are 70 degrees F. or higher. Plants will often self-sow, so learn to recognize the foliage. Take divisions of the clumps in the fall. Plant containerized plants in the spring or fall.

WHERE TO PLANT

Plant cardinal flower along streams, near ponds, in damp meadows, in naturalized areas, or in the flower border. Combine it with other native plants like Virginia sweetspire and native azaleas or water-loving iris (*I. ensata* or *I. pseudocorus*). In the flower garden it provides spikes of bright red late in the season.

HOW TO PLANT

Plant cardinal flower in a moist soil that has been amended with lots of organic matter. If the soil is dry, flowers will not persist. In the flower border, it is best to provide shade from hot late-afternoon sun. A layer of mulch will keep roots cool and retain moisture.

CARE AND MAINTENANCE

Cardinal flower responds well to a soil that is fertile and rich in organic matter. Topdressing once in the spring and then in the fall with a good organic mulch will help keep plants vigorous. No special pruning or fertilizing is required once plants are established. Keep the soil moist throughout the growing season. To encourage plants to self-sow, don't remove the flower stalks until early spring.

ADDITIONAL ADVICE FOR CARE

Lobelia cardinalis is a choice native that occurs throughout the United States. When siting it in your own garden, think about where it grows in the wild—along streams and in swamps and damp meadows. Plant it in combination with the swamp sunflower, or with the native cinnamon fern along the edge of a pond. The cinnamon fern needs a moist but well-drained soil.

ADDITIONAL CULTIVARS AND SPECIES

Many hybrids result from crosses of *L. splendens*, *L. cardinalis*, and *L. syphilitica*. *L.* 'Queen Victoria' grows to 5' with red flowers and bronze foliage. *L. cardinalis* 'Royal Robe,' with red flowers and maroon foliage, is long-lived. *L. gerardii* 'Vedrariensis' blooms later and has velvety purple flowers and green-bronze foliage.

Georgia's Public Gardens

ARDENERS IN GEORGIA ARE A FORTUNATE lot. Throughout the state, high-quality public gardens offer inspiration through aesthetic landscape vignettes, hands-on learning experiences through volunteer opportunities, and basic gardening knowledge through education programs. The following is a listing of the major gardens open to the public. As our gardens change with the seasons, the schedules of these gardens tend to change as well. Call in advance to obtain calendars of gardening events along with standard hours of operation.

Atlanta Botanical Garden
Piedmont Park at The Prado
Atlanta, Georgia 30357
(404) 876-5859

The Atlanta Botanical Garden is a lush garden oasis in the heart of Midtown Atlanta. The ABG features fifteen acres of landscaped gardens, a conservatory which houses endangered tropical and desert plants from around the world, and a fifteen-acre hardwood forest with walking trails. The Atlanta Botanical Garden is an easily accessible gardening resource in the midst of urban Atlanta.

Atlanta History Center
130 West Paces Ferry Road, N.W.
Atlanta, Georgia 30305-1366
(404) 814-4000

On the grounds of the Atlanta History Center, visitors can experience thirty-two acres of gardens, woodlands, and nature trails that show the horticultural history of the Atlanta region. The seven distinct gardens feature a variety of gardening styles from native plantings to formal landscaping with boxwoods and classical statuary. As part of an international effort to promote world peace, a Garden For Peace has been installed. It includes a Soviet Georgian sculpture.

RESOURCES

Barnsley Gardens
597 Barnsley Gardens Road
Adairsville, Georgia 30103
(770) 773-7480

A state historic landmark, Barnsley Gardens features the ruins of a once-grand manor house surrounded by thirty acres of English-style gardens. Godfrey Barnsley designed his gardens in the style of Andrew Jackson Downing, considered America's first great landscape gardener. Barnsley Gardens can boast a past which includes a romantic rescue by a European prince and a present that includes updating for historical accuracy.

Callaway Gardens
P.O. Box 2000
Pine Mountain, Georgia 31822-2000
(800) 225-5292

Located seventy miles southwest of Atlanta and thirty miles north of Columbus, Georgia, Callaway Gardens is a manmade landscape in a unique natural setting. It was conceived by its creators Cason Callaway and his wife Virginia as a place for visitors to discover natural beauty. Today, Callaway Gardens features the largest glass-enclosed butterfly conservatory in North America. Its vegetable garden is the site of the Southern segment of PBS's The Victory Garden television show. In addition, the horticulture center showcases a year-round floral display that integrates indoor and outdoor plant settings. More than a million people visit the 1500 acres of Callaway Gardens each year.

RESOURCES

DeKalb College Botanical Garden
3251 Panthersville Road
Decatur, Georgia 30034
(404) 244-5090

The DeKalb College Botanical Garden focuses exclusively on native plants of Georgia. The garden includes the largest collection of native plants in the state. Approximately 1500 sun- and shade-loving native plants are featured at the DeKalb College South Campus.

Fernbank Museum of Natural History
767 Clifton road, N.E.
Atlanta, Georgia 30307
  and Fernbank Science Center
156 Heaton Park Drive, N.E.
Atlanta, Georgia 30307-1398
(404) 378-4311

The grounds of The Fernbank Museum of Natural History and Fernbank Science Center feature two very distinct garden areas. Adjacent to the Fernbank Science Center is the Fernbank Forest. For many years visitors have walked through the sixty-five-acre woodland. The primeval Piedmont forest contains one-and-a-half miles of paved trail lined with signs identifying the various specimens. The grounds of The Fernbank Museum of Natural History feature a rose garden. Visitors there will see 1300 roses, including some All-American Rose Selections test plants.

RESOURCES

Georgia Southern Botanical Garden
Georgia Southern University
1211 Fair Road (State Highway 67)
Statesboro, Georgia 30460
(912) 871-1114 or 871-1913

The Georgia Southern Botanical Garden is a ten-acre site located two blocks from the campus of Georgia Southern University. The garden features native plants of Georgia, particularly those of the Coastal Plain. The plants are featured in various gardens including a magnolia/holly allee, a butterfly border, and an arboretum. Also within the botanical garden are a children's vegetable garden, nature trails, and seven original farm structures.

Massee Lane Gardens
One Massee Lane
Fort Valley, Georgia 31030
(912) 967-2358 or 967-2722

Beginning with the planting of one camellia plant in 1936, Massee Lane Gardens now serves as the headquarters for the American Camellia Society. The garden, which is located on the site of a former peach farm dating from the early 1900s, also features an education musuem, a rose garden, and a Japanese garden.

Middle Georgia Trial Gardens
Wesleyan College
Macon, Georgia 31210
(912) 751-6338

Under the auspices of The University of Georgia Cooperative Extension Service, the Master Gardeners of Central Georgia operate a trial garden on the grounds of Wesleyan College. New and previously developed varieties of flowers, herbs, and vegetables are cultivated and tested for their response to the Middle Georgia climate.

RESOURCES

The Garden Club of Georgia, Inc. State Headquarters
 and Founders Memorial Garden
University of Georgia Campus
325 South Lumpkin Street
Athens, Georgia 30602
(706) 542-3631

A historic building that dates to 1857 currently serves as headquarters for The Garden Club of Georgia, Inc. On the grounds of
the headquarters is the Founders Memorial Garden. Completed in
1946, the garden was created as a living memorial to the twelve
founders of the Ladies Garden Club of Athens, the first garden club
in America. The two-and-one-half-acre site includes a formal boxwood garden, a perennial garden, and an arboretum.

The State Botanical Garden of Georgia at The University of Georgia
2450 South Milledge Avenue
Athens, Georgia 30602
(706) 542-1244

The State Botanical Garden of Georgia is a 313-acre preserve
under the direction of The University of Georgia. The garden
features five miles of nature trails, an International Garden, and a
three-story tropical conservatory. The State Botanical Garden holds
educational programs year round and has a growing and active
patrons organization.

Vines Botanical Gardens
3500 Oak Grove Road
Loganville, Georgia 30249
(770) 466-7532

Located between Athens and Atlanta in Loganville, Georgia, Vines
Botanical Gardens consists of twenty-five acres of developed landscaped area. Eight distinct gardens showcase several different types
of water features. Sited above the gardens and offering a grand
view is the eighteen-thousand-square-foot Vines House.

Bibliography

*N*O GOOD GARDENING BOOK CAN BE completed without references. The following books have been invaluable to us, and we invite you to discover the tremendous amount of horticultural information contained in them.

Armitage, Allan. 1989. *Herbaceous Perennial Plants: A Treatise on Their Culture and Garden Attributes*. Varsity Press, Inc. Athens, GA.

Bender, Steve and Felder Rushing. 1993. *Passalong Plants*. The University of North Carolina Press. Chapel Hill, NC.

Brooklyn Botanic Garden. *Plants and Gardens Handbooks*, many different subjects. List available from Brooklyn Botanic Garden, 1000 Washington Ave., Brooklyn, NY.

Burke, Ken (ed.). 1980. *Shrubs and Hedges*. The American Horticultural Society. Franklin Center, PA.

Burke, Ken (ed.). 1982. *Gardening in the Shade*. The American Horticultural Society, Franklin Center, PA.

Dirr, Michael. 1990. *Manual of Woody Landscape Plants*. Stipes Publishing. Champaign, IL.

Gardiner, J.M. 1989. *Magnolias*. Globe Pequot Press. Chester, PA.

Gates, Galen et al. 1994. *Shrubs and Vines*. Pantheon Books. New York, NY.

Greenlee, John. 1992. *The Encyclopedia of Ornamental Grasses*. Rodale Press. Emmaus, PA.

Halfacre, R. Gordon and Anne R. Shawcroft. 1979. *Landscape Plants of the Southeast*. Sparks Press. Raleigh, NC.

Harper, Pamela and Frederick McGourty. 1985. *Perennials: How to Select, Grow and Enjoy*. HP Books. Tucson, AZ.

Heath, Brent and Becky. 1995. *Daffodils for American Gardens*. Elliott & Clark Publishing. Washington, DC.

RESOURCES

Hipps, Carol Bishop. 1994. *In a Southern Garden*. Macmillan Publishing. New York, NY.

Lawrence, Elizabeth. 1991. *A Southern Garden*. The University of North Carolina Press. Chapel Hill, NC.

Lawson-Hall, Toni and Brian Rothera. 1996. *Hydrangeas*. Timber Press. Portland, OR.

Loewer, Peter. 1992. *Tough Plants for Tough Places*. Rodale Press. Emmaus, PA.

Mikel, John. 1994. *Ferns for American Gardens*. Macmillan Publishing. New York, NY.

Ogden, Scott. 1994. *Garden Bulbs for the South*. Taylor Publishing. Dallas, TX.

Still, Steven. 1994. *Manual of Herbaceous Ornamental Plants*, 4th edition. Stipes Publishing. Champaign, IL.

Vengris, Jonas and William A. Torello. 1982. *Lawns*. Thomson Publications. Fresno, CA.

Winterrowd, Wayne. 1992. *Annuals for Connoisseurs*. Prentice Hall. New York, NY.

INDEX

INDEX

INDEX

INDEX